THE VICTORIAN GIRL AND THE FEMININE IDEAL

The
VICTORIAN GIRL
and the Feminine Ideal

Deborah Gorham

INDIANA UNIVERSITY PRESS

Bloomington

Copyright © 1982 by Deborah Gorham

Manufactured in Great Britain

Library of Congress Cataloging in Publication Data

Gorham, Deborah.
    The Victorian girl and the feminine ideal.

    1. Women — England — History — 19th century. 2. Women
— England — Biography. 3. Girls — England — History — 19th
century. 4. Mothers and daughters — England — History —
19th century. 5. Family — England — History — 19th
century. 6. Middle classes — England — History — 19th
century. I. Title.
HQ1599.E5G67   305.4'2'0942   82-47944
ISBN 0-253-36258-X   AACR2

CONTENTS

For my mother

PREFACE

Is it a girl or a boy? In all societies, the answer to this question shapes our future from the moment of our birth. It is assumed that our sex assignment at birth destines us to become masculine or feminine adults, and indeed most of us do learn to conform to the gender roles imposed by our culture. The assumptions are readily made; adaptation usually occurs. However, the process by which infants became feminine women or masculine men is complex and not fully understood. It is generally agreed that nature and nurture both contribute, but in what proportion and through what means? In this study, the way in which female infants learn gender roles is examined in a particular social and historical context — the context of middle-class Victorian England. The focus of the work is twofold; it is concerned both with the role that ideas about girlhood played in middle-class ideology, and with the effect that those ideas had on individual experience.

Part One provides an overview of the middle-class girl's experience and an examination of the ideological assumptions that underlay the Victorian perception of girlhood. This analysis of ideology demonstrates that the Victorian perception of girlhood arose not in isolation, but as one manifestation of the Victorian conception of femininity. That conception of femininity played a major role in the construction of Victorian ideology about the family; Victorian ideology about the family, in turn, was a cornerstone of the middle-class world view.[1]

Part Two examines the effect that the Victorian conception of feminine girlhood had on Victorian advice about the rearing of daughters. In the Victorian period, there was a proliferation of such practical, detailed advice, a proliferation that occurred as people became increasingly willing to turn to printed sources for information about all aspects of private life. An examination of such advice provides a way of tracing the influence of Victorian presuppositions about girlhood as they were worked out in concrete discussions of the problems of everyday life.[2]

Part Three analyses the effect that the Victorian concept of girlhood had on actual experience during the early, middle and late-Victorian years. Biographical evidence is used to examine the childhood and girlhood years of a number of individual Victorian women.

This use of group biography illustrates the influence that the idea of feminine girlhood had on the lives of women of the period, an influence that persisted in spite of the changes in the structure of women's lives that occurred over the course of the Victorian decades.

Notes

1. Much of the analysis in chapters 1 and 3 of Part One, the chapters in which the idea of girlhood is analysed, is drawn from Victorian fiction, poetry and art, and from Victorian commentary on family life. Such commentary formed a mainstay of Victorian discourse. It appeared as book-length advice books, and in periodical literature that catered to a wide range of tastes, from well-established periodicals like *Fraser's Magazine* or the *Saturday Review* to magazines especially designed for women and girls. In finding material for the analysis in Part One, several sources were of special help. The Osborne Collection of Early Children's Books, housed at Boys and Girls House, Toronto Public Library, was a valuable source for children's books and periodicals. The catalogue of the collection exists in printed form: *The Osborne Collection of Early Children's Books*, prepared by Judith St. John (Toronto: Toronto Public Library, 1975), 2 vols. Cynthia White, *Women's Magazines: 1693 – 1968* (London, 1970) was of much use in locating titles of women's magazines.

2. In locating Victorian advice material, the Osborne Collection, and White, *Women's Magazines*, were again of help. In locating medical writings about child care and puberty the following was useful: *Index Catalogue of the Library of the Surgeon General's Office*, US Army (Washington: Government Printing Office, 1880 First Ser., 1911 Second Series) (New York: Johnson Reprint Corp, 1972).

3. In addition to the diaries, memoirs and autobiographies that came to hand in the course of the research, the following finding aids proved useful: William Matthews, *British Diaries: An Annotated Bibliography of British Diaries Written Between 1442 – 1942* (Berkeley: University of California Press, 1950); *British Autobiographies Written Before 1951*, compiled by William Matthews (Berkeley: University of California Press, 1955); John Stuart Batts, *British Manuscript Diaries of the 19th Century: An Annotated Listing* (Fontwell, Sussex: Centaur Press, 1976).

ACKNOWLEDGEMENTS

I am grateful to the following people for their advice, suggestions and helpful criticism: Susan Trofimenkoff, Judith Walkowitz, Leonore Davidoff, Naomi Griffiths, Susan Russell, Lynn MacDonald, Marilyn Barber, Ethel Gorham, Diana Pedersen, Florence Hughes, Eta Schneiderman, Angus McLaren and David Keith.

I thank King's College Library, Cambridge, for permission to use Lily Whichelo Forster's diary; the Girls' Public Day School Trust for permission to use their archives; and the archivist and staff at the North London Collegiate School for their help and hospitality. I am especially grateful to Janet Sondheimer, archivist at Westfield College, for introducing me to Constance Maynard's diaries. The librarians at the Osborne Collection of Early Children's Books, Toronto Public Libraries, offered much useful advice. I would also like to thank Frances Montgomery of the Carleton University Library for her advice and assistance.

I am very grateful to Naomi Griffiths, Peter King and Ray Jones, my colleagues in the History Department at Carleton University, for relieving me of some of my teaching duties in 1981.

Finally, I would like to thank Toby Gelfand and Naomi Goldenberg, the two people to whom I owe the greatest debt. I thank Toby for his friendship, and for giving me the benefit of his sound historical judgement, and his patient and thorough editorial criticism. I thank Naomi for sharing with me her insights as a feminist scholar, but most of all for her unfailing support and encouragement.

PART ONE

Chapter 1

WOMEN AND GIRLS IN THE MIDDLE-CLASS FAMILY: IMAGES AND REALITY

If the triumph of industrial capitalism brought about the making of the English working class, it also produced a new middle class, a middle class with a self-conscious identity and a sense of its destiny as the most fitting architect of a new society. The middle class that emerged as a result of industrial capitalism was predominantly urban in character, its male members being engaged in entrepreneurial, managerial and professional occupations. At the highest levels of the class were men engaged in substantial business enterprises, in the liberal professions and in public administration. Its lowest levels included a greatly increased number of clerks, and those employed in the minor retail trades.[1]

A shared set of ideas and beliefs united this diverse group. Of first importance was a belief in the positive value of social mobility. That a man could rise in the world through effort, talent and initiative, and that such a rise in social status was to be commended was the fundamental principle of Victorian middle-class ideology. Fuelling that principle was the gospel of work. As Samuel Smiles put it: 'National progress is the sum of individual industry, energy and uprightness, as national decay is of individual idleness, selfishness and vice.'[2] Smiles expressed a generally accepted belief held by middle-class people that it was they rather than aristocrats or the labouring poor who would most surely possess such industry, energy and uprightness. The virtues of thrift, order, punctuality, all buttressed by evangelical Protestantism, were offered by the self-confident voice of the Victorian middle class as the prescription for individual and collective well-being.

Smilesian self-confidence was not, however, the only feature of the Victorian middle-class outlook. Doubt and anxiety were also part of the ethos of the period. The rapidity with which social and economic change was taking place was both a source of pride and a source of tension. A sense of anxiety is such a pervasive element in Victorian discourse that one historian has seen it as the most important feature of the Victorian 'frame of mind'.[3]

One Victorian response to that tension was to define certain institutions in ways that would allay doubt and anxiety. Having produced
industrial capitalism, the Victorians sought refuge from it. For the
Victorian middle class, the most important of such refuges was the
family. A cult of domesticity, an idealised vision of home and family, a
vision that perceived the family as both enfolding its members and
excluding the outside world, is a major recurring image in Victorian
literature, art and social commentary.[4]

The cult of domesticity helped to relieve the tensions that existed
between the moral values of Christianity, with its emphasis on love and
charity, and the values of capitalism, which asserted that the world of
commerce should be pervaded by a spirit of competition and a recognition that only the fittest should survive. By locating Christian values
in the home, and capitalist values in the public world of commerce,
the Victorians were able to achieve an efficient moral balance. The
home became a shelter for religious values, in their widest context
including the values associated with personal relationships; the world
of commerce could thereby be absolved from the necessity of acting on
Christian principles. Moreover its moral barrenness became bearable,
because the idealisation of the home meant that, at least in theory,
some refuge from the harsh public world was possible.

The creation of a sharp division between the private world of home
and the public world of commerce, professional life and politics, had a
profound impact on the way in which women were perceived in the
Victorian period. Throughout the period, it was customary to refer to
public and private life as two 'separate spheres'. Each of the two
spheres was thought to be inextricably connected either with women
or with men. The public sphere of business, politics and professional
life was defined as the male sphere. The private sphere of love, the
emotions and domesticity was defined as the sphere of women. The
public sphere was the male's exclusive domain, whereas the private
sphere was seen as presided over by females for the express purpose of
providing a place of renewal for men, after their rigorous activities in
the harsh, competitive public sphere.

The cult of domesticity assigned to women both a separate sphere
and a distinct set of roles. Victorian conceptions of the idealised role of
women are epitomised by Coventry Patmore's poem *The Angel in the
House*, the title of which captures its essence.[5] The ideal woman was
willing to be dependent on men and submissive to them, and she
would have a preference for a life restricted to the confines of home.
She would be innocent, pure, gentle and self-sacrificing. Possessing no

ambitious strivings, she would be free of any trace of anger or hostility. More emotional than man, she was also more capable of self-renunciation.

The characteristics of the ideal Victorian woman can be summed up in one word: she was *feminine*. Femininity is a psychological concept, in that it implies a distinctive model for female personality. It is a modern idea and represents a major ideological shift in the justification for the secondary position of females. While female subordination has been a traditional element of Western European civilisation, pre-modern methods of enforcing it had relied largely on brute force or on an appeal to biblical injunction. But since the end of the eighteenth century, the concept of femininity, which is based on a conception of human psychology that assumes that feminine qualities are 'natural', has been the major ideological agent in enforcing the subordination of women.[6] Intimations of the concept are, to be sure, found earlier, but it is only at the end of the eighteenth century that a self-consciously constructed theory about psychological differences between males and females began to be developed. In the Victorian period, the era of the 'Angel in the House', the idea of femininity came to full flower.

Much Victorian idealisation of femininity was concerned with its manifestation by adult women in their roles as wives and mothers. The idealised Victorian home, however, did not consist of husband and wife alone, but of husband, wife and children, and just as the parental role was suffused with intense emotional significance, so also was the role of children. Both male and female children were of importance in idealisations of family life, but daughters had a special significance. Sons would help to determine the middle-class family's place in the world, but daughters could offer the family a particular sort of tenderness and spirituality. As a writer for a late nineteenth-century women's magazine stated:

> Surely there is no thought sweeter or more tender than that which comes with a baby-girl . . . The thought of a man-child has more possibilities of strength and power. It gratifies pride and ambition more . . . But the mother of the little woman-child sees in her the born queen, and, at the same time, the servant of home; the daughter who is to lift the burden of domestic cares and make them unspeakably lighter by taking her share of them; the sister who is to be a little mother to her brothers and sisters; the future wife and mother in her turn, she is the owner of a destiny which may call on

her to endure much and to suffer much, but which, as it also bids her love much . . . is well worthy of an immortal creature . . . A family without a girl . . . lacks a crowning grace, quite as much as a family without a boy misses a tower of strength.[7]

That passage was written in 1887, but similar portrayals of the daughters began to appear by the end of the eighteenth century in advice literature, in fiction, in poetry and in art. This persistence is remarkable in view of the extent to which the actual lives of middle-class girls changed over the course of the nineteenth century. The strength of the imagery and its persistence would seem to indicate that an idealised view of the daughter's role is a crucial feature of the cult of domesticity.

The idealised view of the daughter may have been so powerful because certain features of the idealised view of womanhood could, in fact, more appropriately be applied to daughters than to wives. One of the ambiguities involved in the Victorian idealisation of womanhood is that while the ideal woman was to have womanly strength, she was also to remain permanently childlike, childlike even in maturity:

The perfect loveliness of a woman's countenance can only consist in that majestic peace, which is found in the memory of happy and useful years . . . and from the joining of this with that yet more *majestic childishness*, which is still full of change and promise . . . There is no old age where there is still that promise — it is eternal youth.[8]

The 'majestic childishness' of the ideal woman was a sign of the extent to which she was removed from the vicissitudes of the public sphere. It was seen as necessary that a woman retain a childlike simplicity precisely because it was felt that her life ought to be restricted to the domestic sphere, and her domestic calling was seen as both the cause and the effect of the need to shelter her from the rigours of the public sphere. The Victorians frequently spoke of the way in which males were 'hardened' by their exposure to the rough and tumble of the outside world, but they also believed that, should a woman be so exposed, she too would be hardened. Thus, women were told that they must remain within the domestic sphere both because their duties were to be performed there, and because contact with the wider world would damage their ability to perform those duties.

The idea of the adult woman who possesses 'majestic childishness' reflects the contradictions that existed at the centre of the idealised vision of true womanhood. How convincing could an idealisation be that combined both childlike simplicity with the complex duties of wifehood and motherhood? Even at an overt, explicitly stated level, contradictions existed in the imagery of true womanhood, and beneath the surface, expressed through allusion, were the tensions inherent in the Victorian view of female sexuality. The ideal of feminine purity is implicitly asexual; how, then, could it be reconciled with the active sexuality that would inevitably be included in the duties of wife and mother?[9]

These contradictions could be resolved by focusing on the femininity of the daughter rather than on the adult woman. Much more successfully than her mother, a young girl could represent the quintessential angel in the house. Unlike an adult woman, a girl could be perceived as a wholly unambiguous model of feminine dependence, childlike simplicity and sexual purity. While it might be believed that an adult woman should retain a childlike simplicity, clearly a real child could be conceived of as more childlike than could an adult woman.

The qualities of the Angel in the House, whether she be wife or daughter, were defined as spiritual in nature. For this reason, they took on a universal application, transcending mere material circumstances. The ideal Angel in the House would be able to create a true home wherever she found herself:

> Wherever a true wife comes . . . home is always round her. The stars only may be over her head; the glowworm in the night-cold grass may be the only fire at her foot; but home is yet wherever she is; and for a noble woman it stretches far round her, better than ceiled with cedar, or painted with vermilion, shedding its quiet light far, for those who else were homeless.[10]

In the spiritual realm, then, the true wife could create the desired atmosphere of Victorian domesticity out of thin air. However, middle-class Victorian beliefs about domesticity functioned on levels other than the spiritual. There were, as well, generally accepted standards for the cultural environment of the ideal family, and just as the spiritual well-being of the home was considered a feminine responsibility, so also was the creation of suitable standards of taste and manners.

In its manners and style, the successful middle-class family would, above all else, manifest the quality of *gentility*. The concept of gentility was a legacy of the social structure that had characterised the eighteenth century. Its continued importance in the Victorian period attests to the fact that the middle-class endorsement of social mobility had not been entirely triumphant. The belief that social status could be earned through effort was continually being challenged by the older belief that a particular social status was inseparable from one's rank at birth. This belief was frequently expressed as hostility towards those who had achieved, or who were attempting to achieve, upward mobility. Gentility was not a clearly definable quality but revealed itself in nuances that clearly distinguished members of the established and dominant classes from those who still bore traces of their upwardly mobile progress. Throughout the nineteenth century, whether one was gentle or vulgar continued to be a hallmark of social status.

Two systems of assigning status, then, existed in the Victorian period, one based on material wealth, and one based on the mani-festation of certain personal and cultural attributes. One way in which the conflict between these two systems was managed, if not resolved, was through the family's function as an indicator of status. The family's style of life displayed its tastes and thus its status and its gentil-ity. A man could achieve success through hard work and initiative, and thereby gain economic power, but his social status, if not actually determined through the family he established, was reflected through it. The style of family life, the quality of domesticity achieved, was the final determinant of the niche he occupied in the social structure.

Females played a crucial role in the functioning of the family as an indicator of social status. In the Victorian period, in theory at least, only middle-class men could achieve status. A middle-class woman acquired her status by connection with a man. Indeed no middle-class girl or woman could raise her own status through effort in the world of work, because earning money, for a girl or woman, meant loss of caste. But middle-class females none the less had a role to play in deter-mining social differences. Women, not men, managed the outward forms that both manifested and determined social status. Through the creation of an appropriate domestic environment, and through the management of social life, women at all levels of the middle class were responsible for assuring that the private sphere acted as an effective indicator of status in the public sphere.[11]

Through the family, then, middle-class females played a central role in determining the social status of the males with whom they were connected, just as they played a central role in functioning of the cult of domesticity. Whereas all females, so the theory went, even those who were not middle class, could be perfect wives or perfect daughters, only some could achieve gentility. While all could aspire to 'noble womanhood', only some could be ladies. Those who attempted to be ladies when they could not, according to the arbiters of gentility, truly aspire to the title, came to represent all that was considered objectionable about upward social mobility.

Decisions about gentility and vulgarity were ostensibly made on the basis of such factors as social bearing and education. In reality, they were not separable from wealth. There was a generally agreed upon set of possessions and circumstances, a 'paraphernalia of gentility' that formed the material base upon which the pattern for a successful middle-class way of life rested, an ideal to which all members of the class could be said to aspire, to a greater or lesser degree.[12]

Throughout the Victorian era, this pattern involved ritual, formality and compartmentalisation. Within the privacy of the home such events as mealtimes and family prayers were to take place in an orderly and ceremonial fashion. Members of a household were divided into groups, between which barriers were established; the division between children and other members of the household was to be no less rigid than that between servants and employers.[13] The contacts that the successful middle-class family had with the outside world were, as well, to be carried out in a ritualised way. It was assumed that such a family entertained guests in the home and engaged in the ritual of the formal social call. In order to participate effectively in the rituals of genteel social life, one had not only to know the rules, one had to have the money to pay for the trappings.[14]

One possession necessary for the achievement of a genteel middle-class style of life was a suitable dwelling. While the urban Victorian's nostalgia for the pleasures and moral values associated with rural life assured for the country house its unrivalled place as the most desirable dwelling to which a middle-class individual could aspire, a more attainable goal was the substantial suburban dwelling. A desirable suburban villa would have had an ample number of spacious rooms, and would have been well situated in attractive surroundings.[15]

The employment of domestic servants was also an integral part of middle-class life. Indeed, contemporaries frequently used 'servant keeping' as the chief distinction between the middle and upper classes and those beneath them. It was assumed that middle-class families would employ as many servants as the family income would allow. The generally accepted pattern called for more than one servant. Without two or three servants, it was assumed to be difficult, if not impossible, to create the formal life style that gentility demanded.[16]

While this was the standard of material life generally accepted as the ideal, an acceptance of the ideal presented problems for the majority of those who considered themselves middle class. This ideal material standard, along with the other criteria that were used to determine the presence or absence of gentility, was shaped by the upper middle class. Yet, throughout the nineteenth century, while the middle and upper classes together comprised a quarter of the population, the great majority of middle-class people was clustered at the lower levels of this upper quarter. As a result, while the standards and expectations for the class as a whole were created by its most affluent members, there was no way that the majority of middle-class people could afford to achieve them.[17]

They could not, for example, afford to employ the amount of domestic help considered necessary to produce a genteel ambience. More than one servant was necessary for that, and without at least three, a household was considered to be a modest one. But it has been estimated that even early in the period, a family would have needed an annual income of over £300 to employ more than two servants. Since most middle-class incomes fell in the £150 – £300 range, most middle-class families could employ only one domestic, and perhaps indeed only a charwoman.[18]

A lower-middle-class family could not afford a house suitable for the establishment of a genteel life style. True gentility required sufficient space to maintain the formality that characterised the ideal pattern. An appropriate house would, for instance, have been equipped with a separate nursery wing for the children. A family with a lower-middle-class income, but with genteel aspirations, might call the room in which the children slept the 'nursery' but in a relatively small house, the achievement of the separation of adult and child life that the ideal pattern required would not have been possible. For the same reasons, such features of the genteel life style as the formalities associated with mealtime, or the rituals appropriate to well-bred social intercourse could not have been managed in a small house with a minimum amount of domestic help.

The lack of congruence between the ideal middle-class style of life, and what was actually attainable for most middle-class people affected women more than men because it was they, not men, who were responsible for creating an atmosphere of comfort and gentility, or for failing to create it. The image of the ideal middle-class wife was that of the cultured lady of leisure who was also a careful mother and solicitous wife. While they may well have been careful mothers and solicitous wives, the majority of Victorian middle-class women could not have been cultured ladies of leisure: the majority had to manage a household with, at best, one young maid-of-all-work, who remained with them, on average, for less than a year.[19] Inevitably, this would have necessitated their doing a considerable amount of child-care, cleaning and cooking. Because gentility implied that its possessor did not do manual labour, wives in upwardly mobile middle-class households could have difficulty achieving a balance between performing the physical work of the household and creating gentility. If a wife did too much of the housework, she would appear to be a drudge, and no drudge could be a lady: if she did too little, the house would be ill-managed, and she would be considered lazy or inefficient.

If incongruities existed in the role prescribed for the middle-class wife, so also did they exist in the role prescribed for her daughters, as they moved from childhood to adolescence. The image of the ideal middle-class daughter was that of the sheltered flower, a creature whose role in the home was to adorn it and assist in its maintenance. She would never need to learn how to confront the harsh world outside the home, because it was assumed that she would never enter it. Protected first by the income of her father, and then by that of her husband, she would remain throughout her life within the confines of domesticity.

In reality, the nature of most middle-class incomes meant that the role of sheltered flower, of ornament in the household, was unattainable for many, perhaps for the majority, of middle-class girls. Conflicts between the role and the reality could arise within the family itself; daughters, like wives, could experience an incongruence between the need to appear genteel, and the need to perform real work. And shelter within the household could be altogether impossible. Family necessity might compel a middle-class girl to engage in paid work, and should she never marry, she would have to support herself throughout her life.

In this chapter, several aspects of Victorian middle-class family life have been examined, and their effects on middle-class daughters have been analysed. The spiritual qualities of the ideal family were designed to satisfy moral and emotional needs that were produced by the vicissitudes of capitalist competition. In the construction of the image of the family as refuge and shelter, the conception of femininity was of central importance. But, as we saw, it was not only adult women who were supposed to exhibit the qualities necessary for the 'true home'; the cult of domesticity depended not only on an image of the ideal wife, but also on an image of the ideal daughter.

We have also seen that while the cult of domesticity situated family life in a realm removed from the economic struggle, in truth the family structure of the middle class was rooted in economic reality. The private sphere was not, in fact, separate from the public sphere; it reflected it, and the values of upward mobility were expressed through the family as well as being acted out in the public sphere. In the world of business and the professions, the actors were male; in the world of private life they were female. The myth of the separation of spheres created conflicts for middle-class females, for while male competitiveness was approved of, the struggles for upward mobility waged by females were not overtly sanctioned. In reality, the duties of female members of the middle class did include the enhancement of the family's social status, even though the ideology associated with the cult of domesticity barred them from the inevitable competitive struggles involved in that enterprise. These conflicts affected daughters, once they reached adolescence,[20] as much as they affected wives.

Notes

1. For a discussion of the structure of the Victorian middle class, see Geoffrey Best, *Mid-Victorian Britain 1851 – 1875* (New York: Schocken Books, 1972), pp. 84 – 91; Harold Perkin, *The Origins of Modern English Society 1780 – 1880* (London: Routledge and Kegan Paul, 1969), pp. 176 – 217.

2. Samuel Smiles, *Self Help* (Centenary edition; London: John Murray, 1958), p. 36.

3. Walter E. Houghton, *The Victorian Frame of Mind, 1830 – 1870* (New Haven and London: Yale University Press, 1957).

4. Historians who have discussed the cult of domesticity include Walter E. Houghton; Kate Millett, 'The Debate Over Women: Ruskin vs. Mill', in *Suffer and Be Still: Women in the Victorian Age*, ed. by Martha Vicinus (Bloomington: Indiana University Press, 1972), pp. 121 – 39; Barbara Stein Frankle, 'The Genteel Family: High-Victorian Conceptions of Domesticity and Good Behaviour' (unpublished PhD dissertation, University of Wisconsin, 1970); Leonore Davidoff, Jean L'Esperance, and Harold Newby, 'Landscape With Figures: Home and Community in English Society' in *The Rights and Wrongs of Women*, ed. by Juliet Mitchell and Ann Oakley (London: Penguin, 1976), pp. 139 – 75.

5. Coventry Patmore, 'The Angel in the House', in *Poems* (London: George Bell and Sons, 1906), pp. 1 – 145.

6. The Enlightenment origins of the concept of femininity are discussed by Abby Kleinbaum, 'Women in the Age of Light' in *Becoming Visible*, ed. by Renata Bridenthal and Claudia Koonz (Boston: Houghton Mifflin Co., 1977), pp. 217 – 35.

7. Sarah Tytler, 'Girls', *The Mother's Companion*, I (1887), p. 14.

8. John Ruskin, 'Of Queens' Gardens', in *Sesame and Lilies: The Two Paths and The King of the Golden River* (London: J. M. Dent and Sons, 1907), p. 60. *Sesame and Lilies* was first published in 1865.

Barbara Stein Frankle sees the mid-century as the period when the childlike nature of the Victorian woman was most emphasised. Of women's dress she says: 'For nearly two decades woman was consigned to girlish styles connotive of littleness, sweetness and docility.' Frankle, 'The Genteel Family', p. 92.

9. The conflict between feminine innocence, and the dangers of experience that beset Victorian ideology about female nature is discussed in Peter Cominos, 'Innocent Femina Sensualis in Unconscious Conflict', in *Suffer and Be Still*, ed. by Vicinus, pp. 155 – 72.

10. Ruskin, 'Of Queens' Gardens', p. 59.

11. This interlocking of the public and the private spheres is analysed at length of Leonore Davidoff, *The Best Circles: Society, Etiquette and the Season* (London: Croom Helm, 1973).

12. For a discussion of the 'Paraphernalia of Gentility', see J.A. Banks, *Prosperity and Parenthood: A Study of Family Planning Among the Victorian Middle Classes* (London: Routledge and Kegan Paul, 1954), pp. 86 – 102.

13. On the rituals, see Houghton, *The Victorian Frame of Mind*, p. 341. On the upper-middle-class nursery, see Jonathan Gathorne-Hardy, *The Rise and Fall of the British Nanny* (London: Hodder and Stoughton, 1972), pp. 57 – 9 and pp. 126 – 31, and Theresa McBride, ' "As the Twig is Bent": The Victorian Nanny', in *The Victorian Family*, ed. by Anthony Wohl (London: Croom Helm, 1978), pp. 44 – 58.

14. Banks, *Prosperity and Parenthood*, pp. 48 – 69.

15. 'It was the Englishman's practicality that found in the suburbs the solution to the essentially middle-class problem of escaping the snares of the city without losing control of it. It was his romantic idyll of pastoral bliss that wove in and out of all his plans for taking to the suburbs.' H.J. Dyos and D.A. Reeder, 'Slums and Suburbs' in *The Victorian City: Images and Realities*, ed. by H. J. Dyos and Michael Wolff, I (London and Boston: Routledge and Kegan Paul, 1973), p. 370.

16. Banks, *Prosperity and Parenthood*, p. 76.

17. Patricia Branca, *Silent Sisterhood: Middle-Class Women in the Victorian Home* (London: Croom Helm, 1975), pp. 39 – 45.

18. Banks, *Prosperity and Parenthood*, p. 76; Branca, *Silent Sisterhood*, p. 56.

19. Theresa M. McBride, *The Domestic Revolution: The Modernisation of Household Service in England and France 1820 – 1920*, (New York: Holmes and Meier Publishers, Inc., 1976), pp. 74 – 6.

20. Throughout this work, the word 'adolescence' has been used for the life stage between puberty and adulthood, even though it was not often used during the Victorian period itself. The concept of adolescence was developing during the period; gradually, a conception of maturation as a process that should be measured by rates of physiological and psychological development was replacing the older view, in which youth was a status category. Because views were changing, 'girlhood' itself was defined in an equivocal way throughout the period. If used as a status category, the girlhood of a middle-class girl could be perceived as continuing until her marriage — perhaps until well into her twenties. Only gradually was this definition being replaced by one in which girlhood was deemed to have been completed when the individual had matured, physically and psychologically, into an adult. For an excellent discussion of changing perceptions of male youth see John R. Gillis, *Youth and History: Tradition and Change in European Age Relations 1770 – Present* (New York: Academic Press, 1974).

Chapter 2

THE VICTORIAN MIDDLE-CLASS GIRL:
AN OVERVIEW

Because of the great variations over the century, any picture of a typical middle-class family or typical middle-class girlhood must be both limited and speculative. None the less, such a composite picture will serve as a useful framework for the subsequent questions with which this study is concerned. In this chapter, therefore, an outline of the demography of middle-class families will be presented, along with a general account of what is known about the child care practices of middle-class Victorians, and about the education, training and employment of middle-class girls.[1]

Family size, the first factor to be considered, varied markedly over time, with the significant changes occurring in the 1870s. In the period from the 1830s to the 1870s, the number of children born to middle-class families was between five and seven; by the end of the century, it was between two and three.[2] Along with the change in family size, there were changes in infant and especially in child mortality. At the beginning of the period, infant and child mortality for all classes was high. After 1871, however, there was a decrease in child mortality, and by the 1890s infant mortality as well showed a decrease.[3]

Given these differences, one can contrast the experience of a child born in 1830 with a child born in 1880. The child born in 1830 would, very likely, have had five or more siblings. But it would also have been likely that not all of them would have lived to adulthood. Thus, a child would have been surrounded by sisters and brothers, but also by death. A child born in 1830 would also have had a much greater risk than presently prevails of losing one or both parents before reaching adulthood, both because life expectancy was lower than it is today, and because middle-class Victorians married relatively late, the average age for males being the early thirties, and for females, the late twenties.[4]

In contrast, the pattern of the late-Victorian years more closely resembles the pattern that prevails today. For middle-class people, the family was becoming a smaller, but at the same time, a more stable unit. A child born in 1880 would, on average, have had fewer siblings than one born in 1830, but there would have been less chance of losing one or more of them through death. The late-Victorian middle-class family, in contrast to the early-Victorian family, would thus have been considerably less subject to fragility and impermanence.

While social class caused the greatest variations in mortality rates in the nineteenth century, sex was also a factor. After the age of five, it appears that a girl's chances of death were greater than those of a male child. Male mortality rates were higher in infancy, and in the first years of childhood, but after the age of five, the greater endurance of the female infant was offset by other factors; from early childhood until the mid-thirties, female death rates exceeded those of males. Moreover, there is evidence that these sex differences in mortality were even more marked for middle-class females than they were for girls of the working classes.[5]

This difference in the mortality rates of males and females may have been caused by the female's greater susceptibility to tuberculosis.[6] A variety of factors could have been responsible for this greater susceptibility. In general, middle-class females led a more sedentary life than males, and were more confined to the indoors. Confinement in the home was more unhealthy in the nineteenth century than it is today, if only because the reliance on open coal fires for heat would have rendered the air unhealthy. Female clothing may also have played a part in greater female susceptibility to disease, since it was heavier and more confining than that of males. And there may, as well, have been psychological stresses related to the female role that increased a girl's chances of dying from a disease like tuberculosis, a disease in which the patient's emotional state can be a contributing factor.[7]

When we turn to a consideration of the kind of care that was given to infants and young children in Victorian middle-class families, the variation between levels of middle-class life is more noticeable than variations over time. Major changes in middle-class childrearing patterns had begun to occur in the eighteenth century, when Enlightenment thought had generated a concern with child psychology, and a recognition of the importance of childhood experience. This new outlook had affected only a minority of families by the second half of the eighteenth century, but from that time on, right through to the end of the Victorian period, its influence increased. The pattern itself had been established, however, by the early nineteenth century.[8]

The influence of the new outlook rendered suspect certain child-rearing practices that had been followed by middle-class and upper-class families for centuries. For instance, the practice of employing wet-nurses came under increasing attack, as both unhealthy and psychologically damaging to the child. While some families did employ wet-nurses in the Victorian period, the attacks on the practice were having an effect, and unless the mother was physically unable to do so, it was usual during the Victorian period for women at all social ranks to breast-feed their children.[9]

However, while upper-middle-class Victorian mothers would likely have breast-fed their babies, they would not have been likely to be their children's main caretaker. Throughout the Victorian period, the most notable difference in child care styles between families at the lower levels of the middle class, and those of the higher levels, was the extent to which the more affluent employed domestic servants to take over the day-to-day tasks of caring for infants and children. While it is true that the remote and harsh style of parenting that had been prevalent well into the eighteenth century was giving way to a style that emphasised the importance of kindness and closeness, it was still considered appropriate and usual for middle-class families who could afford them to employ domestics to look after their children.[10]

The more affluent the family, the more servants would be employed, and the more removed the life of the children would be from that of the adults in the family. Both mother and father might be concerned with, and involved in their children's moral and intellectual upbringing. But in an upper middle-class family in which a nurse and assistant nursery maids were employed and in which a separate nursery wing was provided for the children, contact between parents and children had to be limited. Characteristically, throughout the Victorian period, the children of upper-middle-class families lived in a separate world, and they saw their parents only in a formal setting and for brief periods.[11]

Such a pattern of child care was possible only for a small segment of the middle class, although because it was a feature of the family pattern of the elite, it did have an influence on the entire class. For the majority of middle-class families, in which at most one or two servants were employed, the chief caretaker of the children was the mother herself. In the event of her death it was usual for an older sister or aunt to take over the role. In large families, older daughters were in any case involved in the care of the younger children.[12]

There is little general evidence of difference in the physical treatment of boys and girls in middle-class families in infancy and early childhood. Certainly, few such differences were institutionalised or overtly acknowledged as part of general practice. This does not, of course, rule out the probability that there were unacknowledged or unrecognised differences in the way in which female and male infants and small children were fed or physically handled, but the evidence that would allow us to assert with confidence that such differences did exist is not available.[13]

Sex differences played more of a part in determining the toys and books that were provided for children. There were toys that were designed for children of both sexes: for example, the Noah's Ark,[14] popular as a Sunday toy, was designed with both boys and girls in mind, but toys like model railways or dolls were made for one sex or the other. If she had brothers, a girl might play with their toys, but these would still be seen as boys' toys. Many Victorian books and periodicals for children were written to be read by both sexes; others were designed for girls or boys alone. But even when written for children of both sexes, Victorian children's literature emphasised sex differences, and should be seen as one of the period's main agencies for inculcating sex role differentiation.[15]

The proliferation of toys and books designed especially for children is another manifestation of the increased awareness of the importance of intellectual and psychological development in childhood that had its roots in eighteenth-century thought. Some middle-class parents had begun to provide educational toys and specially designed books for their children by the late eighteenth century,[16] and over the course of the nineteenth century, the variety of such toys and books increased and their distribution widened. This development contributed to the construction of a world of childhood experience that became more and more separate from that of adults. Not only was it separate from the adult world, within it, the gap between the sexes widened. For instance, the numbers of periodicals designed especially for boys or girls increased in the last three decades of the century, and their sex-related differences became more marked. In the character of the fiction included, in the didactic tales, and even in the illustrations, these publications presented to their readers separate worlds of girlhood and boyhood.[17]

In the Victorian middle-class family, the main agency through which moral values were inculcated was religion. Religious belief was a central feature of Victorian middle-class life.[18] It was, moreover, an essential part of the fabric of family life. Middle-class Victorians attended religious services on Sunday, but just as important, both for maintaining religious belief and for strengthening family solidarity, were such rituals as family prayers and bible readings, customs that were observed in many middle-class households.

While the great majority of middle-class Victorians were practising Christians, there were those for whom religious belief was essentially a matter of outward form, and there were those for whom it was the centre of their lives. During the period, most of the latter can be classi-fied as evangelicals, whether they were Dissenters or members of the Church of England.[19] Although the social distinctions between members of the Established Church and Dissenters were of impor-tance, from the point of view of religious belief, that distinction was less significant than that between those who were outward observers, and those who were deeply devout.

In the middle-class family, whether religious belief was a matter of outward form, or a matter of intense inward concern, religious instruction began as soon as a child could talk. Children were taught the fundamental beliefs of Christianity both directly and indirectly. Even if it did not deal explicitly with religion, much of the literature designed expressly for children was suffused with it. While a religious orientation was more noticeable in the early than it was in the later Victorian decades, it remained present right through the century. Thus, from the primer from which a child learned to read and from storybooks, as well as from Bible readings and devotional literature, children imbibed a religious outlook.[20] They early became familiar with stories in the Bible, were taught a morality centred on self-sacrifice and duty, were inculcated with an awareness of their own mortality, and were encouraged to recognise the need for salvation. More stress was put on the need for salvation, and on the importance of a conversion experience in evangelical households, than in house-holds where religion was primarily a matter of ritual; in inculcating religious belief in girls, more stress was put on the importance of the duty of self-sacrifice than was the case with boys.

It was primarily through the rhythms of everyday life that a Vic-torian middle-class girl learned the significance of her gender and of her social position. Moral precepts were inculcated through everyday experience, but also through the medium of religious instruction and observance. Formal education was also part of the middle-class girl's experience in the Victorian period, although its place in the average girl's life changed over the course of the Victorian decades, as a new pattern of girls' education began to emerge in the 1860s.

In the early and mid-Victorian periods, the majority of middle-class girls received all or most of their education at home, and their main teacher was a family member, usually their mother.[21] Their earliest lessons — in which their brothers, as well, would share — began when a child was about three years old. By the early-Victorian period, an adult who wished to teach children in the home had sources to go to for advice, and specially designed materials to use. There were, for instance, primers available for teaching reading. Reading would be the first skill taught, but arithmetic would soon be introduced, and for girls, instruction in needlework would begin at a very early age as well.

Such instruction was integrated into the child's day. Because there was no uniform system for the instruction of young children, and its history, like the history of other aspects of intimate family life, is therefore hidden, it is difficult to generalise, but typically, formal instruction would have taken up about an hour in the morning, and an hour in the afternoon, when children were between the ages of three and eight.

While the mother was the usual, and generally considered the natural, teacher of her children, frequently an older sister would teach the younger children. Indeed, in the early and mid-Victorian period, it was not uncommon for middle-class families to send the eldest daughter to school in her early teens. On her return home at sixteen or seventeen, she would then undertake the instruction of her younger sisters and brothers.[22]

In some households, a governess would be employed. Although much has been written about the governess, in fact, only a limited number of families ever employed one, and presumably they were upper-middle-class and upper-class families. Meagre as the salary of a governess could be, even £30 would have been a prohibitive annual outlay for the lower-middle or even the middle-class family.[23]

Assessing the quality of instruction provided by governesses is as difficult as assessing that provided by a mother, sister, father or brother. As was the case with family members, the governess's own education and her aptitude for teaching would determine the quality of instruction she could offer. As a general rule, neither governesses nor mothers received formal training in teaching because such training was not yet considered a requirement for the task.

Most historians who have written about the education of middle-class girls from middle childhood through adolescence in the period before 1850 have assumed that their instruction, whether received in the home, or in school, was uniformly inadequate. Girls, it is assumed,

were given a superficial training in showy 'accomplishments': a
smattering of French, music and drawing, and fancy needlework.
Their acquaintance with more solid subjects like history or geography
is assumed to have been meagre, and their training in basic skills like
spelling and arithmetic was also assumed to have been inadequate.
Historians generally are in agreement that girls did not learn the
classical languages (the hallmark of the educated male) or higher
mathematics.[24]

While these assumptions about the intellectual poverty of middle-
class girls' education in the first half of the nineteenth century have
some foundation, they are not entirely accurate, nor do they tell the
whole story. The most noteworthy feature of middle-class girls' education in the first half of the nineteenth century was its variability. It is
possible to describe an average education, but it must always be kept
in mind that in a situation where there was no standardisation, the
average or typical has limited meaning. While the education of some
girls was completely neglected, a minority received an education that
was both rigorous and extensive. In households where learning was
valued, some early-Victorian girls learned to write, by the middle
years of childhood, in a polished adult style, and read books that
would, in the twentieth century, be considered unsuitable for
children. These comments, made in her journal by a girl who was just
twelve years old, will serve as an example of the level of literacy sometimes achieved by early-Victorian girls:

> Till lately I have never read Spenser, and therefore was not
> personally acquainted with his beauties. Neither do I mean to say
> that now I have read his 'Faerie Queane'; but having accidentally
> met with an extract from his 'Hymn of Heavenly Love', a long
> poem, I went to Papa's study and read the whole poem, which is
> most exquisitely beautiful, and perhaps equal to anything Milton
> ever wrote.[25]

While Emily Shore, the girl who wrote that comment, was unusually
gifted, her experiences were not unique. Many early-Victorian girls
received a first-rate education in 'papa's study'.

That the lack of standardisation in girls' education could, in some
cases, produce better results than the more uniform system that
emerged as a result of the work of the late nineteenth-century educational reformers, was recognised at the time, even by some of the
reformers themselves. As one such reformer wrote:

It was not a good life for the many, the Early Victorian. For the favoured few, it was beautiful. Read *The Gurneys of Earlham* . . . . or a dozen other biographies, and see the splendour of that mysterious thing, a good education, and how it can surround and draw out the very best in a young and growing mind. There were no classes, no herding girls together, but the best was effected for each one singly . . . .[26]

While home education played the most important role in early-Victorian middle-class girls' education, there were, as well, boarding and day schools for girls. It was often assumed by nineteenth-century commentators on the subject that upper-class and upper-middle-class girls were educated at home, by governesses, and that day or boarding schools were used only by the middle and lower-middle class. In fact, some upper-middle-class girls were sent to boarding schools, although such schools were not used extensively by people of high status during the early-Victorian period.[27]

Early-Victorian girls' schools were almost as variable as early-Victorian home education. There were a few large schools for girls,[28] but the typical girls' school during this period was not a school at all in the twentieth-century sense of the word. It was an 'establishment' catering for a small number of girls, run out of a private home, usually by one woman, with two or three assistants. These schools seldom lasted a long time and they were not licensed by any authority. It is therefore impossible to know how many such establishments existed, how many girls attended them, or how long the average pupil remained in attendance.[29]

It is, however, possible to make some generalisations. One can say with certainty that, until quite late in the nineteenth century, boarding school attendance was not a regular part of the average middle-class girl's experience. Only if a girl were orphaned, or if there were other circumstances that made it difficult for her to live at home, did a girl attend boarding school from childhood through adolescence. Usually if a girl were sent to school, it would be for a period of one or two years, when she was in her early teens. Girls were frequently sent to boarding school to mark the transition from childhood to adult life, the school years thus acting as a *rite-de-passage* in the socialisation process.

Some rough generalisations can be made about types of girls' boarding schools in the early-Victorian period. There was, first of all, the really deplorable school, the kind of school that Charles Dickens satirised in his portrait of Dotheboys Hall in *Nicholas Nickelby*. Dotheboys Hall is a boys' school, but such places existed for girls as well. Their purpose is simply stated: they enabled those responsible for unwanted children to get rid of them in a cheap, convenient, relatively respectable manner. It may have been the demographic pattern of the period that produced a demand for such schools. Victorian children were orphaned or half-orphaned more frequently than in the twentieth century, and it appears that often the parent, step-parent or guardian wanted to be rid of the child.[30] Girls were also sent to boarding schools for long periods, even from families where both parents were alive, if the parents found the girl unmanageable.

The second type of early-Victorian girls' school was the religious establishments. These could be Anglican or Dissenting, but in either case they would be managed by a proprietor who was a woman of deep religious conviction. In such schools the religious intensity was high and religious experience, crowned by 'conversion', appears to have been a chief purpose of the school. Girls raised in deeply religious families were frequently sent away to boarding school for a crucial year or two in early adolescence, and would there undergo the experience of conversion.[31]

Aside from the really bad school, whose purpose was to serve as a dumping ground for unwanted children, and the religious school, no other clearly discernible type of girls' boarding school existed. The great majority of such schools were establishments whose main purpose was to teach the girl to function socially by providing her with the 'accomplishments' necessary for a lady. Such schools could be good, bad or indifferent in the quality of their instruction, in the care they gave to the girls and in their physical environment. They ranged in price from those that could be afforded only by the well-to-do, to those that a middle-class or lower-middle-class parent could afford.[32]

The curriculum offered in most such schools was designed to provide a basic English education, with exposure to general knowledge in the areas of literature, history and geography. French was also standard along with music and drawing, although in many schools these latter skills would be provided only as 'extras'. Girls' schools did not normally teach the classical languages or higher mathematics; and one can thus assume that those girls who studied these subjects were educated at home.

Nineteenth-century commentators and twentieth-century historians of girls' education have assumed that the level of instruction in these schools was uniformly low. While this assessment was largely correct, it is, as with home education in the early-Victorian period, a mistake to think that all middle-class girls' schools were dreary and inadequate. There were a number of good girls' schools throughout the century, and by the 1840s some of them resembled in the design of their curriculum and in the level of their teaching the schools that would be established a few decades later, by the educational reformers.[33]

Seen from the point of view of its intrinsic educational value, the quality of girls' education in the early-Victorian period varied widely, from excellent to deplorable. However, the function that education was designed to serve in preparing a girl for life did not vary. Whether they were educated to be learned, or whether they barely learned how to read, most middle-class girls were not educated in a way that would prepare them for the world of gainful employment. Whether they were educated at home or in school, it was assumed that their future lay in a domestic setting. Thus the purpose of any formal education they received was different from the purpose of the education that was given to their brothers. Middle-class males were educated in a way that was designed to prepare them for a life of competition and achievement. For their sisters, achievement was not a central goal. A girl might become a learned lady, or a serious musician or painter, but if she pursued such endeavours, it was to be for her own private satisfaction. As long as she did not violate the norms of femininity or gentility, she was free to pursue such activities, but in her case they would not be seen as a testing ground for further achievement.

In the late-Victorian period, middle-class girls' education underwent a transformation. The changes, which have their origins in the 1850s but which became visible only in the 1860s, have more to do with the development of a new definition of the purpose of middle-class girls' education than with changes in its quality. The main achievement of the educational reform movement was to give credence to the value of an organised, standardised, competitive school experience for girls. The reformers often focused their attention on curriculum reform but it was, in fact, a secondary issue.

The condition of middle-class girls' education was brought to public notice in the 1860s because of the attention paid to the subject by the Schools Inquiry Commission, the Royal Commission appointed in 1864 to enquire into the state of middle-class education. The Commission, under pressure from concerned reformers, decided to include the subject of girls' education in its investigations. The Commissioners took the radical step of hearing testimony from some of the reforming women educators who had been active since the 1850s. Witnesses before the Commission included Frances Mary Buss, Headmistress of the North London Collegiate School, the single most influential pioneering girls' secondary school of the nineteenth century, Dorothea Beale, Headmistress of Cheltenham Ladies' College, a boarding school catering to upper-class and upper-middle-class girls, and Emily Davies, the founder of Girton College.

The evidence given by these women clearly demonstrates both the radical and the conservative qualities of the educational reform movement. The reformers insisted that it was essential to standardise girls' education and to bring it out of the private arena.[34] They testified to the importance of introducing uniform standards and defined goals. While the advocacy of such measures did involve a break with Victorian notions of femininity, with its insistence that females be kept strictly sequestered in the private, non-competitive sphere, their evidence also reflects their basic acceptance of many Victorian beliefs about women's nature. For instance, when defending the use of competitive examinations, the educators were always careful to add the proviso that, in no instance, should girls be 'overworked' or 'overstrained'.[35] Again, all the women witnesses acknowledged that girls ought to be taught domestic skills.[36] Finally their arguments for improving the education of middle-class girls were more frequently based on reasons of necessity — they argued that many middle-class females had to support themselves, and therefore needed to be prepared to do so — or on reasons that accorded well with Victorian views of woman's role. They argued, for example, that well-educated women made better wives and mothers than those who were poorly educated.

The Schools Inquiry Commission Report received considerable public attention and the reformers used the interest that was generated to further their cause. The Report, the admission of girl candidates to the Cambridge, and then the Oxford, Local Examinations and the first steps that were taken towards the admission of women to university mark the 1860s as the turning point in the history of middle-class girls' education in England. In the 1870s and in succeeding decades a new type of middle-class girls' school was established. Schools like those founded by the Girls' Public Day School Company led the way, along with High Schools established in London and in provincial towns.[37] Such schools were 'public' in nature, and formed the most radical break with the past. In addition, many private girls' schools underwent alteration, although it should be noted that girls' schools that conformed to the early-Victorian model continued to exist well into the twentieth-century.[38]

How did the new schools differ from the typical 'Young Ladies' Academy' of the early and mid-Victorian period? First of all they had a curriculum that was modelled on that of a boys' school. The pupils usually learned Latin, sometimes Greek, mathematics, history and the sciences. But of more significance than these curricular changes was the fact that, in the new type of girls' school, classroom work was organised and goal-directed. The students took tests, competed for school prizes, and prepared for public examinations. In addition, there was a sharp break with tradition when it came to the internal organisation of the school.[39] The traditional Young Ladies' Academy, in the words of the Schools Inquiry Commissioners, was 'intended to be more a home than a school.'[40] The new girls' school was designed to be a public institution. At these schools, the girls played competitive games, had their day structured according to a rigid routine, and at some schools, a system of prefects or monitors was introduced, in emulation of the pattern established in the mid-Victorian boys' public or grammar school. The school thus became an institution in which a girl's ability to establish herself in an environment very different from that of her home was developed and tested.[41]

The schools were not, however, exactly like boys' schools. At the North London Collegiate, which was a model for many other schools, there was, for example, a weekly 'Dorcas' meeting, at which all the girls were required to do some sewing. And while the new sort of girls' school encouraged girls to be physically hardy and to develop the temperamental qualities needed in order to function in an impersonal and disciplined atmosphere, they also insisted that their girls exhibit 'ladylike' behaviour. In a variety of ways they encouraged the acceptance of many aspects of Victorian femininity.[42]

The most significant difference between the new girls' school and the old, is that the new school was not designed to be merely a brief phase in a girl's life. The reformers believed that girls should attend school regularly throughout their childhood. And while it cannot be stated with certainty what proportion of middle-class girls did attend school regularly in the late nineteenth century, available evidence does indicate that, by the 1890s, school attendance had become an integral part of life for many more girls than it had been in the 1850s.[43]

Over the course of the Victorian period, occupational patterns for middle-class girls in late adolescence underwent changes that paralleled those in education. In the early-Victorian period, the cult of domesticity had its greatest influence. It was assumed that daughters, like wives, would not engage in paid employment, unless dire necessity compelled them to do so. They were expected to occupy themselves within the household of their parents until they married, and in the early and mid-Victorian decades, this was, indeed, the usual pattern.

A grown-up daughter's years as a 'daughter-at-home' could extend from her mid-teens until her middle or late twenties. The way in which she was expected to occupy her time depended on the family's income. In upper-middle-class households, daughters would learn to participate in the social and charitable occupations with which adult women at this social level were involved. Girls would assist their mothers in dispensing charity to the poor; in religious households, they would take on such obligations as teaching in Sunday School. They would be involved in the rituals of Society, and within the privacy of the home they would participate in the formal routines of family life. They were expected to adorn the household with their skills in music, painting and fancy needlework. At the lower end of the middle-class spectrum, the adolescent daughter might perform some of the functions just described, but in most middle-class and lower-middle-class families, the daughters of the house would be engaged in actual housework: sewing, cooking, even cleaning, in addition to helping with the care of younger siblings, if they had them.

Although the ideology associated with femininity was so pervasive in the early-Victorian period that few were able to recognise the fact, the pattern of daughter-at-home was not financially feasible in many middle-class families. In lower-middle-class families, especially if there were a number of daughters, there would be pressure for daughters, as well as sons, to contribute to their own financial support by mid-adolescence. And while marriage was, in theory, the only acceptable adult role for a middle-class woman, in fact, not all middle-class women did marry.[44]

The possibilities open to a girl whose family could not support her before marriage, or to a woman who never married were bleak indeed, in the early-Victorian period. She could either attempt to support herself, or become a dependent in the household of a relative. While the latter alternative was a respectable choice, a woman who was forced to take it could find herself in the position of an unpaid servant. If she turned to gainful employment her possibilities were extremely limited, if she were not to lose all claim to gentility. Working as a governess was the most acceptable occupation for the middle-class girl or woman, because gentility was a prime requisite for the job, and it was work undertaken in a domestic setting. As an occupation, however, it was poorly paid, and offered no security.[45] Needlework involved more loss of caste than governessing, and could be equally unattractive, in terms of rates of pay, hours worked, and security.

In the mid-century period, the plight of the middle-class girl or woman who had to support herself was brought to the forefront of public consciousness. From the 1840s, articles in the periodical press began to discuss the problem of the 'distressed gentlewoman', and by the 1850s, an organised movement to improve employment opportunities for middle-class girls and women was underway. Both it, and the related movement to reform girls' education, were part of a number of overlapping concerns and causes that made up the nineteenth-century movement for women's emancipation.[46] Reformers worked to change social attitudes and to remove structural barriers. They had to convince Victorian public opinion that some middle-class girls and women both wanted and needed to work, and that the training and occupational opportunities afforded them should be widened. By the 1870s, the employment patterns of middle-class girls and women had, indeed, widened. Was the 'widening sphere', as it has been called, a result of the work of reformers? An analysis of the nature of these broadened occupational choices indicates that while the reformers did help to shape attitudes, the widespread changes resulted from a general alteration in the structure of the economy.[47]

The 'widening sphere' of female employment as it affected the middle class involved first of all an alteration in the traditional female occupation of teaching. In the teaching profession generally, a process of 'feminisation' took place over the middle decades of the century. In 1861, females comprised almost three-quarters of teachers in England.[48] While the greatest increase among all teachers and the most significant area of expansion of opportunities for women occurred in the area of elementary schoolteaching, only a small number of middle-class women entered this occupation in the Victorian period. More important for middle-class women was the demand for teachers for middle-class girls' schools. The schoolmistress in a middle-class girls' school can be said to be the direct descendent of the early-Victorian governess, and the contrast between her position and that of the governess underlines the significance of the changes in the employment patterns of middle-class women that took place in the middle and later Victorian decades. Whereas the governess had been untrained, her sole qualification being her position as a 'distressed gentlewoman', the late-nineteenth-century schoolmistress in one of the new girls' schools sometimes had both a university education and teacher training. Although she did not command a large salary, she did represent a new type: she was a genuine professional woman.[49]

By the late nineteenth century, nursing had become the other major avenue of professional employment for middle-class women. The character of this occupation was completely transformed in the nineteenth century, as the structure of medicine changed. Nursing the sick in a domestic setting had traditionally been one of the functions of females of all social classes, both as wives and as daughters, but nursing for pay had been an occupation undertaken only by working-class women. Even for working-class women, the occupation had not been a respectable one; nurses, it was assumed, were dirty, often drunken, women who took up nursing because they could find no other work. The reforms brought about from the middle of the nineteenth century transformed nursing into an occupation for which rigorous, organised training was required, and one which afforded possibilities, at distinctly different levels, for both middle-class and working-class women.[50]

While the numbers of teachers and nurses did increase considerably in the period between the 1870s and the first World War, they were of less importance numerically than 'white collar' workers. These occupations, which have become the chief employers of females in all industrial capitalist twentieth-century economies, began to develop their twentieth-century character towards the end of the last century.[51]

Office clerk and retail sales clerk were the most important of these occupations. In the early nineteenth century, English business units had been small, the typical organisation being the family partnership. Relatively few individuals were employed by such firms, and those who were hired were presumed to have some chance of advancement to ownership themselves. In the days before elementary education was universal, the skills of literacy, arithmetic and penmanship that such individuals possessed were much more highly regarded than they would be later, when their acquisition became widespread. Accordingly, most employees in business firms were male and middle class.

By the last third of the century, the structure of English business had changed. Firms were larger, more personnel was needed, and the work they did had altered. New technology was introduced — like the typewriter — and the work became both more monotonous at the same time that it offered fewer chances for advancement. As these occupations took on a proletarian character, females began to enter them in significant numbers.

Before the turn of the century, the number of female office clerks had begun to increase, but it was in the area of retail sales that the last decades of the century witnessed the greatest increase. This occupation in fact attracted more females than any other among those that can be characterised as middle class. Conditions of work for sales clerks, either those who worked in large department stores, or those who worked in smaller establishments, were not good. Hours of work were long, working conditions were uncomfortable and often unhealthy, the pay was poor, and the job offered little security. Yet it was this occupation that was the most important single employer of girls and young women who were either middle class, or who had middle-class aspirations.

In assessing the importance of the changes that occurred in the structure of middle-class female employment in the late nineteenth and early twentieth centuries, one historian who has made an extensive study of the subject has concluded that the gains made by women were significant:

> In the mid-nineteenth century, ladies who had to work for their living were a surplus and depressed minority, who were pitied and who pitied themselves. By 1914, middle-class working women, a respected and self-respecting group, were an essential part of the country's labour force.[52]

When one compares their status and earning power with males of the same social class, this optimistic assessment appears questionable: for most middle-class girls and women seeking employment, the 'widening sphere' meant that they could become underpaid sales clerks, nurses, teachers or 'lady typewriters'. But while they remained underpaid, it is true that in comparison to those of their mothers and grandmothers the opportunities for late-Victorian girls were greater. Even an occupation like retail sales clerking offered a young woman more independence than had been attainable by the governess or dressmaker of an earlier generation.

It is certain that, as the structure of employment underwent these alterations, the normal pattern for middle-class girls between mid-adolescence and marriage changed. By the end of the nineteenth century, it had become acceptable and even expected that a middle-class daughter would seek employment during this time of her life. She might even move out of her parents' home and live independently. It is true that even by the 1890s, some daughters, especially if they came from upper-middle-class families, did grow up in an atmosphere in which they were prepared only for domesticity; on marriage they went, as their mothers had done before them, from their father's home to that of their husband having never left the 'private sphere'. But, by the end of the century, this was a waning pattern; in increasing numbers, middle-class daughters were receiving an education that prepared them for paid work, and were spending several years before marriage working in the 'public sphere'.

Notes

1. Harold Perkin, *The Origins of Modern English Society*, and Geoffrey Best, *Mid-Victorian Britain*, help to place the middle-class family in a wider context.

2. D.V. Glass, *Population Policies and Movements in Europe* (Reprint edn; New York: A.M. Kelley, 1967), pp. 70 – 5.

3. Elizabeth Raine Lomax, 'Advances in Pediatrics and in Infant Care in Nineteenth Century England' (unpublished PhD dissertation, University of California, Los Angeles, 1972), p. 259.

4. Patricia Branca, *Silent Sisterhood*, p. 4, p. 20, n. 12.

5. Sheila Ryan Johannson, 'Sex and Death in Victorian England: An Examination of Age-and-Sex-Specific Death Rates, 1840 – 1910', in *A Widening Sphere: Changing Roles of Victorian Women*, ed. by Martha Vicinus (Bloomington: Indiana University Press, 1977), pp. 163 – 81.

6. Ibid., p. 169.

7. Ibid., p. 170.

8. Lawrence Stone, *The Family, Sex and Marriage in England: 1500 – 1800* (London: Weidenfeld and Nicolson, 1977), pp. 405 – 15.

9. The extent of continued use of wet-nurses in Victorian England can only be estimated, but there is agreement among historians that the practice had declined. See the discussion of the question in Branca, *Silent Sisterhood*, pp. 100 – 4.

10. On the use of domestics for child care, see Jonathan Gathorne-Hardy, *The Rise and Fall of the British Nanny*; Theresa McBride, ' "As the Twig is Bent" ', in Anthony Wohl (ed.), *The Victorian Family*.

11. Gathorne-Hardy, *Rise and Fall of the British Nanny*, p. 77. Individual examples of the phenomenon of separation are discussed in chapters 7 – 9.

12. Evidence for the role that elder daughters played comes principally from individual examples. See chapters 7 – 9.

13. Evidence for the probability that Victorian parents did make distinctions can be drawn by analogy from twentieth-century studies, which indicate that parents today make such distinctions without realising that they are doing so. See I.H. Frieze *et al.*, *Women and Sex Roles: A Social Psychological Perspective* (New York: W.W. Norton & Co, 1978), p. 74. For a specific example of a nineteenth-century mother perceiving femininity early in a daughter's life, see Elizabeth Gaskell's comments on her daughter Marianne, then a year old: 'She is very *feminine*, I think, in her quietness. . .' Elizabeth Gaskell, *'My Diary: The early years of my daughter Marianne* (London: Privately printed by Clement Shorter, 1923), p. 15.

14. For the Noah's Ark, see for example, 'Reminiscences of Edith Allen (later

Postgate)', Typescript, North London Collegiate School Archives, Edith Allen was a pupil at the North London Collegiate from 1874 to 1882.

15. The earliest periodicals were produced by evangelicals, to inculcate Christian virtue in children: for example, *The Child's Companion or Sunday Scholar's Reward* (London: Printed for the Religious Tract Society) began publication in 1824. It was designed for both sexes, but the contents encouraged sex differences. This periodical was read by middle-class and upper-class children: some 1,834 issues in the Osborne Collection of Early Children's Literature bear the pencilled initials F.N. (Florence Nightingale) on their front covers. On the development of children's periodicals in the period 1850 and following, see Gillian Avery, *Childhood's Pattern: A study of the heroes and heroines of children's fiction 1770 – 1950* (London: Hodder and Stoughton, 1975) and Patrick Dunae, 'Boy's Own Paper: Origins and Editorial Policies', *The Private Library*, second series, IX (Winter 1976).

16. Lawrence Stone, *The Family, Sex and Marriage*, p. 411.

17. A good contrast is provided by the fiction that appeared in two popular periodicals, both produced by the Religious Tract Society: the *Boy's Own Paper*, which began publication in 1879 and the *Girl's Own Paper*, which first appeared in 1880. The *Boy's Own* contained tales of adventure and stories about sport, whereas the *Girl's Own* contained tales with a moral lesson, tales about self-sacrificing daughters.

18. On the importance of religion for the middle-class family, see, for example, W.L. Burn, *The Age of Equipoise: A Study of the Mid-Victorian Generation* (London: Unwin University Books, 1968), pp. 46 – 7.

19. For the evangelicals, see Charles Smythe, 'The Evangelical Discipline' and Gordon Rupp, 'Evangelicalism of the Nonconformists', in *Ideas and Beliefs of the Victorians: An Historical Revaluation of the Victorian Age* (New York: E.P. Dutton and Co., 1966), pp. 97 – 112.

20. Avery, *Childhood's Pattern*, pp. 52 – 120 *passim*.

21. The evidence for the kind of education girls in middle-class families received is piecemeal and speculative, but there is agreement that daughters were not sent regularly to school in the early and mid-century period: Joan N. Burstyn, *Victorian Education and the Ideal of Womanhood* (London: Croom Helm, 1980), pp. 22 – 4; Branca, *Silent Sisterhood*, p. 45; Joyce Senders Pedersen, 'The Reform of Women's Secondary and Higher Education: Institutional Change and Social Values in Mid and Late-Victorian England', *History of Education Quarterly*, 19, 1 (1979), p. 63.

Evidence from the school register books of the Girls' Public Day School Co. schools indicates that, quite late in the century, even for girls attending such 'modern' schools as these, the pattern of home education in childhood still persisted. For example, the Register Book of the Kensington High School for the years 1874 – 88 shows that, with a mean age at entry of 10.8 years, 36 per cent of the girls had had no previous formal schooling. For the years 1888 – 98, with a mean age at entry of 9.2, 44.5 per cent had had no previous formal schooling. Register Book, Kensington High School, Girls' Public Day School Trust Archives.

22. For positive evidence about the nature of home education, individual examples are our only source of direct information. As one example, there is the education of Frances Ridley Havergal, born in 1836, the daughter of a Church of England clergyman. Frances did go to school, briefly, in her teen years, but her early education was conducted within the home, and it was undertaken by an elder sister:

> We were all taught to read early, and to repeat, by our dear mother; but as I had now left school I undertook this charming little pupil: teaching her reading, spelling, and a rhyme (generally out of Jane Taylor's), for half an hour every morning, and in the afternoon twenty or thirty stitches of patchwork, with a very short text to repeat next morning at breakfast. When three years old, she could read easy books. . .

Maria Vernon Graham Havergal, *Memorials of Frances Ridley Havergal* (London: James Nisbet & Co., 1880), p. 4.

23. For numbers of governesses, see Wanda F. Neff, *Victorian Working Women: An Historical and Literary Study of Women in British Industries and Professions 1832 – 1850* (Reprint edn; London: Frank Cass & Co., 1966), p. 153.

24. For two typical negative assessments of girls' education in the period before 1860, see Josephine Kamm, *Hope Deferred: Girls' Education in English History* (London: Methuen & Co. Ltd., 1965), pp. 136 – 51, and Jonathon Gathorne-Hardy, *The Old School Tie: The Phenomenon of the English Public School* (New York: Viking Press, 1977), pp. 230 – 4.

25. *Journal of Emily Shore* (London: Kegan Paul, Trench, Trubner and Co., 1898), p. 12.

26. Constance L. Maynard, 'From Early Victorian Schoolroom to University: Some Personal Experiences', *The Nineteenth Century* (November, 1914), p. 1,067.

27. This was the point of view taken, for example, by the Commissioners for the Schools Inquiry Commission (Taunton Commission) of the 1860s: 'The wealthiest class very generally do not send their daughters to school; even in the middle class many more girls are wholly kept and educated at home than boys. . .' *Schools Inquiry Commission*, P.P. vol. XXVIII, 13, 1, p. 568.

Frances Power Cobbe, who was born in 1822, is an example of a girl from an upper-middle-class family who was sent to school — briefly — at sixteen. The school selected was a fashionable Young Ladies' Academy in Brighton. See *Life of Frances Power Cobbe, By Herself* (2 vols.; London: Richard Bentley and Son, 1894), I, pp. 57 – 63.

28. Two exceptional schools were the school run by the Society of Friends in York, the Mount School, and the Clergymen's Daughters' School founded at Cowan Bridge in 1824 and later moved to Casterton. The most famous nineteenth-century pupils at the Clergyman's Daughters' School were the Bronte sisters. The 'York Quarterly Meeting Girls' School' — 'The Mount' — was founded in 1831. For its history, see H. Winifred Sturge and Theodora Clark, *The Mount School: York* (London: J.M. Dent and Sons, 1931). For the Clergymen's Daughters' School, see Winifred Gerin, *Charlotte Bronte: The Evolution of Genius* (London: Oxford University Press, 1967).

29. On the variability of girls' private schools, see Joyce Senders Pedersen, 'The Reform of Women's Secondary Education', pp. 63 – 8.

30. A description of one such school dating from the mid-century period is found in Hannah Lynch, *Autobiography of a Child* (Edinburgh and London: William Blackwood & Sons, 1899). Lynch, who published her autobiography anonymously, describes a childhood in which she was physically and emotionally abused by her mother; her stepfather appears to have done little to prevent the abuse. She was born in the early 1850s; when she was seven, she was sent to a small convent school near Birmingham. She says of it: 'Do the ladies of Lysterby continue to train atrociously and mismanage children, to starve and thwart them, as they did in those far-off days?' (p. 144).

31. Examples of this type of school are to be found in accounts of the following lives: Frances Ridley Havergal was sent to such a school — 'Miss Teed's' — at Great Campden House in 1850, when she was fourteen. See *Memorials of Frances Ridley Havergal*, pp. 24 – 30. For an earlier example, see *A Memoir of Miss Mary Helen Bingham*, ed. by Rev. John Bustard (London: John Kershaw, 1827), pp. 10 – 29. Mary Bingham was born in 1809 and died in 1828. The family were devout Methodists; Mary was sent to school at thirteen and underwent 'conversion' there.

For a mid-Victorian example, see the discussion of Constance Maynard's schooling in chapter 8.

32. The school to which Frances Power Cobbe was sent (see above, note 28) was expensive. As she explains, in the 1830s, Brighton was the most fashionable place for fashionable girls' schools: 'there were even then (about 1836) not less than a hundred such establishments in the town, but that at No. 32, Brunswick terrace, of which Miss

Runciman and Miss Roberts were mistresses . . . was supposed to be *nec pluribus impar*. It was, at all events, the most outrageously expensive, the nominal tarif of £120 – £130 per annum representing scarcely a fourth of the charges for "extras" . . . My own, I know, amounted to £1,000 for two years' schooling.' *Life of Frances Power Cobbe*, I, p. 60.

In contrast, the school to which Elizabeth Stevenson (later, the novelist, Elizabeth Gaskell) was sent in the 1820s, was not only much better than Frances Cobbe's Brighton school, it was cheaper. The fees at the school run by the Miss Byerleys were 30gns per annum in 1810: see Winifred Gerin, *Elizabeth Gaskell: A Biography* (Oxford: Clarendon Press, 1976), p. 24.

33. An example of a good school was the 'Miss Byerleys', mentioned in the previous footnote. For its merits, see Gerin, *Elizabeth Gaskell*, pp. 25 – 7.

A school that was in part a 'young ladies' academy' and in part linked to the reform movement was Laleham, whose proprietor was Hannah Pipe. Hannah Pipe opened her first school in Manchester in 1848. She moved the school to London in 1856, where it opened as 'Laleham'. See Anna Stoddart, *Life and Letters of Hannah E. Pipe* (Edinburgh and London: William Blackwood and Sons, 1908), pp. 38 – 57.

34. See, for example, the evidence of Gertrude King, secretary of the Society for the Employment of Women: 'If they were allowed to go in for competitive examinations . . . that would give them a stimulus for work.' *Schools Inquiry Commission*, vol. V, Minutes, pt. II, p. 719.

35. E.g. Emily Davies, in defending competitive examinations, insisted that 'parents and schoolmistresses can easily take care that the girls do not overwork'. Ibid., vol. V, Minutes, pt. II, p. 237.

36. Even Emily Davies, the woman who, of all the witnesses who appeared before the Commission, had the strongest belief in the fundamental similarity of males and females, acknowledged that girls would have to learn household skills: 'I think they ought to have it, certainly, but I think that it is very easy . . . and if they were made sensible women, they would certainly get it for themselves. The most cultivated women are generally also the most efficient in household matters.' Ibid., p. 251.

Frances Mary Buss's more positive assertion, 'I think it is most desirable that every girl should know how to use her needle', (Ibid., p. 254), was also more typical.

37. For the history of the Girls' Public Day School Trust, see Josephine Kamm, *Indicative Past: A Hundred Years of the Girls' Public Day School Trust* (London: George Allen & Unwin, 1971) and Edward W. Ellsworth, *Liberators of the Female Mind: The Sherreff Sisters, Educational Reform and the Women's Movement* (Westport, Conn.: Greenwood Press, 1979).

38. For an account of one such school, 'Queenwood', which was run out of a house in Eastbourne during the last decades of the century (from 1871 to 1906), see Dorothea Petrie Carew, *Many Years, Many Girls: The History of a School, 1862 – 1942* (Dublin: Browne & Nolan, 1967). Queenwood catered to upper-middle-class families. In the nineties, the school still had the 'ambience of a home' (p. 77). The girls' exercise was still restricted to a decorous walk, two by two (p. 68). No Queenwood girl prepared for anything except 'home life' (p. 80) in the Victorian period.

39. For example, on the organisation and instruction at the Girls' Public Day School Co. Schools, see Kamm, *Indicative Past*, pp. 63 – 80.

On the Buss schools — the North London Collegiate and the Camden School — see *The North London Collegiate School 1850 – 1959: A Hundred Years of Girls' Education* (London: Oxford University Press, 1950), chapters 2 and 3.

40. *Schools Inquiry Commission*, 13, 1, p. 547.

41. For a summary of the changes, see Josephine Kamm, *Hope Deferred*, pp. 214 – 28.

42. For a hostile view from a pupil of the 1880s, see M. Vivian Hughes, *A London Family: 1870 – 1900* (London: Geoffrey Cumberlege, Oxford University Press, 1946), p. 165 for dress and p. 188 for the 'Dorcas' meeting.

43. Evidence from the Registers of the North London Collegiate School for the years 1866 – 7, and from those of the Girls' Public Day School Company's Kensington High School bear out this generalisation. At the North London Collegiate, a sample from the Register for 1867 – 8 gives an average age at entry of 12; For the Kensington High School, a sample from the entries for 1898 – 9 gives an average age at entry of 9. Moreover, the Kensington High School sample reveals that of those entering at the age of 10 or over, only 11 per cent had had no previous schooling. Registers in archives of the Girls' Public Day School Trust and of the North London Collegiate School.

44. For a summary of the middle-class attitude to women's work in the early and mid-Victorian period, see Lee Holcombe, *Victorian Ladies at Work: Middle-Class Working Women in England and Wales 1850 – 1914* (Newton Abbot: David & Charles, 1973), pp. 3 – 16. On the leisured woman, see Neff, *Victorian Working Women*, pp. 187 – 243.

45. On the governess, see M. Jeanne Peterson, 'The Victorian Governess: Status Incongruence in Family and Society', in *Suffer and Be Still*, ed. by Martha Vicinus, pp. 3 – 19.

46. The best general account, from the point of the reformers themselves, is still Ray Strachey, *'The Cause': A Short History of the Women's Movement in Great Britain* (reprint ed.; Port Washington, NY: Kennikat Press, 1969).

47. 'The wider employment of middle-class women was certainly necessary and even just, but above all it proved to be expedient. England's rapidly expanding economy created a large and increasing demand for labour, a demand which better educated women could supply as well as men — and at a lower cost.' Lee Holcombe, *Victorian Ladies at Work*, p. 18.

48. Ibid., p. 203.

49. The career of one example of this new type, Sara Burstall, is discussed in chapter 8.

50. Holcombe, *Victorian Ladies at Work*, pp. 58 – 102.

51. For office workers, see Ibid., pp. 141 – 62; for sales clerks, see Ibid., pp. 102 – 40.

52. Ibid., p. 20.

Chapter 3

'SUNBEAMS' AND 'HOYDENS': IMAGES OF GIRLHOOD IN THE VICTORIAN PERIOD

In an earlier chapter, it was suggested that the Victorians developed an image of the perfect daughter; an image of girlhood that represented the quintessence of Victorian femininity. The image of the perfect daughter contributed to the construction of the Victorian ideal of hearth and home, an ideal that was designed to reconcile conflicts and to satisfy longings; to reconcile the conflict between the morality of Christianity and the values of capitalism, and to satisfy the nostalgia for a simple, pastoral past amid the realities of the urban, industrial present.

If the image of harmonious domesticity remained a pervasive ideal that shaped both individual and collective consciousness, so also did a sense of uneasiness about that ideal. Out of this uneasiness, this unspoken recognition that the ideal must, by its very nature, remain unattainable, arose a series of parallel images, images that were negative in character. Thus, alongside the image of the warm hearth arose the image of the cold, neglected, loveless household. And just as the notion of femininity was central to the conception of the ideal home, so also was an image of the unfeminine central to the negative vision of the cold, loveless home. The image of the good wife as the Angel in the House had its counterpart in the image of the self-seeking, selfish, neglectful wife. In the same way, the image of the perfect daughter had its counterpart. The good daughter was gentle, loving, self-sacrificing and innocent: the bad daughter was vulgar, self-seeking, lazy and sexually impure. In this chapter, both the positive and the negative images of girlhood that were current in the Victorian period will be examined in detail, and their roots in the structure of the Victorian middle-class family will be analysed.

The positive image of the daughter at home was expressed through prescriptive and imaginative literature and through art, throughout the Victorian period. The image was most pervasive during the mid-Victorian decades, but its influence persisted right through the century. Because, like grown women, girls were seen as fulfilling their function only as they existed in relationship to others, the image of the ideal daughter at home was most often presented through a portrayal of a girl's relationship to other members of the ideal family. And even though a girl was thought to have a special function in relationship to all the members of the family, her function was thought to be of special significance in relationship to males. It is through the role of father's daughters and brother's sister that the Victorian idealisation of girlhood was most fully expressed.

Two main types of father-daughter relationships appear in Victorian imagery about family life. The first type is the relationship that would exist in a happy, successful family, one in which both mother and father were alive, and in which the father had achieved worldly success, and at the same time possessed the appropriate qualities of masculine strength and sound morality. In such a family, it was suggested that the most important qualities a good daughter could provide for her father were gentleness and cheerfulness. As one writer put it, the successful, hardworking father of a family has a right to expect 'smiling faces, cheerful voices, and a quietly happy welcome which will fall like balm on his harrassed spirit' when he returns home from the outside world.[1] Within the household, his daughters should be 'sunbeams that make everything glad',[2] creatures whose self-forgetfulness, whose willingness to help others, would create a harmonious environment.

After his struggles in the harsh, ugly world of business, the father also had a right to expect that his daughters would adorn the household with their ladylike accomplishments. In an advice book for adolescent girls, published in 1869, the author draws a 'picture of what a girl's home life should be', and suggests that one of the things she will do for her father is provide rest and amusement:

'This has been a tiring day', says the hard-worked, often perplexed father; 'Come, Annie, let me have a little music to rest me. I am so glad you have not gone out this evening. We are getting selfish about you, I am afraid; but I don't know how to spare you, even for an evening.'[3]

The good daughter would always put the claims of home and her obligations to her father first, before any outside concerns. An insistance that this was the daughter's duty continued to be voiced right through the century, even when expanded options were becoming available to adolescent girls. For instance, an author writing in the

1890s, alludes to the admirable qualities of Jephthah's daughter, the biblical figure who was 'A loving, faithful daughter, of whom . . . it is easy to discover that her father's interests were all hers, his sorrows her sorrows, his triumphs her greatest joys.' Even in the 1890s, this author insists, a good girl will emulate Jephthah's daughter:

> It was the daughter's privilege then, and it is the daughter's privilege today, to act the part of sympathiser and interested listener in the home circle. No other claim is greater, no intellectual pursuit should ever be allowed to interfere.[4]

The image of the daughter's relationship to the father in the serene and happy home was important, but the portrayal of the father-daughter relationship in a situation that was less than happy was even more revealing of the kind of femininity that a young girl could uniquely display. In a happy home, the daughter's obligation towards her father was to be a cheerful, accommodating 'sunbeam'. Should the family situation present difficulties, more arduous duties and qualities were demanded of the ideal daughter.

For instance, the good daughter was depicted as having a special role to play when the family experienced financial loss. In novels and moral tales, the good daughter in such a situation provided moral and emotional support to her father as well as genuine practical assistance. Examples from three nineteenth-century tales, all designed to be read by middle-class girls, will illustrate the role of the good daughter in helping a father beset by the vicissitudes of financial reverses.

The first is Maria Edgeworth's story *Simple Susan*, which enjoyed great popularity right through the Victorian period. Susan, Edgeworth's twelve-year-old heroine, is described as a 'sweet-tempered, modest, sprightly, industrious lass, who was the pride and delight of the village'. Susan has a special relationship with both her parents, which enables her to help them through the difficulties that form the basis for the story's plot. Susan's father is an honest, upright, unpretentious farmer, and her family is presented as a model of good behaviour. They make a sharp contrast to the upstart attorney, the villain of the piece, whose evil ways stem from his vulgarity and his social pretensions. As would be expected, the villain's vain, idle daughter is a model of the unfeminine, just as Susan is a model of feminine goodness. When Susan's father experiences financial setbacks, it is Susan who is able to comfort him: 'Happy the father who has such a daughter as Susan! — her unaltered sweetness of temper, and her playful, affec-

tionate caresses, at last somewhat dissipated her father's melancholy.'⁵
As is often the case in such stories, Susan's goodness, in the end, proves
to be not only a comfort to her father: through her charm and virtu-
ousness, the machinations of the upstart attorney are exposed to the
gentlefolk who have the real power in the community, Susan's father's
farm is restored to him, and the attorney experiences a well-deserved
fall from prosperity.

The second example of the good girl's role in the life of a father
experiencing financial reverses is from a tale entitled *The Little
Emigrant*, which was published in 1826. *The Little Emigrant* has two
heroines, the daughter and the foster-daughter of a poor but upright
and honourable curate of an obscure village parish. When the father
loses his curacy through no fault of his own, the two girls do more than
simply adapt cheerfully to the situation. They are resourceful, and
find work doing plain sewing, a skill that the old family servant has
taught them. The plan originates with Annette, the foster-daughter:

> 'Thanks to good Susan', said she, ' . . . both you and I can do plain-
> work, neatly too, I hope. How delightful it would be if we could get
> employment . . . and help to support your dear father and our-
> selves! We will then be more easy; for I can see, though he strives
> before us to be cheerful, that he is far from happy.' Louisa was
> delighted, and immediately asked her father's permission to engage
> in the undertaking . . . He at first opposed it . . . but at length
> yielded.⁶

The plan is put into action in a way that observes the proprieties of the
1820s, a period when girls of gentle birth were not supposed to engage
in paid employment. It is Susan, the servant, who deals with the ware-
house for which the work is done, not the young ladies who work in the
seclusion of their home. But the girls do make money with their sewing
and this enables them not only to experience the joys of being useful,
but also to express their gratitude and support for the story's father
figure.

Our final example of the good daughter's behaviour to a father
experiencing adverse financial circumstances is from a mid-Victorian
tale entitled *The Star and the Cloud: or a Daughter's Love*. Carrie, the
book's adolescent heoine, is a paragon of loving self-sacrifice. As she
says of her love for her family:

> I should love them even if they did not love me; and I should do

anything to show them my love, by taking a great deal of pains to
please them in every way . . . If they should speak hard to me, I
should speak kindly to them . . .[7]

Carrie's family is in fact loving, but the father suffers financial
reverses, in this case largely through his own fault. In the face of these
troubles, it is Carrie who provides the family with both practical and
emotional support. For her father, the emotional solace she provides is
even more important than her practical good sense. In one crucial
scene, Carrie and her father are alone together. Carrie begins to
console her father by stroking his hair:

At first using her hands, and then taking a small comb from her
hair, she drew it gently through his long, dark locks. For a while he
sat motionless . . . under the magnetic influence of that hand and
comb . . .

Carrie's father, in response to these ministrations, says: 'Carrie dear,
thank you, your gentle hand has acted like a charm upon me . . .'
   This passage illustrates the way in which the image of the good
daughter could be used to transcend some of the problems inherent in
portraying the sexuality of the feminine Victorian woman. To a
twentieth-century reader, the above passage has unmistakably sensual
overtones, although to the pre-Freudian Victorians, its sensuality
would presumably not have been obvious: Carrie combs her father's
hair with her own comb, and the hair, the fingers, and even the comb
are described in a covertly erotic manner. Carrie thus offers her father
comfort that is both maternal and wifelike. But because she is his
daughter, and therefore by definition sexually pure and innocent, this
sensual comfort can be offered without overt sexuality, with all its
attendant dangers and contradictions.
   A loss of financial status was not the only difficult situation in which
the daughter could play a special role in relationship to the father. She
could, for instance, be of special importance if he were ill. In such a
case, even a very little girl could play her part. A tale that appeared in
a woman's magazine in 1888 tells the story of the youngest daughter in
a family, who left school to help nurse her gravely ill father:

She had been her father's pet, and with a kind of tender perversity
he chose to be dependent upon her services rather than on those of
his elder children. Her girlish ministrations, with which he could

not dispense, were somehow less mortifying, because almost laugh-able, than the aid of older, and one would have thought, better qualified persons.[8]

Not only could the good daughter soothe her father in physical ill-ness, she could also aid him if he suffered from moral failings. Indeed, the daughter-as-redeemer is the most compelling of all the images of the ideal Victorian girl. Even very little girls could be seen as redeem-ing figures. Usually, if it is a young child who is portrayed as the redeeming figure, it is her helplessness, innocence and immaturity that touch the heart of the selfish, dissolute or wayward father. She has an especial capacity to arouse the conscience if she is in sad circum-stances — ill or half-orphaned. The little girl who is a full orphan can often arouse the sympathy of a father surrogate — an uncle, for example, or a grandfather. The older girl who functions as a redeem-ing daughter frequently displays, in addition to innocence and help-lessness, a well-developed and fully conscious moral purity and strength of character.

The theme of the redeeming daughter is a recurring one in Victo-rian fiction of all types. A didactic story from a late-nineteenth-century woman's magazine will serve as an example of the little girl as a redeeming figure. In this story, the man who is redeemed is a father surrogate — the child's grandfather — but this circumstance rein-forces the point that it is childlike innocence that can best soften the hard father's heart, because the grandfather has earlier rejected his daughter, the child's mother, who had married for love rather than for worldly gain. The child, in winning the sympathy of her grandfather, not only cures him of his pride and worldliness, but is the agent of reconciliation for the whole family, accomplishing, with childish charm, a feat her mother, as a grown woman, could not achieve.

The story employs the familiar Victorian device of concealed identity. The grandfather meets his four-year-old granddaughter accidentally, without knowing who she is. The little girl is described as having a 'sweet face [and] loose tousled curls of fair hair . . .'[9] She gives the old man 'soft kisses' and is able to win his love because she likes him and trusts him. Her trustfulness and helplessness arouse his human feelings which have been suppressed for many years. In the climax of the story, the little girl becomes gravely ill, but her parents are helpless to save her, because they cannot afford the food and medicine the doctor has ordered. The old man offers to help the family, and thus discovers that the little girl is his own granddaughter. In the closing scenes, he is reconciled with his daughter and her husband, and taken in to the warmth of their family circle.

The themes used in this story written by an obscure writer occur also in Victorian fiction that has acknowledged literary merit. Of the well-known Victorian novelists, Charles Dickens was the most frequent employer of the theme of the redeeming daughter. His most interesting redeeming daughter is the heroine of *Dombey and Son*, which first appeared serially in 1846−8. The novel's main theme is the clash between the cold, barren, masculine values represented by the world of commerce, which are the only values that the hero, Dombey, is able to appreciate at the beginning of the novel, and the soft, loving, feminine values, represented by Dombey's neglected daughter Florence.

Florence Dombey is the quintessential redeeming daughter. As a small child, her situation is such as to arouse the deepest sympathy in the reader. After the opening chapter, in which her mother dies giving birth to her brother, she is a half-orphan, and indeed, because her father cannot appreciate her goodness, she is in an emotional sense a full orphan. Throughout the novel Florence is a paragon of self-sacrificing love. While it is her helplessness that is appealing in the opening chapters of the novel, when she is still a very young child, in the later scenes Dickens develops her moral strength. Florence's father rejects her, because, unlike her brother, she cannot gratify his ambitions: we are told that to Dombey, 'a girl . . . was merely a piece of base coin that couldn't be invested — a bad Boy — nothing more.' In the face of this cruel rejection, Florence never ceases to love her father. She in fact behaves as Carrie, the heroine of *The Star and the Cloud*, suggests a daughter should behave in an unloving family; she simply loves with more intensity.

Florence's love is the connecting thread that runs through the novel, and in the end her selfless love redeems Dombey. The redemption scene occurs near the end of the novel when Florence, as a grown woman with a child of her own, returns to comfort her financially and emotionally ruined father. The reconciliation scene begins with Florence asking her father for forgiveness, because she has married for love, against his will. The fact that she would ask for forgiveness, when, in fact, it is he who has wronged her, is characteristic of portrayals of the ideal redeeming daughter. Florence's plea reaches her father's heart, and the reconciliation and redemption take place:

> As she clung closer to him, in another burst of tears, he kissed her
> on her lips, and, lifting up his eyes, said, 'Oh my God, forgive me

for I need it very much!' With that he dropped his head again, lamenting over and caressing her, and there was not a sound in all the house for a long, long time; they remained clasped in one another's arms, in the glorious sunshine that had crept in with Florence.[10]

The image of the ideal girl was expressed frequently through the medium of the father-daughter relationship. Also popular in imaginative and prescriptive literature, and in painting, were images of the sister-brother relationship. The bond between sister and brother represented, for many Victorians, the ideal relationship between males and females. It could have all the emotional intensity of marriage, but at the same time, the issue of sexuality could be avoided, and the relationship could be invested with sacred overtones. A pious poem which appeared in an evangelical mother's magazine in 1851, well expresses the sacredness with which a sister's love was invested during the Victorian period:

> A Sister's Love
> O priceless Gem!
> Surpassing far mere mortal ken!
> To what on earth may I compare
> A sister's loving, anxious care?
> Oh, never may the blush of shame
> Rise at an erring brother's name:
> And never may he cause to fear
> A sister's sigh — a sister's tear.[11]

Throughout the nineteenth century, several aspects of the sister-brother relationship figured in imagery that reinforced the cult of domesticity. There was, first of all, the depiction of the relationship between very young sisters and brothers. An article written in 1887 on the theme of girlhood described the relationship between young brothers and sisters in the following manner:

> He is her chosen champion and hero, while she is pledged to him as his future clever little housekeeper, companion and nurse. In those innocent days neither dreams that there can ever be another, who will come between and usurp the first place in the regard of the boy and girl, become man and woman.[12]

This theme of brother-sister companionship figures frequently in stories for young children. In many such stories, a brother — usually an older brother — acts as a guide for his sister in intellectual and practical matters. In a number of early and mid nineteenth-century tales, the plot involves an account of a brother's departure for school, while the sister remains at home. For the boy, school represents an outlet for male adventuresomeness, and training for the male role. When the boy, in such stories, goes off to school, while he remembers his family, his main attention is turned to his new environment. The sister in such stories remains at home, and continues to focus her attention on her brother, even in his absence. We are told in one such story that the sister passed much of the time, when her brother was at school, in thinking about him and doing things for him: 'In feeding his rabbits, and arranging his garden, she felt she was preparing a pleasure for her dear brother.'[13]

Victorian portrayals of the relationship between the very young sister and brother contained an element of nostalgia. Both writers and painters tended to see the pair as if through the wrong end of a telescope: the image is reduced in size, and bathed in remembered summer sunlight. More than any other relationship, the sister-brother dyad was perceived as free of conflict, perhaps because nineteenth-century ideology about gender prescribed such firmly compartmentalised roles for males and females that, in idealisations at any rate, the possibility of rivalry between siblings of the opposite sex could simply be discounted.

While the relationship between the young sister and brother was portrayed as idyllic, the role of the older sister in the brother's life involved more responsibility. The older sister was supposed to act as her brother's moral guide: 'A sister . . . is that sort of second conscience, which like the fairy ring in an old story, pinched the wearer whenever he was doing anything amiss.'[14] A sister's capacity to act as her brother's moral guide derived from the purity she retained by being cloistered within the private sphere. A brother's task was to go out into the world and shape a public destiny for himself, and this male task meant that 'often he must be wounded, or subdued, often misled, and *always* hardened'. Because she was sheltered from the world, she could be morally uplifting: 'A sister's duties to a brother are of the most important character. Never should she lose sight of the fact that he has more temptations to wander than herself.'[15]

To retain her moral authority with her brother, a sister had to retain her sheltered purity. A brother's love, respect and admiration, it was suggested, ought to be enough to cause a girl to adhere strictly to the canons of femininity: 'A man's *sister* is so sacred and hallowed a being to him, that many things he would pass over in others, he would feel pained by her doing.'[16] Because she was sheltered, she was also in need of protection, and while a good sister was to be a moral touchstone for her brother, she would also defer to him, when she needed guidance in worldly matters, recognising that he knew 'far more of the world' than she could.

Right through to the end of the nineteenth century, when, in reality, large numbers of middle-class girls were themselves of necessity exposed to work in the world, the image of the sister at home, and the conception of her duty to her brother that grew out of that image, retained its force. Indeed, prescriptive writers often insisted that the sister's influence and her duties were so great that if a brother did stray from the path of virtue, a sister could often be held responsible. As an editor of an advice column in a girls' magazine admonished a correspondent in 1892:

> Eleanor: you may yourself be to blame for your brother's bad choice. Are you 'giddy', 'flighty', 'careless about your Sundays'? Sisters have it very much in their own hands to form their brothers' tastes and judgements.[17]

In addition to her spiritual duties as moral guide to her brother, a good sister had practical duties as well. One of these was the duty to make the home a place where the brother would wish to spend his time. Here the girl's duty to her father merged with her duty to her brother. Making the home pleasant for the males who belonged to it was thought to be her highest calling. Both father and brothers warranted such attention, but for different reasons. A father deserved to have a pleasant home as a refuge from those labours that supported the household. In the case of brothers, it was the sister's duty to make the household pleasant so that they would not be tempted to stray elsewhere:

> Make your brothers happy at home, without the aid of those blighting amusements which neither instruct nor improve. Cause your brothers to love the card-table or the drawing-room, and they will soon desert you for open and destructive gaming, and return no more but to reflect on your error and reveal their own degeneracy . . . avoid all that may impair . . . the modesty and virtue which you prize in domestic life.[18]

Like the father-daughter relationship, that between sisters and brothers, although it was suffused with sentimentality, was not in the end perceived as a relationship between equals. The woman's mission of self-sacrifice was meant to be a girl's guiding principle in this relationship, just as it would in future be the guiding principle of her relationship with her husband. That self-sacrifice was the highest duty a girl could perform for her brother was often illustrated by tales about real-life self-sacrificing sisters. One of the most frequently recurring examples, in magazines and books written for girls in the second half of the nineteenth century, was that of Caroline Herschel. Herschel, sister of the astronomer William Herschel, was her brother's collaborator for many years, and, after his death went on to make her own reputation as an astronomer. Yet, when she figures as an exemplar in vignettes written for girls, it is always her self-sacrificing relationship to her brother that is stressed, rather than her own talents, ambitions or achievements.[19]

Although a girl's relationship to her male relatives was more central to the ideology of domesticity than was her relationship to other females, an idealised view of female relationships does also have some importance in Victorian portrayals of domesticity.[20] Prescriptive statements about a girl's relationship to her mother do, for example, form part of the imagery associated with girlhood. As was true of a girl and her father, two main types of mother-daughter relationships figured in Victorian literature and art, one in which the mother fulfilled her maternal functions, and one in which she would not or could not do so.

Throughout the Victorian period, it was generally agreed that a mother should have a special relationship with her daughters. More than any other individual, the good mother could teach a daughter how to be a truly feminine woman. A girl who had such a mother was thought to owe her several kinds of filial duties. In literature describing modest middle-class households, it was insisted that a daughter owed her mother practical assistance in performing household tasks. Many didactic tales portrayed girls from poor households who diligently helped their mothers with domestic work: such tales about girls from households with very little money were designed to develop a sense of responsibility in their better-off middle-class readers.[21] The girl who behaved in a loving and helpful manner towards her mother would be rewarded both with her love and her gratitude:

Sweet is the mother's good-night kiss. She looks back upon the day and sees what anxiety and toil she has been spared through a daughter's love. She folds her arms about her, and draws down the fair head to its old resting-place for a moment — 'God bless you, my darling, my comfort!' . . . Oh! what a peaceful night there is for such a girl, shadowed, protected by so much well-deserved love.[22]

The mother-daughter relationship was portrayed as one in which the daughter always confided in her mother who would be, above all other people, her moral, spiritual and practical guide. The ideal mother, because of her experience and because of her mother love, would retain the respect of her daughters and some authority with them even after they had reached late adolescence. The dutiful daughter would always seek and follow her mother's counsel, whether it was about friendships she should form or about spiritual matters or about what books she should read.[23] The ideal mother-daughter relationship was seen as one of companionship: the mother would be, for her daughters, 'not merely . . . their oldest, but their *bosom* friend'. The relationship at its best would be 'like that of sisters with a subtle difference': 'The point of real weight is the close, intimate companionship, the perfect reliance on either side, the blessed sense of giving and receiving aid as a right, and not as a favour or a purchased boon.'[24]

And what of the daughter who did not possess such a mother? Two themes, that of the motherless girl, and that of the girl with a bad mother, figure in Victorian writing. In the case of the orphaned girl, the mere memory of a good mother is often pictured as having as beneficial an influence as a mother who is actually alive; the sacredness of her memory strengthens her daughter in her determination to be both virtuous and feminine.[25] But in the case of the daughter who has a mother who is ineffectual, flighty or worse still, unwomanly, the good girl's virtuous nature will still triumph. Indeed, nineteenth-century writers frequently used such a situation to demonstrate the inner strength of a good girl. The inference that the reader was meant to draw from such tales was that a good girl's femininity could be stronger than a bad mother's lack of such qualities.[26]

A girl's relationship to the female members of her family — mother, sisters, aunts — was depicted as one of close, supportive companionship, of an intimacy based on the fulfilment of a shared role. Perhaps because, in real life, such relationships figured much more prominently in female experience than did relationships with males, they tended to figure less in idealisations. It was the ideal girl's relationship

of loving self-sacrifice to her male relatives that was central to portrayals of domesticity and of femininity.

Certain images of girlhood figuring in literature and art are not
directly or exclusively related to father, brother or mother. One
particularly resonant and frequently repeated portrayal is that of the
girl who is gravely ill. In this variation of the girl-as-redeemer, the
quality that is often stressed is that of her profound religious devotion,
a devotion that makes her patient in the face of suffering, and more
intensely aware of spiritual matters than a healthy child. A girl suffering from a fatal illness is frequently depicted as achieving an adult
moral sense. She can indeed affect a conversion experience on those
who attend her and change the character of the whole household:

> A sick daughter is often as an angel in the house. Brothers and
> sisters feel how dear she is, and for her sake strive to be good . . .
> and then, if she be a Christian, how much she may do for her
> Master! She may force all the careless ones to confess that after all
> there is something in religion, seeing that it can so elevate her, even
> amid much suffering.[27]

From gentle sunbeam in a happy home, to redeeming angel, even
when she herself was afflicted with fatal illness: in all its many guises,
the image of virtuous, feminine girlhood formed an essential part of
the Victorian cult of domesticity. But, throughout the period, along
with these images of perfect girlhood, were images that arose from
hostile criticisms of the Victorian middle-class girl, criticisms that
were as much a part of Victorian commentary about girlhood as were
the idealisations.

Victorian negative images of girlhood arose from two sources. In
part they simply reinforced the image of the good girl through the
portrayal of her opposite; positive images were presented for emulation, and their negative counterparts were portrayed merely so that
readers could be admonished about attitudes and behaviour that they
should avoid. But negative portraits of middle-class girlhood did not
arise only from the conventions of didactic literature. Just as positive
portraits of girlhood reinforced the cult of domesticity, so negative
portraits played a role in Victorian discourse about the economic and
social structure of middle-class family life.

As we saw earlier, in some discussions of the nature of family life, it
was covertly if not overtly acknowledged that public and private
spheres were not in fact separate, and that the private sphere, like the

public, was an arena of economic struggle and competition. In this struggle, the symbols associated with social status were employed both by the upwardly mobile, and by those who wished to control social mobility. It was the latter whose voices dominated discussions about family life, and for this dominant group, the unfeminine woman came to symbolise much that was objectionable about upward social mobility. In portrayals of the unfeminine, the Victorian middle-class girl, even more than the adult woman, was subjected to harsh criticism.

Among her many admirable qualities, the Victorian ideal girl was dutiful and co-operative. On approaching adolescence, it was assumed that she would become a junior Angel in the House — an aid and comfort to her mother. But in most portrayals of her functions and duties, it was her spiritual qualities that were placed in the foreground. The concrete content of her role, the actual work she ought to do in the household, was rarely spelled out in detail. In portrayals of ideal family life, it was assumed that the amount of domestic work a girl would do would depend on the material circumstances of her family. Whatever they might be, a good girl would unerringly find the appropriate balance between gentility and usefulness that was suited to her situation. One mid-Victorian writer described the ideal girl's ability to be both ladylike and useful in the following way:

> My beau-ideal of a young lady is one who is equally in her place in the parlour and in the kitchen; who can converse pleasantly and rationally with her friends, make her voice and fingers 'discourse most eloquent music', use her needle skillfully for the adornment of her own person or in household matters, or go into the kitchen, and prepare a dinner.[28]

Although this was the 'beau-ideal', much Victorian rhetoric about the failings of middle-class family life assumes that most Victorian girls failed to achieve it. The negative counterpart of the dutiful girl, the lazy, disobliging girl, was a favorite target of hostile critics of middle-class girlhood:

> If a girl is not absolutely compelled to earn her own daily bread, she regards herself as exonerated from any obligation to be useful . . .
> She probably spends a few years in school, and perhaps makes some improvements in an intellectual way; but at sixteen, or eighteen at the most, her 'education is finished', and from that period she is the

veriest idler, lives the most selfishly, in the most useless manner to those around her, of any other class of persons.[29]

That condemnation appeared in a mother's magazine in 1847. The following comments, from an advice book of the 1860s, written for lower-middle-class girls, express the same sentiments:

> Pride and indolence are the crying evils of the present generation of young ladies of the middle classes. They hate work, and don't scruple to say so. They do it in a grudging, ill-tempered way. Everything they touch is half-done. If they lay the table for dinner, a third of the things are forgotten. If they wash a little brother or sister they do it so harshly that the little one cries all the time. . .

Such a girl is described as thinking she is 'too delicate' for domestic work. Instead of helping her mother, she 'creeps about from room to room, strums a little upon the piano, does an inch of fancy work, takes down her back hair, and dresses it afresh, and so passes the day'.[30] The girl in that picture is not only being castigated for being lazy, bad-tempered and disobliging; the author has presented the portrait not merely to warn her readers of how unattractive they would be should they behave in such a reprehensible fashion. The girl is also being criticised for behaving like a fine lady, for giving herself airs, in a household where such a self-concept was inappropriate. Far from achieving the balance that the 'beau-ideal of a young lady' ought to strive for, the girl in this portrait has acquired upwardly mobile aspirations that have outstripped those of her own family, and she has become not merely an ill-bred upstart but a bad daughter.

The critics of the upwardly mobile Miss overlooked the inherent contradictions in the role of the lower-middle-class girl. Achieving a balance between the skills of domesticity and the skills associated with gentility was a problem for the lower-middle-class wife, but it was even more of a problem for her adolescent daughter. The wife, at least, had a role with clearly apparent functions. The role of a daughter-at-home in a lower-middle-class household in the early and mid-Victorian years could be both confining and limited. Unlike girls from better-off households, such a girl could not occupy herself with the rituals of Society, or with charitable works; such activities were not part of the lower-middle-class way of life. Unlike a girl from a less well-off family, she could not occupy herself with paid work. But if she did household work under her mother's direction, how, then, was her status different from that of the young domestic servant who would, most likely, have been employed by such a family?

In an eighteenth-century farmer's or artisan's household, the young girls of the family had customarily learned domestic skills, both for use in the private economy of the household, and for market production. They had learned those skills along with the female domestic servants who had been commonly employed by such families, and who had had a social status not markedly different from the employing family itself.[31] But for a nineteenth-century daughter of upwardly mobile middle-class people, there were circumstances that could have made household work not merely unpleasant, but threatening to her status. If we assume that the hostile criticisms are to some degree a reflection of reality, there is ample evidence that in many upwardly mobile families, daughters became vehicles for the family's upwardly mobile aspirations. They would be educated to be genteel young ladies, and their ability to speak a little French, and to do fancy needlework or play the piano would become evidence of the family's economic and social aspirations, if not of its actual achievements.[32]

Although the hostile stereotype of the upwardly mobile Miss who had been educated 'above her station' at an inferior boarding school was a creation of upper-middle-class commentary, it did have some basis in reality. Many lower-middle-class girls must have received two contradictory sets of messages about how they ought to behave in relationship to household work. Told, on the one hand, that her gentility was an asset to the family, and that she enhanced not only her own, but her family's status by engaging in ornamental activities, she would, on the other hand, have been aware that as long as the family's aspirations to gentility remained aspirations rather than achievements, it would be appropriate for her to help in the work of the household.

According to the hostile critics, the chief reason that the parvenu family educated its daughters 'above their station' was in the hope that they would make upwardly mobile marriages. As one such critic stated:

> If parents would candidly admit their motives [for sending their daughters to boarding schools], we should find that they are generally activated more by a desire for personal improvement than of mental acquirements. In short they wish to see their daughters . . . put in the surest way of making conquests.[33]

The hostile picture of the husband-hunting girl represents the converse of the good girl's selflessness and gentleness, and like the portrait of the lazy girl it was frequently employed by early and mid-Victorian critics of middle-class family life. The portrait arose out of the conflicts that were inherent in the middle-class girl's relationship to marriage. The conflict between the myth that the family was an area sealed off from competition, and the competitiveness that did in fact pervade the 'private sphere' most acutely affected middle-class daughters as they confronted the problem of marriage. In the early and mid-Victorian years, marriage was considered the only truly acceptable adult destiny for the middle-class girl. This idea was so deeply ingrained that in the 1860s, middle-class women who failed to marry were referred to as 'redundant'.[34] But the ideological constructs of domesticity and femininity decreed that a good girl would never *seek* marriage. During the period between childhood and womanhood, she would simply wait, with no unseemly thoughts about her future.

In those portraits of domestic life that buttressed the cult of domesticity, marriage was seen as an event that would inevitably happen to the ideal girl, without any intervention on her own part. It was assumed that the right man would simply appear, and a girl, having performed her function as daughter-at-home, would move on to become a wife. The right man the good girl would marry would always be one she loved — she would never marry for ignoble material reasons — but she would love only a man who was suitable. To be suitable he had to be not only upright and honourable, but it was assumed he would have the requisite social and financial attributes as well.

Such a picture could only be sustained in imagery that ignored the realities of middle-class social structure. While romantic love had ideological power, middle-class values also decreed that marriage be seen as an economic arrangement as well as an affair of the emotions. And for early and mid-Victorian middle-class girls with little or no inheritance to look forward to, marriage was not merely their only acceptable destiny, it was their only sure means of obtaining any possibility of economic security. In Jane Austen's words, marriage was 'the only honourable provision for well-educated young women of small fortune, and however uncertain of giving happiness, must ever be their pleasantest preservative from want'.[35]

The heroine of nineteenth-century fiction would achieve, through marriage, both love and worldly success, and in the process, she would never need to sacrifice the maidenly modesty so essential to femininity.[36]

But in a real world in which middle-class females who did not marry were considered 'redundant', or were said to have 'failed in business',[37] it was covertly acknowledged, if not overtly sanctioned, that a girl might make it her business to marry as well as she could. Unfeminine though it was, she might apply the Victorian business ethic of effort and competition, considered eminently appropriate for her brothers, to the only enterprise open to her.

The converse of the dutiful girl was the lazy girl; the converse of the gentle and selfless girl was the aggressive husband-hunter. There was also a converse of the sexually pure and innocent girl. Although not as freely employed by hostile critics as the image of the lazy girl or the husband-hunter, the impure girl does figure in negative commentary about middle-class Victorian girlhood. In polite Victorian discourse, the idea that a young girl could have any sexual thoughts at all was simply bypassed. It was part of the Victorian belief system that girls were not only innocent of sensuality, they were ignorant of it: indeed, their ignorance was the main safeguard of their innocence. If a girl lost her ignorance, if she became aware of sexuality, she was in imminent danger of becoming unchaste.[38]

The nineteenth-century image of the unchaste girl is frequently linked with those of the idle girl and the husband-hunter. Critics of the husband-hunter often imply that such girls could easily become sexually loose, and fall prey to seduction, or themselves seduce the men they hoped to ensnare in matrimony. As an early-nineteenth-century critic of middle-class girls' education stated:

> The *genteel* education she has received has elevated her above the humble office of housekeeping; she despises her parents, and their vulgar shop or loom garrett; she seeks, in novels and dissipation, some means of escaping from her present condition; and at length, as too frequent experience demonstrates, she falls a victim to seduction. How, indeed, could it be otherwise? Must not the habit of idleness, and all the lessons of pride and vanity which she received at school, tend to encourage a disposition to vice and licentiousness?[39]

This author connects aspirations after false gentility, and the encouragement of 'idleness' in girls with 'debauchery'. In the 1860s, the anti-feminist writer Mrs Lynn Linton, in a successful series of articles about 'The Girl of the Period', accused idle, scheming middle-class girls of being no better than prostitutes:

The girl of the period is a creature who dyes her hair and paints her face . . . in imitation of the demi-monde . . . it cannot be too plainly told to the modern English girl that the net result of her present manner of life is to assimilate her as nearly as possible to a class of women who we must not call by their proper — or improper — name.[40]

But it was not merely boldness in seeking matrimony that was thought to lead to 'impurity' in adolescent girls. 'Impure' thoughts and actions could occur even if the girl had nothing to do with men. This sort of concern focused on a fear of masturbation. Masturbation, which was believed to have adverse effects on mental and physical health, in females as well as in males, was thought to stem from states of sexual arousal that could be produced in morally unsatisfactory circumstances. Ill-ordered domesticity, at any rank of middle-class or upper-class life, was thought to lead to bad mothering. Such parental neglect could, it was believed, take many damaging forms, all of which might lead to sexual stimulation:

> The snowy purity of Christian modesty has been sullied by many a sin in thought, word and deed . . . and it points to one of the greatest defects in the education of our girls. They are never taught to know the difference between purity and impurity . . . Increasing numbers of hysterical cases, and nervous systems shattered without any assignable cause, tell only too surely of the havoc that is the result of knowingly or unknowingly disregarding these moral laws.[41]

The positive and the negative perceptions of girlhood that have so far been the subject of this chapter appear throughout the century in literature and art, but they were at their most flourishing in the mid-Victorian years. During that period, the belief that a middle-class girl's place should be restricted to the confines of the home was largely unchallenged. In the late-Victorian decades, not only had marked changes occurred in the opportunities available to middle-class girls and young women, perceptions of girlhood altered along with those changes. The cult of domesticity and the concept of femininity survived, but they, and the images of girlhood they employed, did adapt to new circumstances. Out of this adaptation there emerged, to take its place alongside the idealised 'sunbeam' and the reprehensible 'girl of the period', an image of the 'modern girl'.

Like its predecessors, the image of the modern girl did reflect the concrete situation of actual individuals, and did form part of individual girlhood experience, but like its predecessors, the image also had an existence as an ideological construct, divorced from objective reality. Positive perceptions of girlhood continued to figure in Victorian efforts to preserve a vision of family life separate from the 'public sphere' and negative perceptions continued to serve as receptacles for anxieties about contradictions inherent in Victorian social and moral values.

The positive and the negative perceptions of the modern girl arose out of discussions of the 'widening sphere' that was opening up for middle-class girls and young women in the last decades of the century. In hostile portrayals, the girl who benefitted from those changes was depicted as loud and aggressive, clumsy and ungracious. Education in large girls' schools, with their competitive, unhomelike environment, and physical activities like cycling, callisthenics and tennis, produced girls who exhibited 'a deplorable degree of roughness, and puerile imitation of the off-hand manners of young men.' To use a word that was common in the late nineteenth century, hostile observers saw the modern girl as a 'hoyden'.[42]

The image of the hoyden did not serve precisely the same function as the image of the lazy, vulgar 'girl of the period'. That hostile image had in part been a vehicle for upper-middle-class fears about lower-middle-class upward mobility. But the hoyden was in no way distinctively lower-middle-class, and the image was not used to express class antagonism. It contained, rather, an expression of antagonism towards the nascent women's movement. It was the 'girl of the period's' unseemly competitiveness about men and marriage that rendered her unfeminine, but the hoyden was unfeminine in a more direct way. Descriptions of hoydenish girls do not imply that they will become husband-hunters, but rather that they will become mannish 'strong-minded' women.

Given what has already been said about Victorian conceptions of girlhood, the hostile response to the modern girl is not to be wondered at. Both the new opportunities and the rise of the women's movement could be seen as threatening to the cult of domesticity. But the resilience of the idea of femininity — and the fundamental conservatism of the nineteenth-century women's movement — are reflected in the fact that it was not only the small minority of late-nineteenth-century feminists who looked upon the new ideas and the new opportunities with favour. Many voices who remained committed to the preservation of Victorian values about family life and femininity developed and wholeheartedly supported their own adaptation of those opportunities and ideas. One symbol of that successful adaptation was the emergence of the positive image of the modern girl, an image that had a secure place in the girls' stories, magazines and advice books of the last decades of the century.

For her creators, the positive image of the modern girl combines the best of the old and the new. She can benefit from the new opportunities: she can receive a modern education, and pursue a profession; she can cycle and play tennis; but she will always remain feminine, both in physical manner and in mental outlook. The ideal modern girl of the 1890s, in short, could achieve the energy and independence associated with the 'widening sphere', but at the same time, she would retain the charm and the selflessness of a sunbeam.

The combination of the old and the new is best displayed in the ideal modern girl's attitude towards marriage. In the eyes of her creators, the ideal modern girl had a more healthy attitude towards marriage than many mid-Victorian girls:

> Thinking . . . for herself, the modern girl grows gradually more self-respecting. She recognises the full indelicacy of being brought as wares to the market to be disposed of to a suitor, and sees no sense in it either . . . She knows that a woman's life is no longer considered a failure simply because she does not marry.[43]

The life of a spinster, then, from being an unthinkable alternative for the ideal girl, had become an acceptable possibility. While singleness was acceptable, however, it was still assumed that the ideal girl would prefer marriage. Her attitude towards marraige represents a transition between the old and the new:

> It is not possible, nor will the true woman wish it were, that any new times can change the conditions of wifehood and motherhood. Woman was made to be a helpmeet to man, and no circumstance can alter this obligation which is at once her joy and duty.[44]

A girl would now seek in a prospective husband a man who could be 'comrade, friend and lover,' but if she were an ideal modern girl, she would also want him to be her 'superior in attainments and talents', and, in spite of the education she had received, or the work she had done, she would, when the time came, give it all up for love:

There is not the slightest fear but that whatever of progress the times will bring to girls, the best and wisest of them will always be ready to meet the lover when he comes . . . How little do those wise people know who will say that the higher education of women will unfit them for the joys and duties of wives and mothers. It may be that they will not mistake gold for brass, and more and more they will demand the gold in character and life; but, when they find it, they will prove themselves — as the best and noblest Englishwomen have ever done — the sweetest, tenderest, most faithful and devoted, and if need be, the most self-sacrificing and self-forgetful women on the face of the earth.[45]

The ideal modern girl represents an adaptation, not a repudiation, of the older values. The fact that Victorian femininity could withstand the onslaught of the competitive examination, the bicycle and the independence that could be achieved through work, testifies to the power that it possessed.

The portrayals of girlhood that have been described in this chapter have been called 'images' because they had a function that was separate from the concrete experience of any individual. They were constructs reinforcing an ideology, and as such, their primary purpose was not to mould the individual girl into a feminine woman, but to contribute to the shaping of the world view of the Victorian middle class. But the images did, as well, form part of individual experience. From the point of view of the individual, there is no opposition between 'image' and 'reality': the image formed part of the individual's experience. Individual middle-class girls, like all members of the class, would have been exposed to all the facets of Victorian middle-class ideology. The images of girlhood, which related so directly to her own situation, would have had a particularly central place in the individual girl's experience.

In addition to the images of girlhood, Victorian writers also generated much specific and detailed advice about the way in which girls should be reared. This advice was influenced by the ideological constructs we have discussed, but it was more directly related to concrete, day-to-day experience than were those more general formulations. It is this body of concrete, detailed advice about the socialisation of middle-class girls that will be the subject of the next three chapters.

Notes

1. *The Mother's Companion*, II (1888), p. 38. *The Mother's Companion* was a magazine directed at middle- and lower-middle-class mothers. It contained articles of advice about child-rearing, recipes, sewing patterns and fiction. It appeared monthly and ran for ten volumes from 1887 to 1896.

2. Marianne Farningham, *Girlhood* (London: James Clarke & Co., 1869), p. 11.

3. Ibid., p. 15.

4. *Our Mothers and Daughters*, I, (1892), p. 166. *Our Mothers and Daughters*, which after the first volume appeared simply as *Mother and Daughters*, was a magazine directed at middle-class mothers and their daughters. It appeared monthly between 1892 and 1898. Its first editor, Mrs G.S. Reaney, was a supporter of the Temperance cause, and the magazine reflects this interest.

5. Maria Edgeworth, 'Simple Susan', in *Tales from Maria Edgeworth*, ed. by Austin Dobson (London: Wells Gardner & Co., 1903), p. 88.

6. Lucy Peacock, *The Little Emigrant* (London: 1826), p. 120.

7. A.S. Roe, *The Star and the Cloud: Or a Daughter's Love* (London and Ipswich: 1857?). p. 19.

8. *The Mother's Companion*, II (1888), p. 58.

9. Ethel Heddle, 'Martin Redfern's Oath', *The Mother's Companion* V (1891), p. 34.

10. Charles Dickens, *Dombey and Son* (London: Oxford University Press, 1950), pp. 844 – 5.

It should be noted that most critics have seen Paul Dombey as the more important of the two child figures in the novel, e.g.: 'Little Paul Dombey, though his part is often played offstage or from beyond the grave, like Christ's role in Milton's epic or in Christian theology, is the pivotal figure of the novel.' Robert Pattison, *The Child Figure in English Literature* (Athens: The University of Georgia Press, 1978), p. 90. This interpretation confuses Dombey's lack of appreciation of his daughter's virtues with Dickens' own perspective.

11. *The Mother's Friend*, IV (1851), pp. 97 – 8.

12. *The Mother's Companion*, I (1887), p. 61.

13. Maria E. Budden, *Always Happy!!! Or Anecdotes of Felix and his Sister Serena. A tale. Written for her Children , by a Mother* (Fourth edn; London, 1820), p. 90. Readers familiar with George Eliot's *The Mill on the Floss* will remember that George Eliot employs the theme of rabbit-feeding there. In that tension-filled portrayal of a brother-sister relationship, Maggie earns Tom's wrath because she *forgets* to feed the rabbits, and they die. George Eliot, *The Mill on the Floss* (London: J.M. Dent & Sons, Ltd., 1972), p. 30.

14. Isaac Taylor, *Advice to the Teens: or Practical Helps towards the Formation of one's own Character* (Second edn; London, 1818), pp. 126 – 7.

15. Matilda Pullan, *Maternal Counsels to a Daughter* (London: Darton & Co, 1855), p. 206.

16. Ibid., p. 207.

17. From the Correspondence Column of *Our Mothers and Daughters*, I (1892), p. 83.

18. *British Mothers' Magazine* (November, 1856), pp. 255 – 6.

19. E.g., in a signed article, written by Millicent Garrett Fawcett, the suffragist leader, the beauty of Caroline's story is said to be that it reveals 'what devoted love can do'. *The Mother's Companion*, I (1887), p. 34.

20. The relationship between females often figures in art: sisterly love, for example, was a favourite theme of Victorian genre painters. E.g., see John Millais, 'The Blind Girl', painted in 1856, which depicts the older, blind girl with her younger sister. In Augustus Egg's series 'Past and Present', which depicts the story of an unfaithful wife,

the second painting (1858) shows the older sister comforting the younger sister after the death of their father. Both paintings are reproduced in Raymond Lister, *Victorian Narrative Paintings* (London: Museum Press, 1966). The Millais is plate 37; the Egg is plate 13.

21. For instance, the following description, which appeared in an Evangelical children's magazine, was meant to encourage all daughters to be dutiful:

> At home she was a very good obedient little girl; she would get up early in the morning to light the fire; she dressed the dinner for the family; and she attended to her little brother when her mother was from home. She was also very handy at her needle and used to earn her victuals when only ten years old. I do hope that the little girls who may read this, will endeavour to follow Mary's example by being attentive to what they are told to do.

The Sunday Scholar's Reward, V (1828), p. 109.

22. Farningham, *Girlhood*, p. 13.

23. For example, even late in the century, girls were told that they should never read anything of which their mother did not approve. See, for instance, the example from a correspondence column: 'Little girls of thirteen are certainly too young to "read novels": — read nothing without [your mother's] leave.' *Girl's Own paper* (October, 1890), p. 16.

24. *The Mother's Companion*, I (1887), p. 94.

25. See, for example, Mrs Newton Crosland, *Hildred: The Daughter* (London: G. Routledge & Co., 1855). Hildred obeys her dead mother's last wish that she give up her dowry, bestowed on her by her unworthy father, who has wrongfully abused the trust of a French nobleman.

26. See, for example, Dinah Maria [Mulock] Craik, *Olive: A Novel*, (1850). Olive's mother is an amoral child-wife, but Olive manages to be moral in spite of her bad example.

27. Farningham, *Girlhood*, pp. 128 – 9.

28. Mrs Roe, *A Woman's Thoughts on the Education of Girls* (London: 1886), p. 14.

29. *British Mother's Magazine* (January, 1847), p. 146.

30. Pullan, *Maternal Counsels to a Daughter*, p. 99.

31. For this older pattern, see Alice Clark, *Working Life of Women in the Seventeenth Century* (London: Frank Cass & Co. Ltd., 1968), pp. 42 – 64: Ivy Pinchbeck, *Women Workers and the Industrial Revolution* (London: Frank Cass & Co. Ltd., 1969), pp. 8 – 16. That it was changes in economic and social structure that had altered the position of the middle-class daughter was sometimes covertly acknowledged by her critics:

> The farmer's wife, who once needed only a stout girl under her, will now keep two or three servants. The daughters learn music, and look back on the making of butter and cheese as the customs of a barbarous age; just as the squire's daughters do, when they hear some lady telling of her exultation over the shirt she made for her brother, when she was twelve years old.

'Defects in the Moral Training of Girls', by A Mother, in *The Church and the World: essays on questions of the day in 1868*, ed. by Rev. O. Shipley (London: 1868), p. 77.

32. As a hostile voice put it, early in the century:

> The shoemaker, the publican, the barber, the tailor, the butcher, the journeyman weaver, send their daughters to boarding schools; and no sooner do they enter those seminaries than they are all at once transformed into *young ladies*.

J.L. Chirol, *An Enquiry into the Best System of Female Education* (London: 1809), p. 233.

Virtually the same points are made in an article which appeared in *Fraser's Magazine*: 'Modern Matchmaking', *Fraser's Magazine*, XIII (1836), pp. 308 – 16.

33. 'Modern Matchmaking', *Fraser's Magazine*, p. 313.

34. W.R. Greg, 'Why are Women Redundant?', *National Review* (April 1862).

35. Jane Austen, *Pride and Prejudice* (London: Collins, 1967) p. 121.

36. For discussions of the heroine in Victorian fiction, see Robert Utter and Gwendolyn Needham, *Pamela's Daughters* (New York: Russell, 1972).

37. 'Married life is woman's profession . . . by not getting a husband, or losing him, she may find that she is without resources. All that can be said of her is, she had failed in business; and no social reform can prevent such failures.' 'Queen Bees or Working Bees', *Saturday Review*, (12 November 1859), quoted in Patricia Hollis, *Women in Public, 1850 – 1900: Documents of the Victorian Women's Movement* (London: George Allen and Unwin, 1979), p. 11.

38. For a discussion of this question, see Peter Cominos, 'Innocent Femina Sensualis in Unconscious Conflict', in *Suffer and Be Still: Women in the Victorian Age*, ed. by Martha Vicinus, pp. 155 – 72.

39. Chirol, *An Enquiry*, pp. 234 – 5.

40. Mrs Lynn Linton, 'The Girl of the Period', *Saturday Review* (14 March 1868), p. 340.

41. 'Defects in the Moral Training of Girls', pp. 88 – 9.

42. *The Girl's Own Paper* (4 October 1890), p. 4.

43. Sarah Grand, 'At What Age Should Girls Marry?', *The Young Woman*, VII (1898 – 9), p. 163.

44. Farningham, *Girlhood* (Second edition; London: James Clarke, 1895), p. 51.

45. Ibid.

PART TWO

Chapter 4

VICTORIAN ADVICE ABOUT THE MANAGEMENT OF FEMALE CHILDHOOD

Even in the early-Victorian years, children in the period from infancy to puberty were seen as having needs that set them apart from adolescents or adults; in the later years of the century, the perception of childhood as a distinct and separate period of life had become even more deeply ingrained than it was in the early decades. Accordingly, this consideration of Victorian advice about the rearing of middle-class daughters will begin with an analysis of commentary about this phase of growth and development.

Because the rearing of infants and children was considered to be pre-eminently the task of the mother, much of the evidence on which this analysis is based comes from advice literature designed for middle-class mothers. A substantial quantity of such advice literature was produced in the Victorian period, because of changes in the conception of motherhood. The Victorian middle-class mother was encouraged to exhibit an unprecedented amount of concern with the child-rearing process. In order to be considered a good mother, a woman would not only be expected to devote time and effort to her role, she was expected to approach that role in a new way. Motherhood came to be defined as a skill that had to be learned, rather than as behaviour that could be acquired simply by contact with other women who had been mothers. As one historian has put it, motherhood was undergoing 'modernisation' in the nineteenth century, and the modernisation of motherhood implied a willingness to seek advice and information from those who were considered to have an expertise based on systematic knowledge.[1]

Middle-class Victorian mothers could obtain such advice from book-length manuals and periodicals designed expressly to aid them in their tasks. In England, from the 1840s, there was a substantial market for such literature, and over the course of the nineteenth century, the market grew. From such publications, mothers could receive advice about the moral and spiritual welfare of their children, their psychological welfare, their physical care and their intellectual and social training. In the early-Victorian period, advice literature dealt more with the child's moral and spiritual welfare than with physical care, and was usually explicitly shaped by evangelical religious belief. By the end of the century, child-care advice, even when it emanated from evangelical sources, tended to be secular in tone, and had come to be more concerned with matters of health and with a child's physical environment than it had been earlier in the century.

The early-Victorian works concerned with the moral welfare of children were sometimes written by clergymen, but more often by women who presented themselves to their readers as pious mothers, whose experience of motherhood and whose piety qualified them to give advice to others. By the later decades of the century, advice about the psychological well-being of children was likely to be written by those who had professional expertise, or presented themselves as having such expertise, either because they were teachers, or because they had familiarised themselves with the study of children. Throughout the Victorian years, advice about physical health was either written by medical practitioners themselves, or was influenced by their beliefs. Nor did medical practitioners restrict themselves to comments about the physical health of children; they also expressed views about their psychological well-being, both in writing for lay readers, and for their fellow professionals. The growing influence of medical practitioners on childrearing in the nineteenth century was in fact one manifestation of the increased prestige that medicine was acquiring during these years.[2]

Victorian mothers, like mothers in all cultures, were expected to perform the task of differentiating between the sexes. Above all, they were expected to teach their daughters to conform to society's definition of femininity. That the successful sex-role socialisation of daughters was considered to be an important task of the Victorian mother and one that began in early childhood, is reflected in the fact that there is considerable explicit discussion of the question in the advice literature. And not only does the question arise as a separate topic, it is also present, implicitly if not explicitly, in the discussion of most of the issues relating to childrearing that were of concern during the period. A concern with the question of sex-role socialisation can be discerned as affecting, in a greater or lesser degree, advice about all the issues which will be considered in this account: physical care; instruction and play; and discipline and moral training.

The physical care of the infant and small child became a central focus of concern in Victorian advice literature in the mid-Victorian period. It is noteworthy that the concern became acute before medical knowledge and other contributing factors had succeeded in lowering the death rate of infants and children to any marked extent.[3] Thus it is not surprising that the prevailing tone in advice manuals about the physical care of infants and children was one of anxiety. As one popular mother's manual put it, an infant's life is 'literally a mere cobweb of strength'.[4]

Mothers could rely on the advice manuals to give them specific advice about the treatment of such common problems as infant diarrhoea or croup, but much Victorian advice about physical care in health or disease was more general in character. Perhaps because medical science could do so little to protect infants and children against the ravages of infectious childhood diseases, the advice literature concentrated as much on attempting to convince mothers to change the general style of their child-care routines as it did on specific questions. Notably, the experts advocated order and regularity, and the maintenance of physical distance between the child and its caretakers. Mothers were advised, for example, to abandon the then common practice of having the infant sleep in the same bed with an adult, a practice that was held to be both unsanitary and dangerous. At worst, it was said to lead to 'overlaying' — the smothering of the child by the adult. At best, it was said to lead to irregular sleep patterns. Mothers were also advised that excessive handling of the infant was unhealthy.[5]

Cleanliness, plenty of exposure to fresh air, and simplicity of diet were advocated both for their health-giving properties, and for their moral significance. This emphasis on the need for a strict routine in handling children, from the time of their birth, and on the need to teach habits of order, cleanliness and self-control, characterised advice about child-care right through the Victorian era. Mothers were told to avoid both overindulgence and neglect, and above all, to be consistent. Consistency, it was said, should begin in the child's infancy:

> From the moment a child takes notice it should be taught by the mother to understand her ways and motions, and it should never be capriciously treated — fondled and caressed at one moment, or treated harshly the next.[6]

If children were treated in an orderly manner, they would come to expect and prefer it, and in this way they would be well on the way to becoming orderly, self-controlled adults:

> A child kept even tolerably and wholesomely clean, will learn almost instinctively the discomfort of dirt . . . When the whole of the operation of her life . . . rising, washing, dressing, saying her prayers, being fed, taken out, put to bed — are done regularly and methodically, as they ought to be done, she will expect the accustomed punctuality and order; will fret against any conspicuous breach of rules.[7]

It is not surprising that Victorian middle-class mothers should have been advised to establish ordered child-care routines. Orderliness, and attention to detail, were advocated as qualities necessary for success in the public world of business and the professions; that they were also seen as necessary for success in mothering illustrates the extent to which the Victorian conception of the nature of the private sphere mirrored its conception of the public sphere. Nor is it surprising that an ordered routine was advocated for female children, as well as for males. While home life was presented as the refuge for the emotions, it was also the training ground for the public sphere. Boys had to be prepared to compete in the public sphere; girls had to be prepared, both as future mothers, and as representatives of their class, to understand, and to be able to transmit, the bourgeois virtues.

While much Victorian advice about the physical care of infants and children was designed to be applicable, without differentiation, to both sexes, sex difference played an explicit part in discussions about dress, diet and exercise. Perhaps surprisingly, in view of twentieth-century assumptions about Victorian practice, the experts of the Victorian period advised that sex differences in regard to these areas be minimised, rather than emphasised. The common twentieth-century image of the Victorian middle-class little girl portrays her as physically restricted and confined, dressed in clothing that impeded her movements, and prevented her from engaging in vigorous play. While there is evidence that many parents did attempt to treat their young daughters as fragile ornaments, expert opinion, throughout the period, was emphatically opposed to such treatment. Such advice either emanated directly from medical practitioners, or was influenced by them, and the view of the medical profession was that from infancy to puberty, children should be provided with a physical regime that did not differentiate in great measure between the sexes. The experts, indeed, believed that parents were all too prone to differentiate between the sexes unnecessarily, to the detriment of the health of their daughters.

This point of view can be seen in discussions of appropriate clothing for infants and young children.[8] The clothing recommended for the period from birth to four was identical for the two sexes. Here, of course, the experts were merely echoing prevailing practice. Up until the early twentieth century, virtually no distinction was made between male and female dress in infancy and early childhood. Boys and girls alike were dressed *as girls*; that is, in petticoats. For infants the experts recommended non-constricting clothing. Mothers were advised that babies should be allowed to 'roll and kick about as much as they will',[9] and that therefore the use of stays or bindings was harmful, although the use of a 'bellyband' (a strip of wadded cloth tied around the infant's stomach) was still being recommended until the end of the century.[10] A baby's clothing should be light and loose, said the experts, and the skirts of its gowns should not be overly long. It was also recommended that the baby be dressed warmly enough, with due consideration being given to the vagaries of the English climate. Early in the century, although infants and young children were often encumbered with heavy dresses and caps, the dresses had been cut low in the neck. By mid-century, loose but high-necked garments were recommended, so that the ill effects of drafts could be avoided.[11]

During the Victorian period, prevailing custom decreed that, at the age of three or four, sex differentiation should be made in children's dress. At that age, boys were ceremoniously put into trousers, and this custom can be assumed to have underscored gender difference. Medical practitioners and lay people who wrote on the subject of children's dress did not challenge this custom, but they did emphasise that between the ages of four and twelve, girls should be dressed in loose, comfortable, unfussy clothing.

The practice that was inveighed against most vigorously was the use of tight stays for little girls. As a popular mother's manual, published in 1879, pointed out:

> They cannot be for the support of the body, for at the tender age of childhood, there is no essential difference in this respect between the frame of the male and that of the female, yet it would be deemed a great absurdity to place stays on growing boys in the same manner as they are employed for growing girls.[12]

Such 'unnatural and unnecessary attire', this author went on to say, is adopted 'for fashion's sake . . . to give . . . a graceful and genteel figure'. It is 'a species of torture' that is damaging to the health of lungs and heart.

Expert opinion was universally negative about the use of tight lacing for pre-pubescent girls. Correct clothing, it was emphasised, should allow a little girl freedom of movement, and keep her warm. Readers of a mothers' manual published in 1866 were offered the following suggestions for dressing their small daughters in winter:

> The following dress for a little girl in winter is *not* a *catch a cold* one, and is sensibly considered — warm woollen stockings, hand-knitted in fine, soft, pretty wool . . . thick double-soled boots, high up the leg . . . a chemise of good, but somewhat stout long-cloth, drawers . . . in the form of knickerbockers . . . a scarlet flannel petticoat . . . tacked or buttoned to scarlet stays* . . . and an upper petticoat of . . . flannel . . . A warm dress with half-high body and detachable sleeves.[13]

That advice illustrates several aspects of mid-Victorian attitudes towards dress for little girls. First, from a twentieth-century point of view, the clothing suggested appears both constricting and overly complicated; the writer assumes, however, that the outfit she is recommending is both less complicated and less confining than the clothing in which many mothers might dress their daughters, without the benefit of her advice. Secondly, it is clear that while the small girl's comfort and physical mobility were to be promoted, distinctions between the sexes were by no means to be done away with. The little girl's stockings should be 'pretty', and while she is to enjoy the freedom and warmth of trouser-like garments under her skirts, she is, none-theless, to wear *skirts*.

Along with sensible clothing, plenty of physical exercise was also recommended. It has already been noted that Victorian child-care experts encouraged mothers to allow their infants free use of their limbs. For small children past the age of infancy, sufficient exercise in the open air was emphasised as essential to health. Here too, as with their advice about clothing, the experts encouraged parents to minimise any sex differences. 'Exercise is indispensible to the health of girls as well as boys', it was said, and throughout the Victorian period, advice book writers clearly believed that they were encouraging their

---

* The 'stays' here referred to were not boned or tight: they were a cotton suspender belt, designed so that other garments could be attached to them. The term 'stays' was used to refer both to this sort of garment, and to the constricting laced corset.

readers to permit their daughters to be more physically active than was normally the rule.[14]

Views about the type of physical activity that was acceptable for little girls did change over the course of the Victorian decades. At the beginning of the period, advocates of a vigorous physical regime for little girls were cautious about the activities they felt they could recommend, and mindful of the need to preserve the proprieties decreed by the early-Victorian conception of appropriate feminine behaviour. A forward-looking writer of the 1830s, for example, while encouraging little girls to play vigorous games, suggested at the same time that boys could play such games in large groups and in public, but that girls should play them only in private:

> Walking and other out-of-door exercises cannot be too much recommended to young people. Even skating, driving hoop and other boyish sports may be practised to great advantage by little girls provided they can be pursued within the enclosure of a garden or court; in the street, of course, they would be highly improper. It is true, such games are rather violent, and sometimes noisy, but they tend to form a vigorous constitution; and girls who are habitually lady-like, will never allow themselves to be rude and vulgar, even in play.[15]

In the 1830s, this writer was ahead of her time. By the late-Victorian years, progressive writers were advocating activity considerably more vigorous than this for pre-pubescent girls. For instance, an expert who wrote for women's magazines in the 1880s, a woman who was one of the first of the pioneer women medical doctors, offered mothers the following advice:

> Let no difference be made between boys and girls, at any rate until the age of twelve, but let the latter have their pets, their garden, their cricket, their wild games, just the same as their brothers. It is merely a question of clothes, and of the girl becoming a 'tom-boy'. . .[16]

Although cricket affords considerably more opportunity for vigorous activity than playing with a hoop, the attitudes displayed by the two writers just quoted are in fact similar. Increased physical activity is recommended in both cases, but both writers perceive such activitiy as 'boyish'. Thus, girls engaging in games or sports were assumed to be behaving *like boys*, and the identification of vigorous physical activity with masculinity was therefore maintained. In both the early and the late-Victorian period, those who recommended 'boyish' physical activity for pre-pubescent girls did so because they thought it would benefit their physical health, but they were always mindful of the need to preserve a girl's femininity.

In addition to advice about clothing and about the physical regime appropriate for infants and young children, Victorian mothers could also go to the experts for information about appropriate diet for their children. For infants, Victorian doctors emphasised that everything should be avoided except breast milk. Nine months was suggested as the appropriate age for weaning.[17] In discussions of infant feeding, no distinctions of gender were made. While advice manuals did make distinctions between the diet appropriate to children after weaning, and that suitable for adults, again no distinction was made between the sexes. Starches, milk and meat were recommended along with a few vegetables and fruits. Mothers were told that girls needed a plain but hearty diet, just as their brothers did, and one medical man, in discussing the subject, was concerned to combat any restrictions in the diet of girls: 'Do we not somewhat imitate the Chinese in the treatment of their daughters' feet? Do we not sometimes withdraw food from a girl for fear she should become too stout . . .?'[18] He goes on to castigate mothers in 'high life' who think it acceptable to have 'ruddy' boys, but who want 'semi-transparent' daughters.

As well as advising mothers about the treatment of their children in health, books and articles also provided advice about the treatment of children in disease. This advice also indicates that medical opinion acknowledged few gender differences in infants and young children in regard to susceptibility to disease. Some medical practitioners, in writing for the profession rather than for lay readers, did note that girls were as a rule more healthy than boys in infancy and as young children.[19] There were only two areas that were thought to provide exceptions to this rule. The first was that of nervous disease. Females were believed to exhibit nervous weaknesses, even as children, more frequently than males.[20] As one medical man put it, girls frequently displayed a 'morbid susceptibility of the nervous system', with the result that once past the age of six, they were more likely to contract chorea (St Vitus's Dance) than were boys. Another physician, writing about nervous diseases in childhood in a household medical manual published in 1881, asserted that girls, but not boys, might well exhibit a pre-hysterical state as young children, if in later life they were 'destined to become markedly hysterical'. This physician described such little girls as possessing a 'peculiar flightiness and excitability of temperament, violent and unreasonable temper, [and a] ready disposition to cry or scream'.[21]

The other malady that many medical practitioners believed was more common in girls than in boys was spinal curvature. The supposed greater frequency of spinal deformity in girls, in both the pre-pubescent and post-pubescent stages, contributed to the controversy over tight lacing.[22] While doctors, throughout the Victorian years, attributed such deformities to improper dress and inadequate exercise, many lay people continued to believe that if a female child or woman was not securely laced, her health would be endangered. The supposed greater fragility of girls may have motivated mothers who continued to tight lace their daughters as much as a desire to make the child appear more graceful or feminine.

Throughout the Victorian period, advice about childbearing reflected a belief that the home was the best place for the intellectual and social training of children, and for the inculcation of moral values.[23] This belief was held in a more unqualified manner in the early decades than it was later in the century; by the later decades, for example, mothers' magazines and advice books were voicing support for the kindergarten movement. But even then, the idea that the home should be the centre and the mother the central figure in all facets of early childhood experience, was not questioned.[24] Again, throughout the period, home-centred socialisation was considered to be of even greater importance for girls than it was for boys.

With respect to instruction in early childhood, both mid-Victorian and late-Victorian magazines and mothers' manuals gave detailed advice about the methods believed to be most suitable for instruction within the home. It was usually suggested that the mother resort to the use of rote learning in the teaching of arithmetic or spelling, but that the child's reasoning powers should be appealed to wherever possible. Such subjects as history and geography, it was suggested, should be imparted in an informal way, through the use of methods that would capture the child's natural curiosity. The author of one best-selling advice book, first published in 1865, explains that she taught geography to her girls and boys in the following manner:

> Geography I taught my children almost wholly in conversations. Three large maps . . . graced the walls of the play-room, and this indeed was our schoolroom . . . We made imaginary visits — first

to our friends in the county we were living in, and then to our relatives in the adjoining county . . . and so we visited all the places that
had anything of interest by which they could be remembered.[25]

When discussing the subject of early childhood education, Victorian manuals of advice always assume that boys and girls would be
educated together in the home. But an integrated routine of study was
thought to be quite compatible with the encouragement of appropriate sex roles. Shared lessons, it was thought, would be but one way
in which brothers and sisters would easily and naturally come to
understand both sex differences and similarities. Moreover, it was
always suggested that the learning of lessons within the home setting
would merge naturally with other activities, in which sex differentiation would play a part. For example, in suggesting recreational
reading matter for children, some sex differentiation was encouraged.
A list of books in one mothers' manual, which consisted chiefly of
moral tales, was designed specifically with girls in mind. While the
author suggests that up to a 'certain period', the list would suffice for
boys as well, in middle childhood, she says, boys would need boys'
books. The titles of the books recommended for boys — *Men Who
Have Risen* and *Famous Boys and How They Became Great Men* are
two examples — reflect the middle-class belief that boys, even as
children, should be encouraged to direct their energies towards
achieving worldly success.[26]

In addition to developing the mind, mothers were told that home
education should also include training in practical skills. In the case of
girls, the practical skills they were to learn were those of housewifery.
Sewing and needlework were considered to be the most essential of
these domestic skills, and right through the Victorian period, it was
advised that training in sewing should begin early in a girl's life. It was
frequently suggested that a little girl begin by learning to cut out and
make up a man's shirt, trying her hand first at making such a garment
for father or brother. A girl who could not sew was considered not only
to lack a useful skill, but to lack one that was essential to her *as a
female*: 'Nothing can be more pitiable than to see a female . . . unable
to ply her needle, her case being somewhat similar to that of a male
. . . who does not know how to read.'[27]

It is remarkable that the importance given to hand sewing in advice
about the training of girls of all classes did not appreciably lessen over
the course of the nineteenth century, although the function of sewing
and dressmaking skills in fact altered radically. Such advances in

technology as the home sewing-machine and commercial dress patterns had, by the last two decades in the century, widened the possibilities for home sewing for women with average skills, but at the same time, the growth of the ready-to-wear industry had reduced the necessity for much of the home sewing that had been done in the early-Victorian period. In spite of these changes in technology and marketing, both plain hand sewing and fancy needlework were still generally seen as essential skills that all middle-class girls should begin to learn early in life, even in the late-Victorian decades. The continued emphasis placed on this skill indicates that its importance was not solely practical: it had, as well, a symbolic connection with femininity.

Teaching a variety of other domestic skills to little girls was also considered essential. Mothers were urged to encourage even the youngest of their daughters to help in the household:

> *Girls* cannot too early be taught the value of knowing how to perform the customary duties of a household; they should be given every opportunity of *seeing* them done, and of *trying* to do them. The lesson will be thus learned pleasantly, continuously and thoroughly. Mothers will have housewives growing up around their firesides unawares.[28]

In play, as in learning, Victorian mothers were advised that within the family, the two sexes should as small children share many activities. Shared play, it was believed, would encourage both suitable similarities, and at the same time, reinforce and develop those sex differences that were assumed to be 'natural'. The general assumption was made that boys were naturally assertive, and girls were naturally gentle and passive. By playing together, each sex would develop some of the traits of the opposite sex — 'the girl's weakness [would be] strengthened, and the boy's roughness softened' — [29] but, as well, each would bring out appropriate behaviour in the other. For a boy, it was suggested that contact with his sisters would develop 'an instinct of protectiveness, which it is well to encourage, since it is the germ of true manly feeling in after life'.[30]

The toys suggested as suitable for each sex reflect both the desire to encourage girls to be active in childhood, and the pervasive assumption that, in adulthood, the roles of males and females would be separate and distinct. Thus, although active games are suggested as appropriate for girls, it is also assumed that all girls will play with dolls. The doll was said to be 'pre-eminently the toy of girlhood'.[31] In the Victorian period, dolls were considered beneficial for girls not only because they would, through doll play, rehearse their future maternal role, but also because they would learn practical skills. Unlike the twentieth-century doll who comes completely equipped with a wardrobe, Victorian dolls provided an opportunity for their young owners to learn needlework. Making clothing for dolls appears, in fact, to have been one of the chief ways in which little Victorian girls engaged in doll play, and Victorian doll play can thus be seen as providing both socialisation for, and training in, the skills of the feminine role.

From the early-Victorian period, right through to the end of the century, Victorian advice literature for mothers had much to say about the correct mode of disciplining children. However, opinion on this issue did change radically over the course of the century. In the early-Victorian years discipline was seen as the most central question in child management. The child's behaviour was seen as directly related to its eternal salvation, and its salvation was regarded as of much greater importance than its happiness, or its physical health. A good mother would be concerned, above all, with her child's spiritual welfare: 'The mother who does not feel for the soul of her child has no more love to it than the white bear to her cub.'[32]

Much evangelical thought during the early-Victorian period was still influenced by the belief, whose origins went back to seventeenth-century Puritanism, that children come into the world possessed of a strong natural will, a will that is inherently sinful, and in need of being 'broken'. A parent's main duty was to control the child's will, a duty that could only be performed by enforcing unquestioning obedience on the child through the use of physical punishment.[33]

The perception of the child as naturally sinful was nearly always accompanied by a belief that the patriarchal model for family organisation was the only correct one.[34] According to that model, a family functions properly only if it possesses a hierarchy of authority. At the top of the hierarchy was the husband and father, who had a God-given responsibility to be head of the family. Both husband and wife, as parents, were responsible for the moral and spiritual, as well as the physical welfare of the child, but while the mother had authority, and indeed had most of the day-to-day responsibility for asserting it, her authority was perceived as delegated to her by her husband.

The fact that within the patriarchal tradition male authority was seen as sanctioned by God, whereas female authority was seen as sanctioned by men, affected the perception of the natures of male and female children and of the discipline they might therefore need. While it was agreed that girls, like boys, had sinful wills, in need of being 'broken', and while harsh physical punishment was advocated for girls as well as for boys, it was implicitly and sometimes explicitly assumed that boys had stronger wills than girls, and passions that were more difficult to control. In fact, it was even assumed that while such gender-related character differences might require that more care and firmness be employed in the handling of boys, the stronger wills of male children would, in the end, make them more manly men: 'Boys early show an impatience of constraint and a taste for ruling which is the germ of their future character, as men to whom God has subjected all created living things.'[35]

Even in the early-Victorian decades, the outlook that perceived the child as inherently sinful, and which advocated harsh punishment, was being challenged by one that perceived the child's character as naturally good, or at least neutral. While these writers also believed that it was the mother's duty to correct the child's passionate tendencies, they suggested that the best way to achieve this goal was through gentleness and the use of reason. Early-Victorian commentators of this type pointed out the contradiction involved in using corporal punishment — a violent act — to correct and control violence within the child.[36]

Those early-Victorian writers who advocated a milder and less authoritarian style of discipline represented the wave of the future. Although one can find advocates of the harsh, authoritarian style even at the end of the century, by the 1870s it was already the case that only the rare child-care expert would advocate 'breaking the will' of the child.[37] By the late-Victorian period, not only was harsh discipline suspect, discipline itself was no longer considered as a spiritual problem that could be seen in isolation, but was part of a more widely conceived set of issues relating to child management. As the 'spare the rod and spoil the child' mentality became discredited, egalitarian notions of communication, rather than the enforcement of authority, became an important goal in the treatment of young children.[38]

Victorian child-care advice about methods of discipline remained consistent in one important respect. Throughout the period, mothers were advised that the purpose of discipline was not simply to control the child, but to teach it to be a moral being. As one writer expressed it, children 'must be taught to dislike what is wrong merely because it is wrong'. Given the religious tenor of the Victorian middle-class world view, it is not surprising that the conception of what morality was, and the means by which it was suggested that morality should be cultivated, was inextricably connected with religion. For most Victorians, religious belief and morality were inseparable.[39]

Perhaps because religious belief was so deeply ingrained, advice about how religious knowledge ought to be conveyed occurs less often than might be expected. What explicit advice there was does indicate that a change occurred over the course of the nineteenth century. In the first half of the nineteenth century, it was considered perfectly acceptable to expose even very young children to vivid pictures of the meaning of evil, the punishment of Hell, and the dangers of dying in a state of sin. Children's stories that met with general approval contained examples of the sad fate that awaited sinners, young or old, who died unrepentent. For example, a widely disseminated early-nineteenth-century children's periodical was full of homilies whose deliberate intention was to instill the fear of sin in the young reader:

> By nature we are all dead in trespasses and sins, careless of our soul; having a carnal mind, which is in enmity against God . . . If we die in that state we cannot be with God, for 'without holiness, no man shall see the Lord.'[40]

Later on in the century it was suggested that a gentler form of Christianity should be presented to very young children, and, in addition, some advice books warned against forcing the young child to absorb long Scripture readings or prayers. As one such advice book writer told her readers:

> I have never wearied my children with long prayers or long Scripture readings or sermons . . . two or three verses sufficed for a pleasant discourse which could be easily remembered and fitted to daily application.[41]

For the most part, the place of religion in Victorian child-care advice was general and pervasive, rather than explicitly focused. The prevailing tone of the advice literature simply assumes that religious sanctions ought to be introduced in instilling moral behaviour in all matters. Even very young children were to be taught that duty, not pleasure, was of first importance, and it was assumed that a commitment to duty world spring from religious belief.

The assumption found in Victorian child-care manuals that morality, duty and religion were interconnected applied equally to girls and to boys. The nature of dutiful behaviour varied according to sex, but the injunction to put duty first, and the belief that children, even when very young, should be taught that they themselves were responsible for their own thoughts and acts, involved no distinction of sex. The fact that the Victorians believed that females, like males, should be encouraged to choose the roles assigned to them out of inward conviction offered a Victorian girl the possibility of developing a sense of self-worth in spite of the limitation of the feminine role.

Even in early childhood, it was suggested that a girl should begin to learn that the feminine role involved self-abnegation and self-sacrifice; but even in early childhood girls were reminded that they possessed an immortal soul, and that their highest duty was to attend to its development. As a mid-century advice book written for girls suggested: 'You cannot think too much of yourself; for you are the germ of an immortal being.' Every action, said this writer, was 'like a pebble thrown in water . . . The most insignificant action you perform, in its influence upon your character will reach through the whole period of your existence.'[42] Paradoxically, then, religious belief both sanctioned female inferiority, by insisting that feminine duty involved self-abnegation, and gave support for the spiritual equality of the sexes. Victorian mothers were told that both aspects of the Victorian conception of feminine duty were to be instilled into girls from their earliest childhood.

Given the fact that adult sex roles were more sharply differentiated in the Victorian period than they are today, the views of Victorian medical practitioners and lay authorities about sex-role differentiation from birth to puberty affords some surprises. As we have seen, Victorian medical and lay opinion advocated that differences in the physical regime of young boys and girls be minimised. Parents were encouraged to dress their daughters in clothing suitable for vigorous play, and to allow them plenty of opportunity for physical development.

While mothers were advised that some sex-role differentiation would be appropriate in early childhood education and training, and in play, here too there was little insistence that the sexes ought to be separated or subjected to a separate regime. Girls, to be sure, were to be introduced to the feminine role even in early childhood — they were, for example, to be encouraged to be 'little housewives' — but up until the age of ten or thereabouts, mothers were told that within the home setting brothers and sisters should learn their lessons together and share their playtime.

These suggestions do not mean that Victorian opinion advocated the eventual minimisation of sex differences. Frequently, the same writers who suggest minimising differences up to puberty advocate sharp differentiation after puberty. It is possible that the enforcement of sex-role differentiation in early childhood was of only minor importance to the Victorians, both because they accorded such early differentiation less importance than it is accorded today, and because they were more certain than we are today about the innate differences between males and females. In the twentieth century, it has been the influence of Freudian psychology that has caused physicians, psychologists and parents to become acutely sensitive to the supposed dangers involved in adoption, even by very young children, of sex-role activity that is defined as inappropriate. The Victorians, in contrast, seemed to have believed that sex differences relating not only to reproductive structure, but to thinking, feeling and behaving, were both innate and unshakable. As one medical practitioner, writing in the 1850s, asserted when describing children from three to seven:

> Another cause of the charm which invests this age . . . is the singular fashion in which children evidently show, by their manner and actions, the sex to which they belong; for it is not true that men and women are similar so long as they play about as little boys and girls, and that training alone makes them different.[43]

A woman physician, writing in 1889 in a women's magazine, urged her readers to allow their pre-pubescent daughters plenty of freedom, so that they would not resent having been born female. Little girls could safely be encouraged to behave like boys without any fear that as big girls they would wish to continue to do so:

> Now, while it is true that a big girl in many respects cannot do as a big boy does, and *usually has no desire to*, it is also equally true . . . that a little girl can do almost exactly what a little boy can, and she usually wants to . . . There would seem to be no good reason why the training and education of girls and of boys should not be essentially identical up to a certain age. Be not in too great a hurry to impose upon your little girl the burden of her sex.[44]

Sex differences, then, were discernible to the Victorians even in early childhood, but it was believed that they would emerge in full flower only at puberty. Then, they would emerge almost inevitably. Since this was thought to be the case, there was no need to enforce differences in early childhood.

Notes

1. As one advice book for mothers put it: it is a mistake to think that mothers can do their work 'without knowledge or instruction of any kind'. This belief, says the author, 'is one of the popular delusions which each year claims a large sacrifice of young lives'. *A Few Suggestions to Mothers on the Management of their Children; By a Mother* (London: J & A. Churchill, 1884), p. vi. For the 'Modernisation of Motherhood', see Patricia Branca, *Silent Sisterhood: Middle-Class Women in the Victorian Home* (London: Croom Helm , 1975), p. 1.

2. For the increased prestige of the medical profession, see M. Jeanne Peterson, *The Medical Profession in Mid-Victorian London* (Berkeley: University of California Press, 1978).

3. Lomax, 'Advances in Pediatrics', p. 259.

4. *Ward and Lock's Home Book: A Domestic Cyclopaedia* (London: Ward, Lock & Co., 1866), p. 417.

5. See 'Overlaying of Children', *The British Mother's Journal* (January, 1858), pp. 43 – 4.

6. Mrs Warren, *How I Managed My Children from Infancy to Marriage* (London: Houlston and Wright, 1865), p. 14.

7. *The Mother's Companion*, I (1887), p. 22.

8. On children's clothing, see Phillis Cunningham and Anne Buck, *Children's Costume in England: Thirteen Hundred to Nineteen Hundred* (London: Adam & Charles Black, 1965).

9. *Ward and Lock's Home Book* (1866), p. 432.

10. Dr Henry Arthur Allbutt, *Every Mother's Handbook: A guide to the management of her children from birth through infancy and childhood* (London: Simpkin, Marshall & Co., 1897), p. 31.

11. Ibid., p. 420. See also Emma F. Angell Drake, MD, *What a Young Wife Ought to Know* (London: The Vir Publishing Co., 1901), p. 51.

12. *The Mother's Home Book* (London: Ward and Lock, 1897), p. 60. See also *The British Mother's Journal* (1856 – 7), pp. 34 – 5.

13. *Ward and Lock's Home Book* (1866), p. 447.

14. Allbutt, *Every Mother's Handbook*, p. 166.

15. Lydia Maria Child, *The Little Girl's Own Book*, (Edinburgh: Robert Martin, 1847).

16. Mrs Atkins, MD, *The Mother's Companion*, I (1887), p. 151.

17. Alfred Fennings, *Every Mother's Book; or the Child's Best Doctor* (London: West Cowes? 1856?), p. 5. Allbutt, *Every Mother's Handbook*, p. 83.

18. Edward John Tilt, MD, *The Elements of Health, and Principles of Female Hygiene* (London: Henry G. Bohn, 1852), pp. 140–1; Allbutt, *Every Mother's Handbook,* p. 151.

19. Tilt, *Elements*, p. 156.

20. Ibib.

21. Mary Putnam Jacobi, 'The Nervous Diseases of Infancy and Childhood', in *Wood's Household Practice of Medicine, Hygiene and Surgery. A practical treatise for the use of families, travellers . . . and others,* ed. by F.A. Castle (London: Sampson Low & Co., 1881), p. 575.

22. 'Perhaps the most common deformity in growing girls is in the spine, which frequently deviates from the straight line in a lateral curve to one side or the other.' A Medical Practitioner, 'The Rising Generation', in *The Mother's Companion*, VII (1893), p. 7. See also Tilt, *Elements*, pp. 161 – 2. Mrs Hoggan, the physician appointed by Miss Buss as the first medical inspector at the North London Collegiate School was very concerned with this problem. See the notebook labelled 'Mrs. Hoggan's Notes', 1882 – 5, North London Collegiate School Archives.

23. See, for example, Warren, *How I Managed*, p. 33; *The Mother's Home Book*, p. 174.

24. E.g., *The Mother's Companion*, I (1887), p. 47; Mrs Matilda Pullan, *Children and How to Manage Them* (London: 1856), pp. 10 – 20; *Mothers and Daughters*, (November 1895), p. 210.

25. Mrs Warren, *How I Managed*, p. 40.

Some writers cautioned against the dangers of forcing children to learn too early: 'When the late Mrs. Barbauld wrote her *Lessons for Children* . . . she unquestionably . . . rendered no good service to the cause of education. Very many things may be, and ought to be taught, at an earlier age than three years, but reading, unless under peculiarly favourable circumstances, is not one of them'. *Englishwoman's Magazine and Christian Mother's Miscellany*, III (1848), p. 644.

26. *The Mother's Thorough Resource Book* (London: Ward and Lock, 1860), p. 177.

27. *The Mother's Home Book* (1879), p. 220.

28. *Ward and Lock's Home Book* (1866), p. 508.

29. *The Mother's Companion*, I (1887), p. 62.

30. Pullan, *Children*, p. 14.

31. *Mother's Thorough Resource Book*, p. 161.

32. *The Mother's Friend*, I (1848), pp. 4 – 5.

33. E.g., 'Alas! Our first step in the study of character confirms the testimony of the experience of six thousand years . . . The human heart is deceitful above all things, and desperately wicked . . . the truth is, that there is EVIL IN THE SOUL.' *Engishwoman's Magazine*, IV (1849), p. 355; and 'If children [are to be] happy in this world . . . and happy in the world to come [they must be] taught to obey you . . ."He that spareth his rod hateth his child, but he that loveth him, chasteneth him betimes".' *The Mother's Friend*, I (1848), pp. 82 – 3.

34. As one writer put it: 'Obedience is absolutely essential to proper family government.' Jacob Abbott, *The Mother at Home: or the Principles of Maternal Duty* (Derby: 1835), p. 27.

35. *The Mother's Friend*, I (1848), p. 153.

36. E.g., these comments about a mother who used physical punishment to control a 'passionate' boy: 'Nor had she any idea that she only *increased* his passions in her strivings to make him submit to her authority, and that *she* herself, really called forth more than half her boy's violence, by her injudicious treatment of locking him up and strapping him.' *British Mother's Magazine*, I (1845), p. 33.

37. It should be emphasised that it was child-care experts who gradually abandoned approval for corporal punishment. One indication that some families, at least, continued to employ harsh physical punishment in disciplining children of both sexes, is the correspondence from readers 'On the Whipping of Girls' which appeared in the *Englishwoman's Domestic Magazine* from 1868 to 1870. My own assessment is that much of this correspondence was bogus, and written with pornographic intent, but some of it was undoubtedly genuine. E.g., 'It seems to me all your correspondents omit the first principle of the usefulness of punishment by whipping — namely that you cannot begin too early . . . as babes in arms my children were never allowed what they screamed for, and at the age of one year I began to chastise them.' *Englishwoman's Domestic Magazine*, VIII (1 February 1870), p. 126. For a discussion of this correspondence, and of two cases involving abuse of female children, see Mary S. Hartman, 'Child Abuse and Self-Abuse', *History of Childhood Quarterly*, II (1974), pp. 221 – 48.

38. For example, an article from the 1890s advocated encouraging children to talk freely, and to abandon the old maxim that 'children should be seen and not heard':

Of course, they must not be allowed to monopolise the conversation . . . still, let them talk when they wish to do so . . . Then the home will be made happier for both parents and children, because confidence between them will be fostered.

Phyllis Browne, 'For Mothers and Wives', *Mother's Companion* VII (1893), p. 100.

39. 'It should never be forgotten that they are tender plants committed to our fostering care, that every thoughtless word or careless neglect may destroy a germ of immortality.' *British Mother's Journal* (January 1856), p. 16.

40. *The Child's Companion or Sunday Scholar's Reward*, VI (1828), p. 106.

41. Mrs Warren, *How I Managed*, p. 47.

42. W. Nicholson, *How to be a Lady: A Book for Girls Comprising Directions for Being Useful and Happy, Accomplished and Agreeable, Loved and Respected in Single and Married Life* (London: n.d. but c. 1850), p. 12.

43. Tilt, *Elements*, p. 105.

44. Lucy White Palmer, 'A Word in Behalf of the Little Girls', *The Mother's Companion*, III (1889), p. 95.

Chapter 5

A HEALTHY MIND IN A HEALTHY BODY: VICTORIAN ADVICE ABOUT THE MANAGEMENT OF FEMALE PUBERTY

Victorian mothers were told that in infancy and early childhood girls and boys should be treated in much the same way; in contrast, the onset of puberty was seen as the period when individuals should adopt the behaviour and physical deportment appropriate to their sex. Although the last decades of the century would bring some modification of these beliefs, throughout the Victorian period, the purpose of a girl's life, after puberty, was defined as preparation for the adult feminine role. In writing about girls during childhood, the girl's future role was kept in the background; in Victorian discussions of female adolescence the fact that girls would, as adults, be expected to embody the Victorian image of femininity assumes a central place. In this chapter and the one that follows the advice that middle-class mothers, and middle-class girls themselves, were given about adolescence will be examined.

In this chapter, it is advice about a girl's physical well-being and her physical behaviour that will concern us. We will begin with an analysis of Victorian advice about the physiological manifestations of female puberty — that is, about menstruation, and the physical changes accompanying its onset. In assessing the significance of the menarche in Victorian perceptions of female adolescence, Victorian reticence about the discussion of bodily processes and sexuality creates problems of interpretation. For example, if we were to rely only on advice books and periodical articles written for young girls themselves, we might think that the Victorians gave these matters little thought, and accorded them little importance in a girl's development; indeed we might be led to believe that Victorian girls managed to become women without undergoing the menarche. In such writings, even in the last years of the century, menstruation itself and the awakening of sexual feelings were referred to only in an allusive manner.

In sharp contrast to its absence from manuals of advice that were written for adolescent girls themselves, was the prominent place that menstruation had in the writings of medical practitioners. Victorian medical men believed that the onset of menstruation was the central event of female adolescence, that it had an effect on a girl's future health in womanhood, and that it was also connected with her psychological and moral condition. The great significance that menstruation had for the medical profession is reflected most noticeably in the professional medical literature, but it may also be found in advice manuals physicians addressed to mothers.

A family owning a copy of *Wood's Household Practice*, a home medical encyclopedia published in 1881, would have been instructed that at the onset of menstruation: 'The pelvis enlarges, hips are expanded . . . the angular and awkward outlines of girlhood . . . are exchanged for the . . . graceful and beautiful'. Mothers were advised to expect accompanying emotional and behavioural changes in their daughters:

> The girl's manners and habits . . . undergo a marked change. She discards the doll that she played with but yesterday; she feels that she is no longer a child, and that duties and responsibilities devolve upon her. She is no longer wayward, romping and careless, but becomes reserved and modest in her deportment. In short, she is now a woman, prepared to love and be loved, and capable of performing the highest and most important functions of her sex.[1]

The medical man who wrote the description expressed a point of view commonly held by members of the profession throughout the Victorian period. Physicians generally held that the physical events of puberty triggered the psychical manifestations of femininity. In the words of another medical practitioner: 'That which makes man more bold, will generally awaken greater timidity in women. Puberty, which gives man the knowledge of greater power, gives to woman the conviction of her dependence.'[2]

This belief that it was the physical events of puberty, and above all the physical event of menstruation, that caused the flowering of the psychological manifestations of femininity has important consequences for the way in which femininity is perceived. If the character traits associated with femininity (traits like timidity, modesty and dependence) are believed to spring directly and inevitably from the physical manifestations of puberty — directly from the menstrual flow, so to speak — any necessity for explaining why girls adopt the traits associated with femininity as they mature is removed.

Victorian medical practitioners generally agreed that the onset of menstruation could bring with it both physical and psychological problems, and that therefore considerable care should be taken as puberty approached. While little girls might be as hardy as their brothers, the maturation process rendered girls delicate and fragile:

> The delicacy of the young female often lays the foundation of many distressing maladies . . . Therefore, it imperatively behoves mothers, and indeed all other persons in the charge of female infancy, to watch carefully and anxiously the important period of incipient menstruation.[3]

Mothers were advised that a girl must be careful of herself, during her menstrual periods. Most Victorian doctors, throughout the century, advised that physical exercise be curtailed, that sea bathing and cold baths be avoided, and that the diet be controlled. Travelling during the monthly period was held to be potentially dangerous for girls; one mid-Victorian medical man advised that railway journeys could have especially harmful consequences. Pleasure and excitement were also thought to be dangerous, because emotional stimulation was believed to have an adverse effect on the menstrual flow.[4] Medical men advised against 'balls and entertainments' during the menstrual period, and also against novel reading. One doctor, the author of a popular manual of advice published in 1882, suggested to mothers that they curtail their daughters' music lessons during the monthly periods: practising the piano, he thought, involved too much physical strain, and in addition, the emotions evoked by the music could be harmful.[5]

Many Victorian doctors extended the dangerous time of menstruation to the entire period of puberty. All of a girl's energies during the period 'so fatal to her sex', as one physician put it, should be devoted to ensuring that healthy womanhood would be achieved. Excessive study, especially, was considered harmful to the adolescent girl:

> During the crisis of puberty, and until puberty is fully confirmed, there should be a general relaxation from study, which might otherwise too forcibly engross the mind, and the energies required by the constitution to work out nature's ends. Even in man the excess of mental labour is known to produce constipation, by some prostration of venous energy; would it not be then likely to have the same effect on girls, besides checking the critical flow which nature contemplates establishing?[6]

In the opinion of Victorian doctors, an extensive number of physical and psychological symptoms exhibited by adolescent girls were associated with a disrupted puberty, and specifically with abnormal menstruation. The physical symptoms included pallor, weight loss, lung disease, stomach disorders, and a tendency to be always ailing. The psychological symptoms identified with abnormal puberty covered a wide range, and indeed, were sometimes contradictory. One doctor, discussing the symptoms of ill-health from which girls with abnormal menstrual patterns might suffer, included the following psychological and behavioural manifestations:

> The patient becomes restless and excited, or melancholy and retiring; listless and indifferent to the social influence of domestic life . . . often a great disposition for novelties is exhibited, the patient desiring to escape from home, fond of becoming a nurse in hospitals, 'sœur de charité' or other pursuits of the like nature, according to station and opportunities.[7]

The two most common labels given to the symptoms attributed to abnormal menstruation were chlorosis and hysteria. Chlorosis covered a wide variety of ailments, the only consistent one being anaemia. As one doctor described it: 'The disease is one of almost universal influence; it is not confined to a particular organ, but affects the entire system.'[8] Thus, as long as a girl displayed any of the symptoms of chlorosis — for example, should she be listless, or overexcitable, or suffer from constipation or diarrhoea — the disease could be held responsible for any other physical or mental ill she might exhibit. The same was true of hysteria, which, although it was seen primarily as a mental or 'nervous' disease, was, like chlorosis, associated with abnormalities in menstruation. Frequently, chlorosis and hysteria were seen as related.

Abnormal menstruation, often seen as a symptom, was also thought to be the specific cause of these illnesses. Victorian medical practitioners prescribed remedies for amenorrhoea, or the absence of menstruation, and dysmenorrhoea, or painful menstruation. According to physicians, amenorrhoea also elicited considerable anxiety on the part of mothers and other relatives. Should a daughter's first menstruation not occur by the time she was fifteen or sixteen, mothers were known to employ a number of traditional remedies, in the form of 'forcing medicines' in order to bring on a daughter's period.

While doctors themselves advocated the use of such remedies in certain circumstances even as late as the 1870s, and some of them in the 1840s and 1850s advocated the use of such drastic procedures as the application of leeches to the vagina,[9] the general tendency of the medical profession was to discourage such practices.[10] By the middle of the century, doctors who wrote about female adolescence knew that the age of first menstruation varied in different parts of the world, and in Britain itself, among different social classes. It was generally agreed that the great majority of British girls would experience first menstruation by sixteen, and that after this age if it had not occurred there was some cause for concern.[11] However, if a girl was not otherwise ill, most doctors advised against intervention no matter what the patient's age. One specialist advised general practitioners that even with a patient as old as twenty, they could 'wait in the confident assurance that all will come right with her betimes' as long as she was, in other respects, healthy.[12]

The usual cure recommended by Victorian medical practitioners for amenorrhoea itself, or for the wide variety of symptoms that were labelled as 'chlorosis' or 'hysteria' was adherence to wholesome living suited to the feminine temperament. Unwholesomeness, in the eyes of Victorian medical men, was associated with the confining and overly luxurious mores of the urban middle and upper classes: rich food, too little exercise in the fresh air, too much stimulation from dances, entertainments and novel reading.[13] An unfeminine life style could also be one in which the girl was involved in serious study, or where she sought to escape from the confines of family life. In short, the best safeguard against abnormal menstruation and the ills that might accompany it, was rigorous conformity to the Victorian ideal of femininity.

If a Victorian adolescent girl exhibited pronounced 'chlorotic' or 'hysterical' symptoms, her family or the medical practitioner attending her might decide in the absence of other evident causes that masturbation was the cause. The topic was rarely discussed, and then only guardedly, in non-medical writing, but quite openly between doctors. Masturbation was held in some cases to be responsible for menstrual problems, and for the entire range of physical and psychological ills that were associated with abnormal puberty. As a last resort, Victorian girls and women were sometimes subjected to the operation of clitoridectomy, which was believed by some doctors to be a 'cure' for masturbation in females. In England, the use of this operation did not receive the support of the medical profession as a whole. The English medical man who publicly advocated its use was I. Baker

Brown, who in 1866 published a book defending the use of this surgical technique in cases where, he believed, the patient's masturbation was leading to otherwise incurable insanity.[14]

Brown was a member of the Obstetrical Society of London. At the Society's annual meeting, following the publication of his book, the issue of the legitimacy of clitoridectomy was raised, and a stormy debate ensued. Brown was censured by his colleagues and expelled. But he was not expelled because of his beliefs about the harmful effects of masturbation. The debates, in fact, reveal that there was a general consensus that masturbation in females was extremely harmful. Brown was expelled on the grounds that he was using a drastic and mutilating form of surgery whose curative powers were untested.[15]

In their treatment of adolescent girls, Victorian medical men were primarily concerned with their physical health, not with their psychological well-being, nor with imposing conventional sex roles upon them. None the less, medical men for the most part shared the views of their time, and these views did influence their medical thinking. Their belief that there was a connection between normal puberty and what they saw as healthy behaviour caused them to advocate behavioural changes in their patients. And from the descriptions associated with abnormal female puberty, it is evident that the behaviour that medical men perceived as normal closely reflected the Victorian ideal of feminine girlhood. A well-adapted young Angel in the House would not be 'listless', nor would she be 'irritable', nor would she desire to 'escape from home', nor, above all, would she be unchaste or sensual. By linking feminine behaviour with the prevention and treatment of physical ailments, medical men reinforced the ideology of femininity.

In the late-Victorian decades, when the movement to improve the education of middle-class girls had begun, the views of medical men about the dangers of female puberty were used as a weapon in the battle to oppose that movement. Brain work was held to be dangerous to a girl's health, and also to her future capacity to bear children. The competition that was introduced in the new girls' schools, and that a young woman would unavoidably encounter should she go on to pursue higher education, was held to be physically damaging, and there were doctors and others who opposed the strenuous games and exercises that were often engaged in at the new girls' schools and at the women's colleges.[16]

In countering such criticism, progressive educators could by the 1870s call on the support of a small number of doctors who had begun to question the prevailing views of the Victorian medical profession about the dangers of female puberty. Prominent among these practitioners were the handful of women doctors who entered the profession in the last three decades of the century. In their writing, and in their practice, such doctors treated menstruation itself in a more matter-of-fact manner than had been customary and both directly and indirectly challenged the belief that girls, on reaching puberty, became fragile and delicate.

In 1877, for instance, Mary Putnam Jacobi published her book *The Question of Rest for Women During Menstruation*. While Jacobi did not entirely discard the notion that menstruation depletes a woman's strength, she strongly questioned the prevailing notion that a girl or woman will inevitably suffer harm if she works or studies during the time she is menstruating.[17] And Elizabeth Garrett Anderson, also working in the 1870s, went on record as opposing drastic treatment in cases where young girls suffered from dysmenorrhoea.[18]

At the North London Collegiate School, the Headmistress, Frances Mary Buss, not only introduced vigorous gymnastics in the 1870s, but also, in the early 1880s, took the radical step of employing a physican to oversee the health of the girls. Miss Buss thought it essential that the physician be a woman, and accordingly one of the first of the women physicians, Mrs Hoggan, became the North London Collegiate's first medical inspector. Mrs Hoggan's opinions about the supposed dangers of menstruation are revealed in the records she kept; during her term as medical inspector, girls at the North London Collegiate were only excused from gymnastics during their menstrual periods if they complained of dysmenorrhoea.[19]

Views of doctors like Jacobi, Anderson and Hoggan represented an important challenge to the Victorian conception of female puberty as a difficult and potentially dangerous time, but they had limited impact on society as a whole. Much of the advice available to middle-class mothers, and to middle-class girls themselves, continued to propagate traditional views about menstruation.

Victorian doctors believed that menstruation was the central event of female adolescence, and encouraged mothers to regard their pubescent daughters as physically fragile and vulnerable. What Victorian middle-class mothers were actually advised to tell their daughters about the physical changes accompanying puberty, or about sexuality, is difficult to say since advice books broached such matters only through veiled hints. Writers insisted, however, that the mother had a responsibility to say something. As one writer of the 1830s commented, when dealing with 'delicate subjects . . . mothers are the only proper persons to convey such knowledge . . . A girl who receives her first ideas from shameless stories . . . has in fact prostituted her mind by familiarity with vice.'[20]

In the late-Victorian decades, the social purity movement did have an influence on sex education, but the work of such reformers did not dispel the notion that these were 'delicate subjects'. Social purity reformers did wish to encourage the dissemination of information about sexuality, especially to boys and young men, but they were primarily concerned to emphasise the dangers of sexuality.[21] The attitude that information about sex should be mainly admonitory applied even more to girls than to boys. Even at the end of the century, any information about sexuality was believed to be inherently dangerous, and there was a belief that a girl should only be told of such matters in order to protect her from the even more dangerous possibility that she would learn about them from evil sources. As one well-known social purity reformer commented, in 1899:

> How far direct teaching on matters of sex should be given to our girls has been a far greater perplexity to me than in the case of boys. In the present state of our schools and our streets our boys must get to know evil. Hitherto it was possible to say that our girls *might* get to know evil, and between that 'must' and 'might' lay a great and perplexing chasm. We do not want our garden lilies to smell of anything but pure dews and rain and sun warmed fragrance. But is this ideal possible any longer, except in a few secluded country homes?[22]

The author of this advice book for mothers concludes by telling her readers that, given the 'conditions of the present day', it was no longer possible to keep daughters in a state of 'ignorance and unconscious innocence'. She does not, however, give any guidance about what exactly a mother ought to tell her daughter; it is clear that she thought the subject too dangerous for explicit elaboration.

Given Victorian taboos about sexuality, it is not surprising that Victorian advice that was written expressly for girls themselves, and much that was written for mothers, simply avoided the subject, or passed over it as quickly as possible. However, advice books and periodicals did discuss less intimate physical matters in considerable detail; dress, exercise and hygiene were all dealt with. Mothers and daughters were advised by these sources that adolescence should, indeed, bring with it significant changes in a girl's attitude towards her body and in her deportment.

In general, such advice both encouraged girls to become more restrained than they had been in childhood, and impressed on them an increased obligation to care for their own health. Girls were told that for reasons of health and decorum, they must accept physical constraints as they moved towards womanhood, but at the same time, they were cautioned against allowing the constraints that went with the feminine role to damage their health. Although there was a belief that, after puberty, girls were more 'delicate' than boys, no one who gave advice to middle-class families recommended behaviour that would encourage such delicacy, or lead to permanent invalidism. The romantic image of the consumptive, doomed girl, too ill to leave her sofa, a martyr to her intense emotions and to her physical weakness, was certainly present in nineteenth-century art, poetry and fiction, but the cultivation of such an image was not encouraged by those who gave advice to the middle classes; they were aware that, in reality, middle-class girls would grow up to be women with tasks too difficult and too essential to permit chronic invalidism.

In the Victorian period, a change in style of dress was the most obvious physical sign of a girl's transition from childhood to 'young ladyhood'. At some point in her early or mid teens, a girl assumed adult female dress and hair styles. Throughout the century, no matter what the fashion epoch, such styles were constraining and confining.

For females in childhood, it will be remembered, advice books recommended non-confining styles that were not radically different from the styles recommended for male children. When it came to offering suggestions about dress for girls after puberty, the tone of Victorian advice changed sharply. Adolescent girls should adopt adult female dress and the limitations that such clothing placed upon vigorous physical activity, especially activity connected with play. For example, while 'tight-lacing' was condemned, the use of some sort of constraining corset, once a girl reached adolescence, was considered both necessary from the point of view of fashion, and healthful:

> The corset, or to use the old English word, 'stays' . . . forms a comfortable, healthful garment, as used by sensible people; made to fit them, and pressing nowhere in an injurious manner. Moreover, it enables our dressmakers to make a better fit of our dresses . . . To fit a dress on a person without a pair of stays is like endeavouring to make a down pillow into shape.[23]

It was assumed that over her corset, an adolescent girl would wear a considerable weight of material in the form of petticoats and skirts. Writers did not condemn these practices. All they did was recommend that heavy skirts be suspended from the shoulders, rather than from the waist or hips, and that stays should be fastened from the bottom up, so as to support rather than to constrict the internal organs. In the words of a doctor writing in a girls' magazine in 1883: 'The corset should on no account be too tight . . . The framework of a growing girl needs support — but not modelling, remember!'[24]

Victorian attitudes towards 'tight-lacing' in adolescence illustrate the tendency, present in much of the advice given to adolescent girls, to insist that girls must accept constraints, but at the same time to blame them if they carried these constraints too far. While stays were appropriate and necessary, stays that were too tight were reprehensible. Young girls, it was said, laced themselves too tightly out of vanity, and thereby endangered their health:

> Young girls delight to compress themselves until they attain that height of their ambition, a small waist — a deformity which not only detracts from the pleasingness of their appearance, but also inevitably destroys their health. Many sudden deaths have occurred solely from tight-lacing.[25]

In regard to exercise and exposure to the cold or to wet weather, girls were given the same sort of advice as they were given about dress. They were to avoid 'hoydenism', but at the same time, they were not to indulge themselves or seek to be too comfortable. While rough play was considered inappropriate for a girl who had reached adolescence, long vigorous walks were highly recommended:

> It is well . . . not to acquire the habit of coddling, as in a climate as changeable as ours, it is impossible wholly to escape draughts and damp. The best safeguard is to strengthen the constitution as much as possible.[26]

But if a girl took a long vigorous walk on a damp day, and caught cold, then she was guilty of 'criminal negligence':

> A young girl exposes herself to violent vicissitudes of temperature, and goes out on a wet day with thin boots and fine stockings, and she gets a cold and is laid up on a sick bed . . . If . . . she becomes a confirmed invalid, let her not think that this sickness was inevitable.[27]

Victorian advice books generally assumed that girls themselves looked forward to the changes that adolescence would bring, in spite of the constraints that would accompany those changes. In this respect, the Victorian girl would have been confronted by a dilemma that exists in most cultures: to earn the status of adulthood, a girl child must accept constraints on her behaviour, whereas a male child, by growing older, gains more freedom. Many writers were mindful of the negative effects of a too rapid assumption of the adult role, and urged both mothers, and girls themselves, not to hasten the process. As one writer of the 1860s said, in addressing girls themselves:

There are certain privileges belonging to the more advanced teens which young people are very ambitious of enjoying, and there are not many prouder moments in life than those in which a girl discovers that she is at last old enough to wear long dresses. It is such a comfort to be a child no longer . . . and not to be considered too young to attend evening parties, or lectures, or concerts . . . not too young to be of some importance in the world . . . [But] we would respectfully inform our young friends who at fourteen or fifteen are desirous of arriving at nineteen or twenty, that with the privileges there are responsibilities, that with the mirth and excitement there are graver duties . . . Dignity is one. Women do not forget that they have left their play-time far back out of sight, and though if they are wise they will never leave off being cheerful and sprightly, yet the hoydenism, the frolic, and the exuberant mirth will now become unseemly, and therefore will be exchanged for a soberness of manner.[28]

Victorian adolescent girls, right up until the end of the century, were subjected to physical constraints in the form of confining dress and mores that condemned 'frolic and exuberant mirth' as unseemly. Yet, while the constraints remained, there were changes. By the 1880s, encumbered as they were by long skirts and tight bodices, girls and women were riding bicycles and playing tennis, and in girls' schools the girls were playing such team sports as hockey and cricket. These new activities were taken up only gradually, and they by no means met with immediate acceptance, but they did have great significance; girls and women were to gain from them both increased physical strength and increased mobility, and they did help to contribute to a gradual alteration in the way in which the female body was perceived.[29]

The reforming educators at the new girls' schools were largely responsible for making sports acceptable as an activity for adolescent girls. Provision for physical activity in the new girls' schools began with gymnastics, rather than with team sports. For instance, at Miss Buss's North London Collegiate, 'gentle callisthenics' were introduced in the 1850s. At first, the activity took up only fifteen minutes each day, but by the late 1860s, more extensive gymnastics were part of the school day, and by the 1880s, the North London Collegiate had a proper gymnasium.[30]

Miss Buss, and the other pioneering Headmistresses who followed her lead were mindful of the criticisms that would inevitably be directed against them. They were well aware of the fact that the programmes they developed for their girls violated many of the accepted tenets about the socialisation of female adolescents. Competition and excessive 'brain work' were not only considered to threaten the femininity of girls, they were thought to represent a threat to health. Gymnastics were introduce in the first instance as a health measure, to counteract the tension produced by study, rather than for the amusement of the girls, and while such exercises were designed to promote physical vigour, they were also meant to encourage feminine grace.[31] The girls did the exercises decorously, in their ordinary clothing, and there was no suggestion that the competitive atmosphere associated with team sports should be encouraged.

In spite of the cautious manner in which gymnastics were introduced in the new girls' schools, they only gradually met with acceptance. For instance, one mid-Victorian writer, counselling girls on the need for exercise, acknowledges that callisthenics may be 'beneficial', but suggests that 'the simpler method of doing some portion of the housework'[32] would be even more beneficial, as well as more useful. By the 1880s, however, gymnastics were meeting with approval even from moderate or conservative observers. Girls' magazines began to voice support for physical training, although such support often stressed the health-giving properties of such activities, and linked a healthy physical regime with a girl's future needs as a wife and mother:

> If . . . the importance of duly training the body in conjunction with the mind is . . . recognised in the case of our boys, surely the future wives and mothers of England — for such is our girls' destiny — may lay claim to a no less share of attention in this respect.[33]

Callisthenics were thus gradually seen as compatible with socialisation for femininity. The acceptance of team sports came much more slowly. While gymnastics were seen as 'moderate bodily exercise, taken under supervision',[34] team sports were thought to encourage 'hoydenism' — to make girls boisterous and unfeminine — and were introduced only in the late 1880s and the 1890s. Even then, only the bolder and more radical of the pioneer educators were prepared to make affirmative statements about the character-building or psychological benefits of team sports. Dorothea Beale, the Headmistress of Cheltenham Ladies' College, for instance, remained concerned, even in the 1890s, about the unfeminine nature of such activities, and she would not let her girls compete against other schools: 'I am most anxious that girls should not over-exert themselves, or become absorbed in athletic rivalries, and therefore we do not play against other schools.'[35]

Throughout the Victorian period, those who gave advice to the middle classes about the socialisation of their daughters regarded the physical development of girls as a central feature of adolescence. The coming of puberty was thought to alter the physical needs of girls from the point of view of their health, and it was also believed that on entering this new stage of life, a girl should adopt physical deportment compatible with the grace and modesty associated with femininity. While it was always insisted that vigour and hardiness were compatible with femininity, the girl's future role as wife and mother became, from the time of puberty, the determining factor in defining what was acceptable for her in respect to dress and physical deportment. This fundamental definition remained influential in spite of the fact that by the last decades of the century, such pursuits as organised sports and cycling were gaining some acceptance as respectable activities for middle-class young ladies.

Notes

1. A. Reeves Jackson, MD, 'Diseases Peculiar to Women', in *Wood's*, II, p. 539.
2. Edward John Tilt, *The Elements of Health, and Principles of Female Hygiene* (London: Henry G. Bohn, 1852), p. 173.
3. Samuel Mason, MD, *The Philosophy of female health: being an enquiry into its connection with, and dependence upon, the due performance of the uterine functions; with observations on the nature, causes and treatment of female disorders in general* (London: 1845),p. 5.
4. Edward John Tilt, MD, *On the Preservation of the Health of Women at the Critical Periods of Life* (London: John Churchill 1851), p. 20ff.
5. Lionel Weatherly, MD, *The Young Wife's Own Book: A Manual of Personal and Family Hygiene: Containing Everything that the Young Wife and Mother Ought to*

Know Concerning Her Own Health and that Of Her Children at the Most Important Periods of Life (London: Griffith and Farran, 1882), p. 24.

6. Tilt, *Elements*, p. 209.

7. I. Baker Brown, *On the Curability of Certain forms of Insanity, Epilepsy, Catalepsy and Hysteria in Females* (London: Robert Hardwicke, 1866), pp. 14 – 15.

8. Samuel Ashwell, MD, *A Practical Treatise on the Diseases Peculiar to Women* (London: Samuel Highley, 1844), p. 22.

9. 'The application of leeches to the os and the cervix uteri . . . will frequently produce menstruation; but it is somewhat difficult so to employ them . . .' Ibid., p. 75.

10. E.g., 'The non-occurrence of menstruation at the usual time frequently gives rise to much anxiety on the part of the girl's friends — especially of the mother, who is quite likely to use various domestic remedies of a stimulating sort . . . no means for coercing nature should be used, no matter what the age of the patient may be.' A. Reeves Jackson, MD, 'Diseases Peculiar to Women', in *Wood's*, II, p. 543.

11. Tilt, *Preservation*, pp. 26 – 7.

12. Sir James Y. Simpson, *Clinical Lectures on the Diseases of Women* (Edinburgh: Adam and Charles Black, 1872), p. 608.

13. E.g., Jackson, in *Wood's*, II, p. 543. See the discussion of this issue in Carroll Smith-Rosenberg 'Puberty to Menopause: The Cycle of Femininity in 19th C. America', in *Clio's Consciousness Raised: New Perspectives in the History of Women*, ed by Mary Hartman & Lois Banner (New York: Harper Torchboooks, 1974), p. 27.

14. Brown, *On the Curability*. For the Brown case, see Elaine Showalter, 'Victorian Women and Insanity', *Victorian Studies*, vol 23, no 2 (winter, 1980), pp. 176 – 9.

15. The mutilation involved offended the Society's members more than any other feature of the operation. It is clear that many felt that the operation made a girl 'damaged goods': 'There are a number of young women upon whom this operation has been performed without the perfect knowledge of themselves and their relatives; and these young women are in as deplorable a condition as can be imagined. They are in this position, if they are honourable, and if any proposal of marriage comes to them . . . [they] are obliged to tell the person proposing that she has been mutilated.' Dr Tyler Smith, from the Report of the Special Meeting of the Obstetrical Society, *The Lancet* (6 April 1867), p. 439.

16. 'Some of our hapless little girls, in consequence of having been subjected early to strain of masculine drill, hockey, cricket . . . are more like colts . . . than they are like charming human maids.' Arabella Kenealy, *Feminism and Sex-Extinction* (London: T. Fisher Unwin, Ltd, 1920), p. 87.

17. Jacobi believed that much distress during menstruation is psychological in origin: 'Persons without occupation suffered at menstruation in a much larger proportion than those who were occupied' (p. 61). She concludes that 'There is nothing in the nature of menstruation to imply the necessity or even the desirability, of rest, for women whose nutrition is really normal' (p. 227). Mary Putnam Jacobi, *The Question of Rest for Women During Menstruation, The Boylston Prize Essay, Harvard University, 1876* (New York: G.P. Putnam & Sons, 1877).

18. Elizabeth Garrett-Anderson, 'On Dysmenorrhea', Abstract of the Proceedings of the British Medical Association, Friday, August 6, 1875, *The Obstetrical Journal of Great Britain and Ireland*, III (1875 – 6), pp. 469 – 72.

19. See 'Mrs. Hoggan's Notes' in the North London Collegiate School Archives.

20. Lydia Maria Child, *The Mother's Book* (London: Thomas Tegg, 1832), p. 187.

21. On the Social Purity movement and sex education, see Edward Bristow, *Vice and Vigilance* (London: Gill, 1977).

22. Ellice Hopkins *The Power of Womanhood or Mothers and Sons: A Book for Parents and those in Loco Parentis* (London: Wells Gardner, Darton & Co., 1899), p. 141.

23. The Lady Dressmaker, 'Recent Ideas on Dress Reform', *Girl's Own Paper* (18 October 1890), p. 35.

24. Medicus, 'Things that Every Girl Should Learn to Do', *Girl's Own Paper* (3 November 1883), p. 71.

25. Mrs Pullan, *Maternal Counsels to a Daughter* (London: Darton & Co., 1855), p. 107.

26. Ibid.

27. Ibid., p. 99.

28. Marianne Farningham, *Girlhood* (London: James Clarke & Co., 1869), pp. 20 – 1.

29. For a helpful general summary of these developments, see Paul Atkinson, 'Fitness, Feminism and Schooling', in *The Nineteenth-Century Woman: Her Cultural and Physical World*, ed. by Sara Delamont and Lorna Duffin (London: Croom Helm, 1978), pp. 92 – 133.

30. For an account of athletics at the North London Collegiate, see Mrs Roscoe Mullins, 'The North London Collegiate School for Girls', *Sylvia's Journal*, September, 1896, p. 500 (in the North London Collegiate School Archives).

31. 'It is perfectly evident that now, when a girl's mind is by advanced competitive examinations put to a strain which heredity has scarcely yet enabled it to endure, that we need to bring to the question of bodily training all the help that modern skill and science can suggest.' Alfred Schofield, Esq., MD, 'Notes of a Lecture on the Physical Education of Girls, with Special Reference to the Use of Calisthenics in School', June 1889, p. 3. Girls' Public Day School Trust Archives.

32. Pullan, *Maternal Counsels*, p. 103.

33. Mrs Wallace Arnold, 'The Physical Education of Girls', *The Girl's Own Paper* (17 May 1884), p. 516.

34. Ibid.

35. Quoted in Josephine Kamm, *How Different From Us: A Biography of Miss Buss and Miss Beale* (London: The Bodley Head, 1958), pp. 222 – 3.

Chapter 6

THE PROPER YOUNG LADY: VICTORIAN ADVICE ABOUT CORRECT FEMALE BEHAVIOUR IN ADOLESCENCE

In the preceding chapter, we saw that for the Victorians, the physical changes that accompanied female puberty were believed to lay the foundation for the chief purpose of a girl's adolescence: preparation for, and acceptance of the adult feminine role. The Victorians believed that the physical changes of puberty should be accompanied by changes in a girl's outward behaviour, and in her thoughts and feelings. Throughout the period, both middle-class parents and middle-class girls themselves were exposed to detailed advice from many sources about the way in which the transformation from child to woman should take place. Advice about the intellectual, practical, and emotional content of that transformation is the subject to which we shall now turn.

The adult role for which the Victorian middle-class girl was supposed to be preparing herself was that of wife and mother. It was believed that some preparation for that role should begin even in childhood; while mothers were advised that in childhood the differences between girls and boys should be minimised, still, even during those years, girls were to learn to be 'little housewives'. While they could be physically active, it was still assumed that they would play with dolls. After puberty, a Victorian girl was expected to give up both vigorous physical activity, and play. When she put up her hair and donned long skirts, she was to begin to prepare herself with adult seriousness for adult femininity.

In the early and mid-Victorian years, literature of advice directed at adolescent girls was emphatically explicit about one central feature of this adult role; it meant accepting limits and restraints, and recognising male superiority. In the words of Sara Stickney Ellis, author of *The Daughters of England*, one of the most popular early-Victorian manuals of advice for middle-class girls: 'As women, then, the first thing of importance is to be content to be inferior to men — inferior in mental power, in the same proportion as you are inferior in bodily strength.'[1] In adolescence, the testing ground for adulthood, girls were to accept that they must keep a tight rein both on their aspirations and on their behaviour. Whereas boys, in adolescence, were encouraged to develop their independence, girls were encouraged to accept dependence on the male as a natural and inevitable part of the feminine condition:

> Woman is so formed as to be dependent on man. The woman who is considered the most fortunate in life has never been independent, having been transferred from parental care and authority to that of a husband . . .[2]

Girls were to be reared for domesticity, and prepared, in adolescence, for a dependent and subordinate position in relationship to males. But the domestic role that the Victorian middle-class girl was told she must prepare for was a multi-faceted one. It was not the simple domesticity of the thrifty yeoman's wife, skilled only in housewifery that was held up to her as a model, but rather the complex role of Angel in the House. In addition to the skills of housewifery, she was told that she should prepare herself to bring to her role as wife and mother both aesthetic and intellectual qualities. As a writer on girls' education commented:

> I conceive that a woman's mission is twofold. While it is clearly her duty to superintend and arrange those things which form the physical comforts of the home, and administer to the temporal wants of those who look to her to supply them, it is also her duty to adorn that home with the refinements of intellectual culture, to make herself a suitable companion to her husband, a mother competent to train her children, and a mistress fit to rule and guide her household.[3]

Even in the early and mid-Victorian decades, it was acknowledged that a girl would need some education if she were to provide her future home with 'the refinements of intellectual culture'. But early and mid-Victorian advice books took pains to emphasise to girls that they should always keep in mind the ultimate purpose of their education; it was to make them pleasant and useful companions to men, and responsible mothers to their children. In order to achieve this goal, girls were told that their attitude towards their studies was as important as anything they might learn.

A responsible, feminine girl, said the advice books, would neither be frivolous about her studies, nor would she be over-serious. In the same way that they were told they must be responsible about their health, middle-class girls were told they should take responsibility for their studies. In respect to their health, they were neither to ignore the inevitable fragility that was thought to accompany puberty, nor were they to indulge that weakness. In respect to their studies, they were told that they must apply themselves diligently during the period when they were receiving instruction, either at home or at school. After their formal education was over, their responsibilities became even greater. Throughout the Victorian period, manuals of advice and articles in girls' magazines impressed on their readers that a daughter at home should devote a portion of each day to private study. A girl should not regard her education as 'finished' when her formal lessons came to an end; instead, she should realise that she now had the responsibility for self-education:

> How self-education is to be taken up . . . how to divide the time which, after the performance of home and social duties is left for intellectual pursuits — these are questions which are very difficult to settle, and which constitute a serious problem to many an earnest, thoughtful girl. And yet they must be decided, for self-education is a duty of the gravest import.[4]

But while girls should be serious about improving their minds, they should always be aware of the need to preserve their femininity, and many Victorian commentators thought that too much learning of the wrong sort would damage it:

> By an exclusive attention to the solid branches, and that in a high degree, the character is rendered too masculine. There is need of the softening influence of those pursuits which are designed chiefly to embellish.[5]

Many Victorian commentators on girls' education insisted that the only reason that girls should learn anything at all about 'masculine' subjects was so that they could become better listeners when in male company. For example, Mrs Ellis in *The Daughters of England* told her readers that science, if studied for its own sake, would damage their 'feminine delicacy'. Scientific studies were only justifiable as part of their education because such knowledge would 'render them more companionable to men'. and Mrs Ellis emphasised that possessing such knowledge did not mean that a girl should display it: 'I must again observe, it is by no means necessary that we should *talk much* on these subjects.'[6]

As another writer put it, while a 'girl is none the less feminine because she has serious interests in life', girls must always remember that they should 'look up to men', and they should *never* become 'strong-minded'. In the second half of the nineteenth century, the epithet 'strong-minded' was often directed against the overly learned girl or woman. A strong-minded girl, according to the writer just quoted, was one who was 'dogmatic and presumptuous, self-willed and arrogant, eccentric in dress and disagreeable in manner'. While this mid-Victorian writer does acknowledge that there have been genuine 'learned ladies', she warns that the line between the learned lady and the strong-minded female is dangerously thin. And in any case, while learning is a good thing: 'In a general sense, woman's truest mission is otherwise than this, and while marvelling at what learned ladies have done, we are by no means sure that learned men could not, and have not, done much better.'[7]

Throughout the Victorian period, many commentators suggested that it was more important for a girl to become familiar with poetry, art and music than with the more 'masculine' areas of knowledge. A knowledge of these subjects would be more useful to a girl in the performance of her feminine task of complementing the roles of men. If they could play the piano, if they were familiar with art and poetry, middle-class girls and women could enrich the lives of their men, who, given the exigencies of capitalist competition, could 'know no relaxation from the office or counter'.[8] But even art, music and cultural activities had dangerous possibilities. They too could be pursued in an over-serious manner. In the early and mid-Victorian periods, when it was not accepted that middle-class females should ever venture outside the private sphere, girls were warned against developing tendencies to approach the study of art or music in a professional way. Such talents were to be used as 'the means of home enjoyment', and never as a 'medium of display':

> Who would wish a wife or a daughter, moving in private society, to have attained such excellence in music as involves a life's devotion to it?[9]

In the early and mid-Victorian period, then, it was generally agreed that middle-class adolescent girls should develop some familiarity with intellectual pursuits and considerable familiarity with cultural pursuits, and that they should approach their studies with seriousness of purpose. But their attitude towards learning should always remain a 'feminine' one, and this meant that in fact that they were advised that they should never be interested in learning for its own sake. The mid-Victorian view was that there was a feminine and a masculine way of acquiring skills and knowledge, and that the feminine way represented a softened, more emotional, but also more constricted version of the masculine. Learning and achievement were seen as masculine attributes; however, middle-class girls, in order that they might become true complements to middle-class males, were to take part in these pursuits, but in a feminine way.[10]

These early and mid-Victorian views about the role that education should play in the socialisation of middle-class girls corresponded well with the actual structure of middle-class girls' education during these decades, acquired as it was largely within the confines of home, and not designed to prepare girls for gainful employment. But in the last decades of the century, the structure of girls' education changed. Not only did school itself become an integral part of the experience of middle-class girls, the school curriculum altered to take account of the fact that girls ought to be prepared to function in the 'public sphere'. Given the extensive changes that took place in the structure of girls' education, it is all the more remarkable that the early and mid-Victorian ideas about the ultimate purpose of that education were not abandoned by the reforming educators of the last decades of the century. While new attitudes developed alongside them, the ideal of the cultured Angel in the House still remained one that was of central importance to the educators themselves, and one they sought to impose on their pupils.

The strong influence that these ideals retained can be seen in the very arguments that were given for reforming girls' education in the first place. For example, Annie Ridley, one of the teachers at the North London Collegiate School, was involved in the campaign to raise money for the school's expansion in the early 1870s. In a pamphlet written for fund-raising purposes, Ridley explicitly stated that the chief reason she was soliciting support for an improved education for middle-class girls was so that they could be better fitted for domestic life. 'A woman's natural destiny is marriage', Ridley insisted, and the most noticeable weakness of the majority of girls' schools was that they provided an inadequate preparation for the role of wife and mother.[11]

Ridley believed that both mid-Victorian home life, and mid-Victorian schooling for lower-middle-class girls especially, did not teach them the self-discipline and self-control that would be necessary to them as grown women. Unlike working-class girls who were 'fit for the continued discipline of daily toil by the duties of their life', and unlike upper-middle-class and upper-class girls who had the benefit of 'high culture', the majority of middle-class girls, on finishing an inadequate formal education at fifteen or sixteen, simply frittered away their time while waiting for marriage, 'the one hope of their existence':

> From no fault of their own, there are thousands of girls destitute alike of the physical life of the class below them, and of the mental culture and social advantages which enrich the life of the class above them.[12]

As the new girls' schools grew in strength and numbers, and as more of their pupils went on to skilled employment or even to university, the educators responsible for these new achievements did display pride in them. From the 1860s, the pioneer educators were forthright in their insistence that girls had a *right* to a good education, and that they had a contribution to make to society. A minority among the educators even became involved in the early women's rights movement, some going far as to support causes as radical as votes for women. In expressing approval of the academic and professional achievements of their girls, the educators were, without doubt, creating new patterns. By the 1890s, if not before, a new model for the socialisation of adolescent middle-class girls was emerging, a model that allowed and even encouraged girls to be ambitious, and to develop their intellectual capacities without restraint.

In spite of their contribution to the creation of new attitudes, none of the pioneer educators entirely abandoned the older views. For all the changes this group of people initiated, they still encouraged girls to regard the role of wife and mother — the role of Angel in the House — as the highest and most desirable role a woman could hope to fulfil. Nor was their support for the Victorian concept of femininity merely something to which they paid lip service in public, in order to soothe the fears and the hostilities of those opposed to the movement for improved middle-class girls' education. They disseminated these values to the girls themselves. For example, Sarah Burstall, a product of the North London Collegiate, and of Girton, and one of the first women to receive a Degree from the University of London, returned to her old school in the 1880s to become a mathematics mistress. In addition to her teaching duties, Burstall took on the task of overseeing the school magazine. The pieces she wrote for the magazine reflect her wish to encourage the school's pupils to remember that, even as they entered into school life, with its lessons, tests and examinations, they ought to be developing their capacities to fulfil 'woman's mission'. In one issue of the magazine she even extolled that classic paean to Victorian femininity, Coventry Patmore's poem *The Angel in the House*. It 'ought to be on every girl's bookshelf', she told her readers.[13]

Headmistress Buss herself was a lover of Patmore's poem. As she told her girls in one of her weekly addresses to the assembled school: 'The *Angel in the House* places before every girl the mystery of that loveliness which emanates from a refined and cultivated mind, from the gentle, self-forgetful, sympathising, innocent heart.'[14] In many of her weekly addresses, Miss Buss encouraged the girls to adopt the values of femininity rather than those associated with ambition and a competitive spirit. From the examples she chose to employ, it is clear that for Miss Buss herself, ambitious achiever though she was, the image of the Victorian ideal girl was a powerful and persuasive one. On one occasion, she urged her pupils to be good daughters in language whose resonance is indistinguishable from that of the mid-Victorian rhetoric out of which came the image of the daughter as sunbeam:

A good daughter is a well-spring of gladness and help in any home. Fondly her parents lean on her and love her . . . . This is true of those *good* daughters who repay the care and money expended on their education, and minister in a thousand ways to the comforts of home. It is not true of those who are satisfied if they can manage to get through their lessons with as little trouble as possible, whose thoughts are centred on themselves, who waste their father's money by carelessness or extravagance in dress, who are utterly selfish about their lessons and never think of contributing in any way to the comfort of home . . .[15]

Constance Maynard, founder of Westfield College, and another pioneer woman educator, also remained wedded to Victorian ideas about woman's role. Maynard supported excellence and achievement for girls and women, but at the same time, she too believed that 'woman's mission' was fundamentally different from man's:

The place of women in the general order of things is determined by elemental facts . . . One half of the human race are to be fighters, rulers, explorers, discoverers, and builders, and the other half are to make — body, mind and soul — those of the coming generation who are to fight, rule, explore, discover, and build.

For Maynard, there were two justifications for expanding the field of women's education and women's work. First there was the necessity of providing work for the unmarried daughters of professional men and second there was the need to improve the quality of motherhood. 'Motherhood needs immense expansion if it is to be true and noble', she said, and an improved education for girls was the way to improve the quality of motherhood.[16]

The fact that the pioneer women educators of the late nineteenth century clung so tenaciously to the Victorian ideal of femininity meant that their contribution to ideas about the socialisation of adolescent girls contained inherent contradictions, contradictions that were never resolved in their own thinking.[17] The educators were in effect suggesting to girls that they should develop two opposing sides to their personality, an achieving, ambitious, striving side, and a side that accepted the ideal of feminine selflessness and self-sacrifice. Moreover, in any contest between the two opposing sets of values, they believed that femininity should triumph over purposeful, self-fulfilling achievement.

This opposing set of values was disseminated to middle-class adolescent girls in the late nineteenth century through sources other than the written and spoken words of Victorian educators. Much late-Victorian fiction for girls was, for example, permeated with this conflict of values. A favourite plot construction in such fiction involves an ambitious girl, who has been given a modern girl's education, and who wishes to strike out on her own and centre her life on achievement rather than domesticity. While the authors of such stories are usually sympathetic to the girl's strivings, in the end, the heroine is always made to realise the superior value of femininity and of a life dedicated to domesticity.

In one such story, revealingly entitled 'The Mother's Chain: or the Broken Link', which was published serially in a magazine in the 1890s, the young heroine, Margaret Armytage, is the eldest daughter in a poor but genteel family. Her widowed mother is an ideal Victorian mother: loving, strong and self-sacrificing. Margaret, encouraged by a silly, shallow woman who lives in the neighbourhood, decides that she wishes to leave home to take a job. She tells her mother:

> 'I should like to be independent, to earn my own living; and I am
> offered a situation as companion to an only child of rich parents,
> who is to attend classes at Queen's College, and I am to share the
> benefit and help her in her studies; and then if she goes to
> Newnham or Girton I am to go with her, and I am to have a
> hundred a-year; Mother, think of that!'

Her mother's reply is meant to illuminate the older virtues:

> 'I think you are making a mistake, Margaret. In my young days,
> girls of your age were content to remain at home, and make home
> duties their calling till they married. I should be thankful, when the
> right time comes, to see you . . . married; but I do not wish you to
> leave home.[18]

The conclusion of 'The Mother's Chain: or the Broken Link' finds
Margaret, chastened by her difficult experiences as a paid companion, accepting an offer of marriage from a man of whom her mother
heartily approves. In this story, the values of femininity unequivocally
triumph over those of ambition.

Throughout the Victorian period, middle-class girls were told that
education was necessary to them, but that its primary purpose was to
fit them for their future duties as wives and mothers. In the early and
mid-Victorian years, this view of the purpose of girls' education
was expressed unequivocally. The educational reforms of the late-
Victorian decades did create challenges to this conception of the
purpose of girls' education — in these years, the value of achievement
for its own sake was also disseminated to middle-class girls. But the
new values never triumphed over the older ones, and were generally
expressed only in an equivocal fashion. At the end of the century, girls
were still advised, even by those most committed to their education,
that they should perceive that education as a preparation for 'woman's
mission': for femininity and domesticity.

Education was not the only way in which the Victorian middle-class
girl was advised that she should prepare for feminine adulthood. The
management and direction of her future home would also depend on
her practical skills, and throughout the Victorian period, preparation
for the practical part of her future role was considered indispensable
to her upbringing. In childhood, girls were encouraged to develop

domestic inclinations through early lessons in sewing, and through play that developed their skills as 'little housewives'; in adolescence, lessons in housewifery were to be taken up with more seriousness.

As we saw earlier, the amount of actual housework that a middle-class girl or woman was expected to do varied according to her place within the middle class, the aim always being to achieve an appropriate balance between necessity and gentility. But whether or not they did any actual housework, all middle-class wives were considered to be responsible for the management of their households. For this reason, training in housewifery was considered essential for all middle-class girls. Even upper-middle-class girls, it was thought, should be familiar with some of the domestic skills. These included sewing, cooking and even cleaning. Even if, as adult women, they would never be called upon to perform such tasks, it was still believed necessary that, as females, they should be familiar with them. The writer of an article that appeared in a woman's magazine in 1848 neatly summed up the standard arguments that were given to justify the teaching of housewifely skills to all girls:

> Let a girl — no matter what her station — learn herself to perform well every household duty commonly entrusted to servants . . . This would not be a waste of time, even should she never afterwards be required to do it for herself; for how much better a mistress could guide her household . . . But who could guarantee it would never be required in these days of commercial reversals?

In giving specific suggestions about exactly how girls should learn the skills of housewifery, this author illustrates the way in which a girl's social class was to be reflected in her relationship to housework. As the following quotation suggests, even upper-class girls should *know* something of these matters, although they, unlike their middle-class sisters, need not actually learn how to perform them:

> I would urge that *all* classes should *learn*, and the middle classes uniformly *practise* the performance of all the minor duties which contribute to their personal comfort. Would it be derogating from the dignity, or seriously abridge the comfort of a young lady, were she trained to keep her own *room* in order, as well as her own person — even to make her own bed, dust her own toilet?[19]

A best-selling mother's advice book, published in the 1860s, which was written expressly for lower-middle-class families, gives specific details about the author's methods of teaching her teen-aged daughters domestic skills. The author explains that she wanted her daughters to become 'economical and industrious, but not fussy, housekeepers'. When the two girls had reached the ages of seventeen and eighteen, the family deliberately reduced its domestic staff, in order to make it necessary, rather than simply a matter of form, for the girls to learn domestic tasks: 'We even discharged our cook, and took a good general servant; this not being done so much from a motive of economy, but in order to make my girls good housekeepers.'[20]

Training in housewifely skills continued to be seen as necessary in the late-Victorian decades, just as it had been earlier. The late-Victorian girl could go to school and train for a profession, but she was also to be taught how to sew, cook and clean. Sewing and cooking became part of the programme even at the most academic of the girls' schools, and, as well, advice books and magazines continued to suggest that adolescent girls should help with the housework in their own homes. Such home tasks were seen as 'splendid training for their own homelife of the future' and they also encouraged girls to be helpful and co-operative during their adolescent years.[21]

Middle-class Victorian girls were advised that in adolescence they should develop both their intellects and their practical skills in order to prepare for their role as adult women. In addition, the Victorian girl was also told that she must strive to perfect her moral nature; her future tasks as wife and mother, indeed, could be properly carried out only if her moral sense were properly developed. The inculcation of moral values in adolescence involved a continued emphasis on the precepts that governed their inculcation in childhood. The moral outlook that was presented to middle-class girls was influenced by Christianity and by the general moral values of the middle class as well as by those values associated specifically with the middle-class conception of femininity.

As good Christians, girls were expected not only to observe the outward forms of religious observance, but even more important, to strive for a commitment to duty that could spring only from a well-developed conscience. In the discussion of advice about the rearing of girls in childhood, it was noted that specific direction about the inculcation of a religious outlook did not figure as a major element in advice to parents. Nor did it figure in the foreground of advice to adolescent girls. Instead, it was a pervasive and continuous part of the background of all other advice about how a girl should behave; so essential and so fundamental was it considered to be that it needed little elaboration.

More explicit and detailed attention was given to the importance that the bourgeois virtues should play in the development of a girl's character in adolescence. Throughout the Victorian period advice literature encouraged girls to develop habits of self-discipline, a business-like sense of order, and self-control. These were the character traits that figured prominently in the socialisation of middle-class males; boys were told that they must develop them in order to prepare for their manly tasks in the public sphere. In spite of the fact that the feminine role was conceived of as radically different from the male role, self-discipline, order, regularity and self-control were advocated as being as necessary for girls, in their own way, as they were for boys. Victorian middle-class opinion, it would appear, while cherishing the feminine because it was seen as a refuge from the mechanistic business world, still insisted that the order and routine of that world be imposed on the middle-class home. Therefore, in order to prepare to be a good middle-class wife, a girl was told that she too, must exemplify these middle-class virtues.

Girls were, for example, told that they must use their time wisely. Victorian manuals of advice warned girls about the dangers of time wasting that could result from their position as adolescent daughters at home. In *The Daughters of England*, Mrs Ellis stressed that girls, during this period of their lives, must develop a careful schedule for their activities. She suggests that a girl's time should be precisely parcelled out, 'the exact amount proportioned to every occupation'. A girl's obligation to organise her time was primarily a moral one, according to Mrs Ellis: 'time, this great ocean of wealth', she says, 'is ebbing away from us day by day . . .'[22] The advice literature also warned girls that they must learn to control their 'impetuous and unregulated feelings'; control over their emotions was necessary to them as girls, and would later be necessary to them as mothers of children. In respect to the development of their practical skills, in preparation for the role of household manager, it was suggested that girls should learn order, method and regularity: 'Without in the least degree allowing girls to adopt masculine views, or inculcating within them a wish to obtain duties only fitted for the other sex, we can and ought to make them thoroughly businesslike.'[23]

Victorian commentators on female adolescence devoted much attention to suggestions about the intellectual, practical and moral qualities that a middle-class girl needed to develop in order to prepare for her future role as wife and mother. Another issue that often figured in manuals of advice was the question of how a girl should conduct friendships during adolescence itself. Although home was seen as the centre of a girl's life, friendships outside the family circle were none the less acknowledged to play an important part in her development. From the late-eighteenth century, the idea that friendships with other girls should form part of girlhood experience was well accepted; by the early-Victorian period, writers of advice books were adopting a favourable attitude towards such friendships. A girl's desire to establish friendships with girls of her own age outside her family circle was not only regarded as legitimate, her ability to make such friendships was seen as a mark of her depth as a person. A girl who could not make friends was regarded with a degree of suspicion: 'We never think very highly of the woman who cannot count upon the love . . . of one staunch friend of her own sex.'[24] The first serious female friendship in a girl's life was seen as a significant turning point in her adolescent development. As one writer suggested, 'perhaps not even the acceptance of a lover is a more important era in the life of a young girl than her first serious choice of a friend'.[25]

Victorian advice books, however, expressed approval of girlhood friendships only if they were 'serious'. While friendships between girls were important, they could also be dangerous, and girls were advised to choose their friends with care, and to distinguish between the slight, unimportant, giddy friendship and the deep, intimate one. Girls were warned that if they had too many friends, they were probably being frivolous and shallow: 'A girl without a friend is a lonely being; a girl with a great number of friends is nearly as bad. It is impossible to have a close and real friendship with a great many.'[26] Girls were advised to choose their friends for their inward qualities, and not merely because they were 'good looking, or merry, or accomplished', and they were warned to beware of a tendency, seen as all too common in young girls, to 'take a sudden and violent liking which expends itself in a little while'. Girls' friendships, it was believed, should foster the feminine qualities of empathy and expressiveness, and should develop the capacity for sustained intimacy.

Victorian advice book writers were especially concerned with the dangers of schoolgirl friendships. Such friendships were often 'lightly entered into'. There was even a danger that when a girl left school and returned home, she might engage in wasteful, time-consuming and even morally reprehensible letter writing, with friends made at school:

Few schoolgirl friendships endure for any long period after the
parties are separated; nor is it desirable that they should unless they
have some more solid foundation than propinquity . . . the silly
chitchat and often pernicious gossiping in which young girls
indulge, is a serious evil.[27]

The best way to guard against the formation of undesirable friendships was for girls to consult their mothers. Even in the late-Victorian
period, girls were told that they should never correspond with anyone
without the 'sanction' of their mothers, and never write anything in
letters that they would be hesitant to show to her.

In the new girls' schools of the late-Victorian period, the opportunities for girls to make friendships independent of adults were
increased. Those responsible for the new schools recognised the fact,
but even in the later decades, maintained the right of parents to sanction or prohibit a girl's friendships. At the Girls' Public Day School
Company schools, for example, girls were only allowed to walk home
from school together if both sets of parents gave their permission. The
sanction was designed to assuage fears that the girls at the schools,
coming from a wide range of middle-class homes, would form socially
unsuitable friendships.[28] And yet, those who supported the new educational opportunities for girls argued that the companionship nurtured
in the school or college environment was one of the important benefits
accruing to the students. In an article that appeared in a girl's magazine in 1883, describing Westfield College, which had opened the year
before, the companionship that the college atmosphere fostered
received special praise:

At the college . . . there is bright companionship in study, together
with the charm of English home life, and it would be hard to find a
happier group of girls than the fourteen students now in residence.
Affecting neither strange opinions nor strange attire, they pass
from the lecture room, to the tennis court, or country ramble; from
the social tea-party to the quiet hour of reading, each in her own
pretty study by her own fireside . . . One afternoon all amused
themselves making marmalade, and very good marmalade it was,
as I can assure those who doubt that domestic accomplishments
could flourish on such soil.[29]

That description of the girls at Westfield College highlights one
important aspect of the perception of girlhood friendship that existed

throughout the Victorian period. Friendships between girls, like so many other aspects of a girl's life, were meant to foster femininity. Whereas friendships between boys and young men were seen as developing 'manliness', group loyalty, and the ability to fight battles in the public arena, girls' friendships were seen as important because they would encourage the development of a personality capable of intimacy and the mutual sharing, with other girls and women, of a domestic environment.

Victorian commentators accepted that close friendships between girls — for all their potential dangers — would play a part in female development during adolescence; they were much more uneasy about contact between the sexes. Although, as was seen earlier, adolescent girls were meant to be preparing themselves for marriage and hence finding a husband was a girl's business, she was never supposed to appear to be actively pursuing a mate. This ambivalent attitude affected the advice about girls' behaviour during the phase of their lives when they would be experiencing a sexual awakening, and in which they would be faced with the need to prepare themselves for the future.

In the early and mid-Victorian period, it was generally agreed that, with the exception of her contact with brothers, girls should not have regular relationships with males. But while such contact was frowned on, there was an awareness of the fact that girls in their teens might well be experiencing an interest in the opposite sex. The care that advice book writers took to condemn flirtatious behaviour is clear evidence of such an awareness. Girls were warned to maintain a strict propriety in all their relationships with males. As a writer of the 1850s put it: 'Many a girl has been ruined in consequence of a very slight deviation from propriety, which has led to others of a more serious nature.'[30] Another mid-Victorian writer, Eliza Warren, explained that she gave the following advice to her own teen-aged daughters on the subject of flirtatious behaviour:

'I hope and trust that neither of you will ever know from experience what flirting means. It is destruction to a girl. No man cares to marry a flirt, whose modesty has exhaled, and whose purity is smirched by levity of manner. A girl courts to win contempt.'[31]

But if a girl was not supposed to seek a husband, how was she to find one? Meeting suitable men could be difficult, especially for mid-Victorian girls from lower-middle-class households, and much

Victorian opinion was insensitive to the dilemma in which such girls could find themselves. While flirting was condemned, so also was the failure to find a husband:

> Married life is woman's profession: and to this life her training — that of dependence — is modelled. Of course by not getting a husband, or losing him, she may find that she is without resources. All that can be said of her is, she has failed in business; and no social reform can prevent such failures.[32]

Some advice book writers offered more constructive suggestions to middle-class parents than that reflected in the above comment. Mrs Warren, for example, fully recognised the problems that girls from modest middle-class families might face. When her daughters had reached their late teens, she confronted her husband with the dilemma the girls were facing:

> 'It is the concealed hope of all girls to marry, to be happy . . . and yet, how is a girl to find a husband if she have no opportunity of mixing with the opposite sex? We have been so happy in our home, so selfishly wrapped up in its comforts, so lovingly idolised by our children, that we have forgotten to associate with other families more than what has been absolutely necessary. What youth have we ever invited here to make acquaintance with our daughters — to see them as they are, with loving natures, with simple manners, and truthful bearing?'[33]

Although her husband at first accused her of being 'indelicate', and of engaging in 'husband-hunting', Mrs Warren did begin to entertain, in a suitably modest way, and in consequence, both daughters found husbands.

Mrs Warren's *How I Managed My Children from Infancy to Marriage* was first published in the 1860s. The widened employment opportunities that opened up to girls and young women in the last decades of the century did alter general views about the place of marriage in a girl's life. Marriage was no longer seen as the only possibility for a middle-class girl, and with this shift in attitudes toward matrimony came a recognition that the mores governing contacts between young men and young women had changed to some degree. There was, for instance, a recognition that as middle-class girls left school to go to work, the workplace might afford opportunities for meeting a possible future husband.

An article that appeared in 1895 in a magazine designed for middle-class girls and young women who had recently left school discussed this question in considerable detail. The author pointed out that a girl who had experienced independence would make an excellent wife — 'it is just the girls who have had to fight the battle of life on their own account that are most appreciative of protection'. Men, however, were not so quick to recognise this fact, and a girl who pursued a career might well find that she had damaged her matrimonial chances. The author goes on to point out that, on the other hand, the workplace provided many possibilities of meeting men. School-teaching and office clerking were both favourable fields: 'In certain callings where men and women are employed together, as in business-houses, or as teachers in schools, a considerable proportion of marriages result from their intercourse.'[34] Nursing, says this author, used to provide excellent opportunities for meeting young men, but it had become, by the early 1890s, less likely for a young nurse to meet a possible husband through her work:

In early days, when the lady-nurse was an exceptional creature many nurses became engaged to and ultimately married young doctors whom they met during their time of training, but now in numbers there is safety — for the doctors.[35]

Although there is evidence of a more relaxed attitude towards contact between young women and young men in the last decades of the century than had been the case earlier, Victorian manuals of advice still insisted that girls and young women had a responsibility to observe the proprieties in their relationships with young men, and urged them to exercise extreme care in their choice of a mate. The correspondence columns that were a popular feature of late-nineteenth-century magazines for girls and women provide a good source of evidence for the sort of specific advice about relationships with men that was offered to the middle-class girl. Answers to queries include, for example, advice about the appropriate age for marriage. A correspondent to the *Girl's Own Paper* was sternly informed that she was too young to marry:

Seventeen is too early an age for marriage in this country. Physically, your bones are not hard till past twenty or twenty-one. Mentally, you are too inexperienced; and in such matters more especially, you cannot be sure that you know your own mind.[36]

Correspondents to advice columns who wrote asking for guidance in their selection of a mate, might receive a reply like this one:

> Jenny T — E —. Give him up. A girl is mad to marry an avowedly 'unsteady man'. No, you will not be able to reclaim him. Cast aside the thought and be sensible. I am so sorry for you, but run from your infatuation as if for your life.[37]

Such responses indicate that by the last two decades of the century, it had become acceptable for girls to meet men outside their enclosed family circle, and to seek advice about their personal lives from sources outside the home.

This change in attitude about a girl's relationships with young men is but one indication of a more general shift in opinion about the appropriate amount of independence from her family that a girl should have. In the early and mid-Victorian period, it was assumed that the proper place for a girl, in the years between childhood and marriage, was her parents' home. Only in the case of severe financial necessity would a girl leave home to go to work, and then it was assumed that she would find work as a governess or lady companion, and live in the home of her employer. By the last decades of the century, middle-class girls were taking up employment that would allow them to live apart from their families.

The question of whether or not such activity was appropriate, respectable or advisable was frequently discussed in advice books and periodicals. Some commentators were very much opposed to the idea that girls should leave home. Such behaviour, they suggested, was both selfish and unwise:

> The girl at home should stay there as long as she may, even though she may have less money to spend than other girls of her acquaintance. There is a temptation to do otherwise now. Many girls who are really needed at home to help the mother and look after the children get appointments for the sake of the freedom and the cash. It is much better to yield to the home discipline and to learn how to make the money suffice.[38]

Other writers were more sympathetic to the late-nineteenth-century girl's desire for independence. Although there was general agreement that if a girl were needed at home, she should stay there, there was also a recognition that where her presence was not necessary, she had a right to follow her own inclinations. Two separate answers that appeared in the same correspondence column in 1892 illustrate the way in which distinctions were made according to family circumstances. To one query the following reply was given:

> Obedience to parents does not mean for girls to spend their years in enforced idleness. The command is, 'Children obey your parents in the Lord'. The qualification of obedience is opposed to idleness, selfishness, and luxurious ease. Certainly obey your heart's instincts . . . and find your life mission in service for others. With 'three older sisters at home' you need have no compunctions about leaving your parents.

In contrast to this encouragement of independence, the editor gave the following response in reply to the second query:

> Your place is at home. Your work and mission are there. God can accept no service which is self-imposed while positive duties are neglected. I am sorry your father's tastes and yours do not agree about music; but you owe the cultivation of your talent to his money and should certainly humour his fancies.[39]

In the 1840s, Victorian middle-class adolescent girls were advised that they must be content to be 'inferior to men'. If they were to be considered properly brought up young ladies, they would accept both the limited confines of domesticity, and a very narrow range of public self-expression. If they were to achieve gentility, they should never be gainfully employed, or indeed, experience any necessity for independence. If they needed to seek work, they were considered unfortunate; if they wished to seek work or independence for its own sake, they were considered outlandish. If they were seen to step beyond the intellectual boundaries of accomplished young ladyhood, they risked being labelled 'strong-minded'.

By the 1890s, middle-class girls could pursue study that was both serious, and directed towards the achievement of externally imposed goals. Some voices of course continued to condemn the education of middle-class girls but by the 1890s, a middle-class family would not have been perceived as eccentric if it provided a sound education for its daughters. On leaving school, a middle-class girl could even take up employment. Again, while there were those who continued to believe that girls should not work before marriage unless it was economically imperative that they do so, employment before marriage had, at least, become respectable. Moderate if not conservative voices assured the late-Victorian girl that it was acceptable for her to ride a bicycle, to play lawn-tennis, and even to get to know the young men whom she might meet at her place of work.

Yet, amid all the many undeniable changes that took place in attitudes towards the behaviour of middle-class girls and young women, the values of Victorian femininity continued in full force. In a magazine that informed young women about opportunities in medicine, journalism and other masculine professions, the reader would still encounter statements like this: 'Girls should be like daisies — nice and white, with an edge of red if you look close; making the ground bright wherever they are.'[40] In the most modern and pioneering of the new girls' schools, girls who won prizes for excellence in Latin or Mathematics would be given books like *The Romance of Woman's Influence*,[41] books that extolled the virtues of feminine self-sacrifice rather than of goal-directed achievement. Prevailing views about the socialisation that was appropriate for middle-class girls, indeed, adapted themselves to changing circumstances, but few voices raised any sustained challenge to the Victorian conception of male and female roles. Even at the end of the century, most people, including those involved in the education of middle-class girls, would have agreed with the writer who exhorted girls to remember that 'influence is woman's "work" ':

> Let each fill their separate sphere of usefulness, and there need be no detraction of worth on either part; but interfere, or tread one on the other's ground, and we have the result in a feminine man, or a masculine woman; either, or both, of which is an aversion to both sexes.[42]

Notes

1. Mrs [Sara Stickney] Ellis, *The Daughters of England, their Position in Society, Character and Responsibilities* (London: Fischer, Son & Co., n.d. but 1843), pp. 11 – 12.

2. Edward John Tilt, *Elements of Health, and Principles of Female Hygiene* (London: Henry G. Bohn, 1852), p. 15.

3. Mrs Roe, *A Woman's Thoughts on the Education of Girls* (London: 1866), p. 39.

4. Clare Goslett, 'The Duty of Girls in Regard to Self-Education', *Our Mothers and Daughters*, I (1892), p. 8.

5. W. Nicholson, *How To Be a Lady* (Wakefield: Wm. Nicolson & Sons, *c.* 1850), p. 253.

6. Mrs Ellis, *The Daughters of England* (London: Fischer, Son & Co., 1843), p. 113.

7. Roe, *A Woman's Thoughts*, p. 6.

8. Ellis, *The Daughters of England*, p. 169.

9. Matilda Pullan, *Maternal Counsels to a Daughter* (London: Darton & Co., 1855), p. 81.

10. 'A woman, in any rank of life, ought to know what ever her husband is likely to know, but to know it in a different way . . . a man ought to know any language or science he learns, thoroughly, while a woman ought to know the same language, or science, only so far as may enable her to sympathise in her husband's pleasures, and in those of his best friends.' John Ruskin, 'Of Queens' Gardens' in *Sesames and Lilies* (London: Dent, 1907), pp. 64 – 5.

11. A.E. Ridley, 'Pearl or Sea Foam? Or Some Thoughts on Secondary Education for Girls' (Privately printed, 1871), p. 6. North London Collegiate School Archives.

12. Ibid., p. 10.

13. *North London Collegiate School for Girls: Our Magazine* (June, 1877), p. 175.

14. Grace Toplis, ed., *Leaves from the Note-Books of Frances M. Buss: Being Selections from her Weekly Addresses to the Girls of the North London Collegiate School* (London: Macmillan & Co., 1896), pp. 46 – 7.

15. Ibid., pp. 44 – 5.

16. Constance L. Maynard, 'From Early Victorian Schoolroom to University', *The Nineteenth Century* (November 1914), p. 1061.

17. For a discussion of this question, see Sara Delamont, 'The Contradictions in Ladies' Education', in *The Nineteenth-Century Woman*, ed. by Sara Delamont and Lorna Duffin (London: Croom Helm, 1978), pp. 134 – 63.

18. Emma Marshall, 'The Mother's Chain: Or, the Broken Link', *The Mother's Companion*, IV (1890), p. 20.

19. *British Mother's Journal* (May 1848), p. 111.

20. Warren, *How I Managed My Children* (London: Houlston and Wright, 1865), p. 60.

21. E.g., an article in the North London Collegiate School Magazine humourously described the benefits that would be derived from the cooking classes that had been introduced as an 'extra' at the school: 'Each pupil may become, in her own way, the centre of a small cooking-world; and, at all events, when mamma goes away for a week or two, her algebra-hydrostatical daughter, now, with soups, entrees, and omelettes at her fingers' ends, will no longer, in agonizing despair, address cook with the words, "What *are* we to have for dinner?" ' *North London Collegiate School: Our Magazine* (April 1876), p. 139.

22. Ellis, *The Daughters*, p. 42.

23. *Ward and Lock's Home Book* (1866), p. 218.

24. Farningham, *Girlhood*, p. 55.

25. Pullan, *Maternal Counsels*, p. 192.

26. *Girls, Their Work and Influence* (London: W. Skeffington & Son, 1877), p. 35.

27. Pullan, *Maternal Counsels*, pp. 56 – 7.

28. See clipping from the *Pall Mall Gazette*, dated 16 May 1885, in the papers for 1875 – 94 in the North London Collegiate School Archives: 'History of the School'.

The writer expresses support for girls' high schools, but criticises the schedule at some GPDST schools — four hours in the morning, with the girls then returning home: this unsatisfactory timetable 'was devised to meet social prejudices . . . Parents, it was assumed, would not send their girls to schools to which all classes were admitted, except on the understanding that they meet only for lessons. Hence the midday meal in common which prevails in most boys' day schools was pronounced impossible . . . and all lessons were crowded into the morning. So servilely has this spirit of social exclusiveness been deferred to that in some of the Company's schools it is a punishable offence for one girl to address another . . . a system which fosters . . . the worst features of English middle-class society . . .'

29. 'The Dream of Princess Ida', *Girl's Own Paper* (15 December 1883), p. 171.

30. Nicholson, *How To Be a Lady*, p. 71.

31. Warren, *How I Managed*, p. 70.

32. Warren, *How I Managed*.

33. Warren, *How I Managed*, p. 61.

34. Mrs Esler, ' "Between Ourselves": A Friendly Chat with the Girls', *The Young Woman*, IV (1895 – 6), p. 105.

35. Ibid., pp. 105 – 6.

36. *Girl's Own Paper*, (1882 – 3), p. 32.

37. *Mothers and Daughters*, IV (1895 – 6), final page, May 1896.

38. Farningham, *Girlhood*, II, p. 41.

39. *Our Mothers and Daughters*, I (1892), p. 183.

40. 'Mr. Ruskin's Message to Girls', *The Young Woman*, I (1892 – 3), p. 168.

41. Alice Corkran, *The Romance of Women's Influence* (London: Blackie, 1906) was given as a prize book to a girl at a Girl's Public Day School Co. school, *c.* 1913. The book is in Janet Sondheimer's possession.

42. E.B. Leach, 'Woman: What is her Appointed Position and Work?' *Girl's Own Paper* (March 1884), p. 340.

PART THREE

Chapter 7

EARLY-VICTORIAN GIRLHOOD EXPERIENCE

In this chapter and the two that follow, we turn from a general analysis of Victorian middle-class girlhood to an account of the girlhood experiences of individual Victorian women. In this chapter it is the early-Victorian period with which we will be concerned. The women selected for inclusion here were all born between 1819 and 1834. During their girlhoods, the ideals of femininity, and the specific advice about childrearing that have been discussed in the preceding chapters were in their early stages of development. The idealisation of feminine girlhood had begun to have an influence, and concrete advice about the rearing of their daughters would have been available to the parents of these women. But any woman born before 1835 would have reached maturity well before she could have been influenced in girlhood by the changes in opportunities for middle-class girls, and in ideas about them, that characterised the last decades of the century.

The five women whose lives are the focus of this chapter came from diverse social backgrounds, and were of diverse temperaments. Three of them — Florence Nightingale, Emily Shore and Anne Jemima Clough — came from affluent, well-connected families. Florence Nightingale, born in 1820, became famous in adulthood as the chief architect of the modern nursing profession. Her painful childhood illustrates both the opportunities that were available to an intelligent, ambitious, early-Victorian girl and the constraints that femininity could impose. Emily Shore's whole life was her girlhood — born in 1819, she died of tuberculosis in 1839. Emily Shore, like Florence Nightingale, was unusually intelligent, and like Florence Nightingale, she received an excellent home education. But in contrast to Nightingale, she experienced little conflict between her intellectual ambitions and the values of femininity. Anne Jemima Clough, born in 1820, was the first Principal of Newnham College. The sister of the poet Arthur Hugh Clough, she was similar to him in temperament. Their experiences in childhood and youth illustrate the contrasting effects that a commitment to duty rooted in evangelical Christianity could have on a female and a male from the same family.

The two other women, Frances Mary Buss, born in 1827, and Mary Anne Hearne, born in 1834, both came from much less affluent families than Nightingale, Shore or Clough. Frances Buss was the founder of the North London Collegiate School and the Camden School for Girls. Mary Anne Hearne had a career as a minor writer of advice literature, and was editor of the *Sunday School Times*. The girlhood experiences of Buss and Hearne illustrate the problems faced by early-Victorian girls from households so modest that the ideal of sheltered femininity was never a possibility for them.

Florence Nightingale wrote a passionate protest against the constraints to which early-Victorian girls and young women of the middle and upper classes were subjected:

> What form do the Chinese feet assume when denied their proper development? If the young girls of the 'higher classes' . . . were to speak, and say what are their thoughts employed upon, their *thoughts* which alone are free, what would they say?[1]

She was already in her early thirties when she wrote 'Cassandra', the essay from which the quotation is taken, but her status was still that of a girl; she was still restricted by the demands of her family, still 'chained to the bronze pedestal',[2] as she herself put it. For Florence Nightingale, the family and its demands were a pernicious force, sapping her strength, time and talents:

> The family uses people, *not* for what they are, nor for what they are intended to be, but for what it wants them for — its own uses . . . . If it wants someone to sit in the drawing-room, *that* someone is supplied by the family, though that member may be destined for science, or for education, or for active superintendence by God, i.e. by the gifts within.[3]

Florence Nightingale was not a typical middle-class woman; her personality was extraordinary, as were her achievements and her family background. But the conflicts between the conception of feminine duty that custom and her family imposed on her, and her own ambitions and desires, were similar to those experienced by many other upper-class and middle-class women who came to maturity in the early-Victorian period. Victorian female adolescents of the 'higher classes' were shaped both by the contemporary conception of femininity, and by the constraints and opportunities afforded by their social status. For some, the process of growth was untroubled, the girl passing from childhood into womanhood with little conflict. For others, the passage was stormy.

With Florence Nightingale herself, the conflicts she experienced in adolescence and young womanhood stemmed from her early childhood. Born in 1820, into a rich, well-connected family, Florence, and her elder sister Parthenope (born in 1819), had parents whose own personalities contained unresolved conflicts. Both William and Fanny Nightingale came from backgrounds that valued the life of pleasure that money and good connections provide, but at the same time, they were products of that upper-class English tradition that placed a great value on duty and seriousness.[4] From early childhood, the Nightingale sisters were presented with both models of behaviour simultaneously; the family led a life of leisure and ostentation, but at the same time, the children were raised in a moral atmosphere calculated to develop a careful conscience. They were, for example, given the sort of evangelical reading matter designed to induce both a sense of duty and a sense of guilt.[5] For Florence, it was the earnestness of the Nightingale heritage that had the most influence in shaping her character.

The Nightingale's wealth meant that Florence and her sister were raised in the formal style appropriate to their class. While both mother and father were concerned and careful parents, the day-to-day care of the children was left in the hands of nursemaids and governesses.[6] The Nightingales did live in the country — they had two sizable country estates — so that the girls, in childhood, did enjoy plenty of vigorous outdoor play; they freely explored the gardens, rode ponies, and kept a succession of pets.

The interpersonal difficulties that beset the Nightingale family and affected all of its members throughout their lives, were established early. Parthenope and Florence were the only two children in the family. Both girls were intelligent and attractive, but even as little girls, Parthe, the elder, was less energetic and less assertive than her sister, and her jealousy of Florence manifested itself early on in their lives. Thus, while the sisters were close, it was a closeness filled with tension.[7] Again, the pattern of the girls' attachments to their two parents were established early in life. Florence, even as a small child, was intelligent and strong-willed, but she was also self-conscious and acutely sensitive. Fanny Nightingale found Parthe, the more ordinary of her two daughters, the easiest to understand, and she was always closest to her.[8] Florence, in return, never felt easy with her mother; she established close attachments to other adult women — to her governess and to a favourite aunt — but with her mother she was constrained. But while her relationship with her mother was, from early childhood, a difficult one, she was, in contrast, her father's favourite.[9]

The divisions within the family became clearly evident in 1832 when William Nightingale, himself a serious private scholar, decided to devote his energies to his daughters' education. Although the Nightingales continued to employ a governess to teach the girls music and drawing, their main lessons came from their father. His programme of study included Greek, Latin, German, French, Italian, history and philosophy; the girls were required to spend several hours a day at their lessons. The rigorous regime suited Florence, but it did not suit Parthenope, and as a result Florence became her father's 'companion in the library' while Parthenope became her mother's 'companion in the drawing-room'.[10]

With an education as rigorous as that of any young man, one might suppose that Florence escaped the conflicts between feminine and masculine values. Nevertheless, Florence encountered opposition from all the members of her immediate family over her desire to pursue her intellectual development. By her late teens, Florence became seriously interested in the study of mathematics, and by the time she was twenty, her wish to pursue this interest in an organised fashion led to a painful conflict with her parents. What she wished for was a mathematics tutor. Her mother who had for some years been fearful and resentful of Florence's seriousness of mind, was very much opposed; Florence's 'destiny was to marry', she said, 'and what use were mathematics to a married woman?' Even her father, as it turned out, was opposed. Although he had taught her the Classical languages, subjects of study that were generally considered to be unfeminine, he had not included the serious study of mathematics, and also did not encourage Florence's wishes in this case. Except for a brief interlude, when lessons were arranged by her favourite aunt, Florence had to study mathematics unaided, making time for her exploration of the subject in the early hours of the morning or late at night.[11]

Florence's conflicts with her family over mathematics were part of a larger conflict over what she wished to do with her life. From her late teens, when she came out into Society, Florence found herself torn between two opposing possibilities. On the one hand, she did participate successfully and even with enjoyment in the social engagements that were part of upper-class life, attending balls and parties and travelling abroad.[12] On the other hand, her inner life was one of turmoil. The conception of duty inherent in evangelical religion was the strongest acknowledged force. Never completely acknowledged was a driving sense of personal ambition. Florence felt a compelling wish to serve God, and in fact, before her seventeenth birthday, she had received what she believed to be a 'Call': 'On February 7, 1837, God spoke to me and called me to His service.'[13]

Many years were to pass before Florence found a suitable outlet for her desire for useful work. Outwardly, she had conflicts with her family, even in her early twenties, when she became too zealous over visiting the poor in the cottages surrounding one of the family estates. While such activity was considered proper for a young woman in her position, the work was never supposed to take precedence over one's duty to one's family.[14] Both her mother and her sister complained, as they were to do for many years, that Florence neglected her primary duty to the family to engage in other matters. Inwardly, Florence suffered great pain over what she saw as her own shortcomings. She was especially ashamed of her tendency to day-dream, a weakness she saw as peculiarly feminine; she speaks of that 'perpetual day-dreaming, which is so dangerous', and says 'it is the want of interest in our life which produces it; by filling up that want of interest in our life we can alone remedy it.'[15]

Florence Nightingale's adolescence and young womanhood can without exaggeration be characterised as tormented, with much of the torment being directly attributable to conflicts between her own ambitious drive and conception of duty and the notions of femininity adhered to by her family and by society. She did not succeed in 'filling up the want of interest' in her life until she was over thirty, and her family finally agreed to let her take up nursing. In the 1850s. Nightingale became a national heroine because of her work in the Crimean War; after the war, she became a tireless and formidable worker in the cause of public health. As she achieved fame and the satisfactions that came from achievement, she put the torments of her youth behind her. She also put aside her early concern with the plight of middle-class and upper-class women. As she became a powerful, much respected figure Nightingale developed a mistrust of other women, and she gave only half-hearted support to the nascent Women's Movement; having found her own private solution to the conflict between femininity and ambition, she closed her mind to the general nature of the problem.[16]

The demands of femininity caused Florence Nightingale acute psychic pain in adolescence and young womanhood; on Emily Shore, they did not weigh heavily. Emily was born in 1819, the eldest child of a Church of England clergyman who, although well-connected, did not rise in the Church because of his religious doubts.[17] The Shores lived in Bedfordshire, the household containing not only the father, mother, five children and several servants, but also a series of young male pupils whom Thomas Shore educated as a way of adding to his income. There could be five or six such boys in the household at any one time.[18]

In 1830, when she was eleven, Emily began keeping a journal in which she continued to make regular and lengthy entries until her death in 1839.[19] From this extensive, detailed record we are able to gain direct knowledge of her intellectual and creative development, of her emotional life, and of her perceptions of her own family and of the social context in which she lived. During her childhood and early adolescence, the main insights that the diary provides are into Emily's intellectual and creative development. She was educated exclusively at home, no governess ever being employed.[20] In Emily's case, her main teacher was her father, and perhaps because of this, and because she had her lessons in company with her brother closest in age, she received an education that, according to the standards of the day, could be considered masculine in content as well as in thoroughness.

Before she was thirteen, Emily learned Latin and Greek; she read voluminously, and widely, being interested in everything from literature to economics. Her most consuming intellectual interests in childhood were geology, botany and zoology. Even as a young child, she had the scientist's precise mind, and love of categorisation. She spent much of her time out-of-doors, observing and collecting plants and animals, and making careful written records of what she saw.[21]

Her diary does not indicate that she was considered to be a tomboy, or that her interests were too masculine, and it is evident that, as a child, Emily did not feel that any activities were closed to her either because of her sex, or because of her age. She read and commented on learned articles in the *Quarterly Review*; she consulted the *Boy's Own Book*[22] for information about what to do for a sick pet lark; she regarded the family cook as a 'great coward' because she was 'afraid even of slugs, snails and mice';[23] Emily herself prepared stuffed specimens of birds and animals. She also had mechanical dexterity; she constructed a home telescope, and when she was only eleven years old, she made an elaborate pasteboard model of a steam packet on which the family travelled during her first sea-side holiday: 'I made it very correct and furnished and painted all the cabins, even to the staircases. I also rigged it and put the rudder and boat to it, with the paddles, seats, railings and flags.'[24]

All of these activities received full support from her family and there is no indication that they were thought to be in any way unsuitable. The Shores knew that their eldest daughter was unusually talented, but they did not regard encouraging her interests, during her childhood, as in any way jeopardising her development as a girl. And, in fact, Emily also learned the feminine skills appropriate to a girl of her social class, and appears to have enjoyed them: each day, in addition to her other lessons, she did needlework.[25] She also helped with the amusement and instruction of her younger sisters and brothers, even before she reached adolescence, and she also was involved, before she was twelve, in the kind of charitable activity that was considered suitable for the young daughter of a comfortably off Church of England clergyman.[26]

Emily Shore's diary provides evidence of the way in which an intelligent early-Victorian girl could, as a child, simply ignore both her age and her sex, in developing a perspective on the world in which she lived. For example, the description she wrote of the social structure of her own Bedfordshire village could have been composed by a gentleman of fifty, rather than by an eleven-year-old girl: 'The principal persons in Potton, besides papa and Mr. Whittingham, the Vicar, are Mr. Keal and Mr. Moore, surgeons; Mr. Youd, a wool merchant; and Mr. Smith, a rich farmer.'[27] Emily thoroughly understood the social system of which she was a part, from the perspective of the adult males who dominated it. Her identification with their position was so complete that, as a little girl, she seemed oblivious to the fact that her own position, as a female, would be a different one. It was for this reason that she could, for example, develop an interest in Cambridge after she made a visit there in 1832, when she was twelve. She asked her father to explain the workings of the University to her, and in her diary she describes, in minute detail, the College system, the examinations for degrees, and the University system of government, all the while seemingly oblivious to the fact that, as a girl, she would never be able to attend Cambridge herself.[28]

A girl can adapt to the disabilities related to her sex during childhood, simply by ignoring them, as Emily Shore did. In most cases such a strategy becomes more difficult to sustain in adolescence. In Emily's case, however, it continued to be possible. For her, adolescence brought with it no sharp break; as a child she had been educated exclusively at home, and this continued to be the case during her teen years. Her studies simply became more complex and exacting as she grew older. The routine of her life was established when she was thirteen, and it continued throughout her teen years:

> I rise as soon as I can wake, which is usually as late as half-past seven, and employ myself in doing my Greek and Latin, and learning whatever I have to get by heart. After breakfast I feed the birds with breadcrumbs, and from about that time till twelve o'clock I am usually employed in teaching the children [her younger brothers and sisters] and in some of my own lessons.

After an interval for dinner, Emily then usually read aloud to her mother and did needlework. In the mid-afternoon, she would take a walk. Then, she and her brother Richard would 'finish our Greek and Latin for papa', and after tea, they would have their daily lesson with him.[29]

In addition to her formal lessons, Emily continued with the self-education she had begun in childhood. Her interests continued to be more characteristically masculine than feminine. For instance, at sixteen, she recorded a consuming interest in manufacturing:

> I long exceedingly to become thoroughly acquainted with every manufacture in England. I read carefully every account of any one which I can light upon, and I am much interested by those given by Babbage in his *Economy of Manufactures*; but alas, we have very few books on this subject, and I doubt whether many exist.[30]

That her parents did not object to, but in fact encouraged, these interests, is indicated by the fact that Babbage's *Economy of Manufactures* had been a present they had given her for her thirteenth birthday.[31]

Emily realised she was a learned girl. By early adolescence she also knew how the typical young lady of the day was thought to behave, and she was anxious to avoid all traces of such behaviour herself. For example, an entry in her diary made in 1834 about drawing, reflects her desire to avoid the usual young ladies' style: 'I cannot bear what the *Quarterly Journal of Education* calls the neat sampler-like style practised by so many young ladies.'[32]

Reading in the periodicals to which the Shore family subscribed also influenced Emily's views of young ladies' boarding schools. In 1833, she recorded in her diary information she had gathered on the evils of 'tight-lacing', and on the connection between that bad habit and the boarding school:

> The *Penny Magazine* . . . contained a highly interesting and valuable article on the horrible . . . effect of tight-lacing and want of exercise. The whole body is diseased, every function depraved by this fatal practice. Boarding-schools are nurseries of illness; few girls come from them in health; and in one in particular, all who had been there two years were more or less crooked.

Living a relatively isolated life, within the shelter of a loving and supportive family, Emily could, in her mid-teens, manage to be both a young lady herself, and at the same time avoid any identification with the stereotypes of the early-Victorian 'Miss'. Although her comments are not free of that self-righteousness and priggishness that charac-terised many intelligent nineteenth-century and twentieth-century adolescents, still, the distance that she was able to maintain between her own situation as a middle-class girl and the supposed characteris-tics of girlhood that were foreign to her nature, gave her the freedom to develop her personality in a strong and positive fashion.

At fourteen, Emily did have a brief encounter with the more usual pursuits of early-Victorian young ladies when she was sent to relatives in the North of England to have lessons in French and dancing. During her stay there, she recorded a good-humoured conversation she had with one of the young ladies of the household about proper behaviour at dances. Informed that one did not talk about either science or natural history, Emily replied: 'How horrid! How can you like it? What a very great waste of your time, when you ought to be learning and improving your mind, to go to balls and talk nothing but nonsense!'[33]

On her return from Rutlandshire, Emily resumed her home activ-ities: studying, having lessons from her father, teaching and reading to her younger sisters and brothers, spending time reading and doing needlework with her mother. But a fever she had contracted while visiting her cousins marked the beginning of the consumption that was to take her life before she was twenty, and the illness, in gradual stages, altered the course of her life. Her mid and late adolescent years were dominated by a growing awareness of her approaching death.

Despite this shadow over her last four years, Emily's vitality, her curiosity about life, and her good humour did not diminish. Both the illness and her increasing maturity did, however, cause her thoughts to become deeper, more tinged with emotion, and less exclusively cerebral. For the first time in her life, she turned seriously to religion, as she struggled with the inevitable despondency of disease. In July, 1836, she first recorded her response to her illness: 'I prayed earnestly for submission to the Divine will, and that I might be prepared for death; I made up my mind that I was to be the victim of consumption.'[34] A few months later, she was even more despondent, and wrote that she believed God had caused her illness because she had been too 'attached to the world and estranged from heaven': 'Has He not chastised me by withdrawing me from those things which chiefly formed the delight of my life?' She went on to reflect on what she perceived to be the weaknesses of her nature, expressing a self-doubt and self-hate that were unusual with her:

> There is completely a world within me, unknown, unexplored, by any but myself. I see well that my feelings, my qualities, my character, are understood by no one else. I am not what I am supposed to be; I am liked and loved far more than I deserve. I hate — yes, I truly hate myself; for I see the depths of sin within me, which are hidden from all other eyes.[35]

Emily managed to recover from this despondency, and adjust to the limits that her illness imposed on her. Her interest in learning continued right up until her death in December 1838, although in the final years, she was more interested in literature than she had ever been before, and in what it had to say about the emotions and about human relationships. Her own relationships became increasingly important to her, both those with her family, and with friends she made outside the home. She made two intense friendships with young women, and she even had a brief romance, which was put aside, on the advice of her family, because of her illness.

Emily Shore's intelligence, courage and vitality transcend the category of sex. But her sex, like her social class, did shape her experience and her relationships to her parents, her sisters and brothers and her friends. Unlike Florence Nightingale, Emily adjusted to the limits inherent in the early-Victorian female role. In sharp contrast to Florence Nightingale, she registered no complaints about having to spend time in the drawing-room. She even accepted that it was necessary for her to learn to dance, and to become an 'accomplished' young lady. She took seriously her position as older sister, willingly teaching the younger children, and amusing them.

The contrast between Florence Nightingale and Emily Shore could have arisen from differences in their own temperaments, and in the temperaments of other members of their respective families. Perhaps, as well, the great affluence of the Nightingale family, compared to the solid, but relatively modest comfort of the Shore household, increased the irksomeness of the social demands made on its daughters. The contrast between the two women could also have arisen from the fact that the nature of their ambition differed. Nightingale wished to strive for achievement in the public world; Emily Shore had no such ambitions, and probably would not have developed them. Had she lived, she would probably have become a writer — even before her early death, she had achieved her first publication — and professional writing was one of the few intellectual occupations a middle-class woman could pursue, in the early and mid-Victorian period, without violating the norms of appropriate feminine behaviour.

The girlhood of Anne Jemima Clough, who was born in 1820, provides both contrasts and similarities to those of Nightingale or Shore. A major contrast is that, while Anne was born into an affluent family, its wealth was more precarious than that of the Nightingales or the Shores. Anne's father was a Liverpool cotton merchant, and when his business failed, in 1841, Anne had to adjust to the effects of downward mobility, just as she was on the threshold of young womanhood. In temperament, Anne Clough, like Florence Nightingale, suffered considerable psychic pain during adolescence, but her struggles were inward, and rarely openly expressed. Like Florence Nightingale, Anne Clough too was strongly influenced by evangelical Christianity. In intellectual interests, she provides a contrast to both Shore and Nightingale; while intelligent and conscientious, she did not possess their spontaneous love of learning.

Most of the first sixteen years of Anne's life were spent, not in England, but in Charleston, South Carolina, where James Clough moved, for business reasons, in 1822. During her earliest years in Charleston, Anne and her three brothers formed an isolated, inward-looking group, of which their mother formed the centre. Mrs Clough was determined that her children would remain English, and not be contaminated by what she perceived as the vulgarity of American mores, and she kept them as separate as she could from Charleston society. The family employed an ample staff of servants, but Mrs Clough attended to the children's lessons herself, and oversaw their upbringing. Their father's importance in their lives was limited, since he was away for long periods at a time.[36]

Although Anne had the company of her three brothers in childhood, the difference between the two sexes was early underlined for her, because the boys were all sent 'home' to England to be educated well before they reached their teens. Anne, however, was never sent to school, either in Charleston, or in England. During Anne's later child-hood years, and in her early adolescence, it was she and her mother who formed a unit, a unit separate from that of the males of the family.[37] But although Anne and her mother found themselves tied to each other, held together by a bond that extended well into Anne's adulthood, when she became the maiden daughter and mainstay of an invalid widowed mother, the relationship between mother and daughter was not an easy one. Anne was never her mother's favourite child; that place was reserved for Arthur, the eldest son, who had been born in 1819. Even as a child, he occupied a special, privileged place in the family.

Anne began to keep a regular diary when she was nineteen, but for several years before that, she had kept some record of her experiences.[38] Three concerns stand out from this written record of her adolescence and young womanhood. Anne was, first of all, pre-occupied with religious questions, and with moral choice; secondly during these years, she was confronted with the stirrings of sexual and romantic feelings; finally, she was concerned with how she could best employ her time. Often, throughout her adolescence, these concerns were in conflict with one another.

She was twelve years old when, as she put it, 'religion took a deep hold on my mind'.[39] The Cloughs were members of the Church of England and in Charleston they attended one of the city's fashionable Episcopalian churches. But at twelve, Anne began to attend Revival meetings, where she experienced religious observance in a more intense and emotional atmosphere than that of well-bred Episcopalianism. This intensity soon came to characterise her religious commitment, as this entry from her diary suggests:

> I have not felt so well in mind, so much more tender-hearted and softened for ages as on Sunday. For a long time I have felt like ice at my prayers and everything else, but now my heart has been thawed. I could really believe and felt yesterday that God was my Father.[40]

That entry was written at a time when she felt satisfied with her inner state. More often, she was dissatisfied with herself. She worried that her inner feelings were unworthy, and, in the privacy of her journal, she analysed her failings, and her attempts to remedy them.

Many of her worries about her spiritual state were connected with her feelings of inadequacy as a female. For Anne, the Victorian ideal of femininity presented itself as a compelling model for behaviour, a model to which, more often than not, she felt she failed to conform. Anne strove to be calm, gentle and self-effacing, but she often believed herself to be by nature aggressive and uncontrolled:

> The worst thing that has grown in me is a sort of wild, boastful feeling, which would lead me to give way to a great deal of wildness if I had the opportunity and did not try to keep myself in. Yes, I am sure it would lead to a great deal of wickedness.

She was 'wanting in quietness and gentleness', she felt, and in patience towards other family members, especially towards her mother.[41]

As early as fifteen, when she was living in Charleston, feelings that she saw as conflicting with her religious and moral nature began to preoccupy her. She began to have romantic fantasies, and to think about the possibilities that might await her as an adult woman. After a trip she took at fifteen, she said:

> It seemed as if a great change had come over me, through the excitement of so much travelling and change and getting acquainted with so many new people; in fact, being grown up. Girls of fifteen married in Charleston, and I was nearly fifteen.[42]

Her romantic inclinations flowered in her mid-teens. As a friend from her Charleston days put it, in a letter she wrote to Anne in 1838:

> I think you are the most romantic damsel I ever knew. Here is nearly a whole page of your last letter occupied with the beautiful theory of shutting your affections in an impregnable castle, which I suppose is never to be stormed, but to open its gates and surrender at discretion when the right cavalier appears.[43]

Her romantic feelings caused her such guilt and anxiety that at one point she even put aside the poetry of Byron because of the emotions it aroused.[44] But when she actually came into contact with men, she felt shy and awkward. In the late thirties, when the Cloughs were still well enough established both socially and financially so that Anne had opportunities for meeting young men, she found that she did not know what to say to them: 'I cannot talk the common flirting slang or nonsense . . . I do not like to speak about books, and so I seldom find a subject.'[45] By April, 1841, she felt like a failure in relation to men, and this increased her shyness:

> My winter's going out is ended. I believe I have found out that I am not at all to suit the general taste. Scarcely anybody ever thinks of dancing with me twice; in short, I am considerably stupid, I never can find much to say. I think I am growing shyer; I do not like to talk to gentlemen, I always feel bothered.[46]

It appears that, in 1841, when she was just twenty-one, Anne Clough repressed her romantic thoughts. In any case, such references no longer appear in her journal.

If romance was not possible, work was, and in her late adolescence, Anne attempted to repress her 'bad thoughts' and control what she saw as a tendency to 'indolence' through hard work.[47] The kind of work she sought, and her thoughts about that work, poignantly illustrate the dilemmas faced by a young middle-class girl in the early-Victorian period. Anne's life, during these years, had no well-defined outward form. She did not attend school and, of course, the avenue of paid employment was not open to her. Thus, she had to shape her life herself, and she attempted to do so both through outward service to the community, and through private study.

Outward service began early in 1837, soon after the family had settled in Liverpool, when Anne began teaching in a school for working-class children. Her position as a junior Lady Bountiful provides an example of the way in which a middle-class girl's social superiority could modify the lack of status connected with being young and female. In February 1837, Anne was not quite seventeen, and very shy. The experience of becoming a figure of authority to a group of poor children, and to their parents as well, was a mixed one. She entered into the work with a sense that it was both worthy and expected of her, and she gained in maturity from doing it, although there were aspects that she found especially difficult. She did not, for example, enjoy visiting the children's parents, and only did so because others did it. But she did like the sense of self-worth she received from the children's approval: 'The children know me, and speak my name. This was delicious to me and more worth than a thousand praises. This was one of my grandest days; it was almost too much for me.'[48]

Teaching the children of the poor and visiting their households aroused an awareness of social inequities in the young Anne Clough:

'There is fierce indignation in my heart at all the sufferings of the poor, and at the wrongs and oppression too, I may say.'[49] But when it came to working for deep-going social remedies, Anne found herself confronted by the limitations of her sex. While it was appropriate and acceptable for her to teach working-class children, and visit the houses of the poor, she could not go beyond this traditional feminine role of noblesse oblige. Even as a girl of seventeen, Anne realised that more thoroughgoing remedies were needed if the injustices of society were to be removed: 'If I were a man, I would not work for riches, to make myself a name or to leave a wealthy family behind me. No, I think I would work for my country, and make its people my heirs.' The refrain, 'if I were a man' occurs frequently in Anne Clough's adolescent journal. She felt the stirrings of ambition, but was thwarted by the fact that there seemed to be no legitimate outlet for such feelings:

> I have a lofty ambition. I sometimes fancy I shall do great things but will it not all come to nothing? Yet I should like never to be forgotten, to do something great for my country which would make my name live forever. But I am only a woman.[50]

If public activities more extensive than Lady Bountiful philanthropy were not open to her, learning was, and during these years, in addition to her good works, Anne also strove to develop self-discipline through private study. While she did enjoy such study, her chief reason for embarking on learning was to achieve a satisfactory spiritual state. She set up a formidable schedule for herself:

> This month I want to do over one book of Euclid, as far as the 80th page in the Greek grammar, translate book II of Virgil from the German, read 2nd and 3rd volumes of Milman's *History of the Jews*, Milton over again, and the second volume of Wordsworth. Working hard at these things may perhaps be of no particular use to me so far as knowing these things goes, but I can at least hope to acquire industrious habits and strength of mind, which I lack terribly.[51]

A girl could set herself such a schedule, but the psychological barriers to carrying out the programme were great. Only a natural scholar with a spontaneous love of learning — only someone like Emily Shore — would find it easy to keep to such a self-imposed schedule. Anne continually scolded herself for not working hard enough. In May, 1840, she wrote: 'Up at 6 — not early enough. Euclid and German: no time for Arnold's Sermons . . . Very lazy; want of sharpness.'[52] What would lead a young woman of twenty, who had no fixed occupation, and who lived in a household with several servants, to feel guilty because she did not rise until six in the morning? Only a belief that time, 'that great ocean of wealth', was slipping away, and that it was her duty to fill it worthily. But although Anne often felt that no amount of work would be adequate, at other times the work itself seemed pointless to her:

> I am beginning to grow tired of study. I think I might as well take my pleasure and be lazy if I like. I do nobody any harm, and if I were to be industrious, should I do anyone any good?[53]

Soon after she wrote that entry, the conflict between Anne's sense of duty, and the fact that she had no fixed goal towards which to direct it, was solved for her. In 1841, when James Clough's business failed, Anne's life as a sheltered young lady came abruptly to an end.[54] The immediate effect of the father's business failure was a move to a smaller house, with fewer servants. Reduced to a minimal amount of domestic help, Anne and her mother had to undertake much of the household work. For many years thereafter, Anne was responsible for her mother. Even before her father died in 1844, she had, in spite of the family's uneasiness about their only daughter taking on any financial burden, opened a small school run from the family home.[55] With the death of James Clough, Anne's management of the household, and her ability to support herself and her mother through teaching became an absolute necessity.

Both the conflicts that Anne Clough experienced as a sheltered young lady, and the responsibilities she was obliged to shoulder after 1841, provide a poignant contrast to the experiences of her brother Arthur. As they grew up, the two developed a similar religious and moral outlook. The conscientious scrupulousness that characterised Anne's personality also characterised that of Arthur. The differences between them lay not in their impulses, but in the scope within which they could act upon them. Anne's field of action, as we have seen, was circumscribed. In contrast, Arthur, from the age of ten, was out in the world, testing himself.

Arthur Hugh Clough attended Rugby School during the initial period of Thomas Arnold's reforming Headmastership. Arnold's Rugby became the model for the new, distinctively Victorian, public school, which came to be seen as the best training ground for producing masculinity in upper-class and middle-class boys. At Arnold's Rugby, masculinity meant moral earnestness, an ability to compete fairly, and the development of a capacity for leadership. Arnold's goal was to produce 'Christian gentlemen.' During his years at Rugby, Arthur Clough thoroughly internalised Arnold's conception of the Christian gentleman. He excelled as a student, but he also exemplified Arnold's ideal of moral leadership. As a senior boy, he was encouraged by the system to take his responsibilities very seriously indeed, perceiving himself as the moral and spiritual guardian of the other boys at the school.[56]

Arthur also assumed the role of moral guardian with his younger brother George, and with his sister. But there was a decided contrast between the advice he gave to George, and that which he gave to Anne. Whereas he urged George to take on the duties of manhood,[57] he encouraged Anne to develop a seriousness that would be distinctly feminine. He did help her with her studies, but he was always critical should she exhibit any tendency to act assertively, or to pose as a learned woman. Anne, in return, was acutely sensitive to any criticism from Arthur, especially criticism about behaviour Arthur saw as overly forward.[58]

Anne's feelings about Arthur reflect many of the qualities of the idealised sister-brother relationship that was analysed in an earlier chapter. Anne always looked to Arthur as a guide, as her connection to the outside world. She respected and even feared him, and wanted to please him.[59] She also identified closely with him, devoting much thought to his concerns.[60] Arthur never had this sort of identification with Anne. While he loved his sister, and helped her throughout his life, it was not an evenly balanced relationship. She thought much more about him than he ever did about her. For Arthur, his sister 'Annie' was merely a loved part of the background of his life.

A lower-middle-class girl, even if she was a member of a loving family, would never have had the opportunity to experience either the pleasures or the constraints of the role of the sheltered daughter at home. Frances Mary Buss, born in 1827, founder of the North London Collegiate School for Girls, grew up in such a household. Frances's father was an engraver and illustrator, and the family lived in the Mornington Crescent section of Camden Town, an area of London that was, during that period, an artists' enclave. The household had a limited income and few servants, and Mrs Buss not only looked after her children, but did much of the housework herself. From an early age, Frances, the only daughter in a family with several brothers, learned and accepted the fact that it was she who was expected to help her mother with the affairs of the house; to help with the care of the younger children, for example, and to help with the cooking.[61]

For the most part, Frances helped willingly, even as a small child. However, she also loved reading, and sometimes she would take her book and hide under the sofa so that she could read without interruption. Frances's biographer records that the mother had considerable sympathy with her daughter's wish to have time to herself, 'kindly shutting her eyes to those surreptitious studies under the sofa, instead of calling on her only girl to take her part in amusing the younger children'.[62]

In a household of this sort, the learning of such feminine tasks as sewing was not merely part of the training that a mother would give to a daughter as a necessary part of her upbringing, but they also could be genuinely useful to the family. For instance, before Frances was ten years old, she had learned to sew a man's shirt, a valuable skill in a family with four males. Out of this sharing of housewifely tasks, a strong bond developed between mother and daughter, a bond that extended through Frances Buss's adolescence, and was sustained until her mother's death.[63]

Frances's capacity for hard work and self-sacrifice grew as she entered adolescence. Her own formal education was minimal. As a child, she did attend a little day school in Camden Town, but her school days came to an end at fourteen. At that time, Mrs Buss decided to open a school of her own, with Frances's help, and at this early age, the girl began her life work. According to her biographer, Frances accepted the need to work cheerfully, being fully in accord with the family's decision to educate her brothers, rather than their only daughter:

> Like so many other sisters, this girl would watch her brothers going off to school or college for the studies in which she — *being a girl* — could have no share. But, like many a good sister before, and since, she would contentedly put aside her own dreams or desires, doing her best to help her brothers. Such sacrifice was taken simply as the highest duty, and thus turned to deepest delight.[64]

In her late teens, Frances was fortunate enough to meet the Honourary Secretary of the Governesses' Benevolent Association, and before she was twenty, she had become, through his good offices, one of the earliest students at Queen's College. She attended the College's

'Lectures for Ladies' for some years, earning a diploma by the time she was twenty-three.[65] These studies demanded dedication and determination. She worked all day in her own school, and then after a hard day's work she attended classes herself.[66] But the education she gained and the contacts that she made enabled her to transform the school she ran with her mother from the usual young ladies' establishment it originally was, into the pioneer school it became.

From evidence drawn from later periods of her life, we know that Frances Buss believed that girls should be taught to embody feminine qualities of self-sacrifice and, at the same time, be encouraged to pursue externally measurable goals. In her own adolescence, it appears that she herself achieved a balance between ambition and self-suppression. Through hard work, and luck, and because her goals suited the needs of the time, she was able to become more than the obscure teacher or governess that the great majority of her contemporaries who were similarly situated became. Comments she made about her own work during her most productive period indicate that she did not subscribe to the values of Victorian femininity in an unreflecting manner. She saw the difficulties that could confront the lower-middle-class girl or woman; it was because of such difficulties that she had devoted herself to improving their education:

> As I have grown older, the terrible sufferings of the women of my own class, for want of good elementary training, have more than ever intensified my earnest desire to lighten . . . the misery of women brought up 'to be married and taken care of', and left alone in the world destitute.[67]

Mary Anne Hearne's household was so modest that she was not brought up 'to be married and taken care of'. She was born in 1834, and grew up in a Kentish village where her father was a small tradesman who also served as village postmaster. Given the father's occupations, we can place the family at the lowest levels of the lower middle class. The Hearne family employed no live-in servants at all.[68]

Mary Anne was the eldest in a family of five. In her autobiography, she depicts her childhood as a happy one, although it was never totally carefree. The mother was at the centre of the children's lives, providing them with emotional and moral training, teaching them to read, and teaching the three girls of the family the skills of housewifery: 'Most lessons came from our parents, chiefly, of course, our mother. She taught us to sweep and clean, sew and knit . . . all the household arts.'[69] Mary Anne describes herself as a 'rollicking, mischievous child' with a love of nature. Like Frances Buss, she also had a love of reading. But her desires to roam the countryside, or to spend time reading were often checked by her mother:

> The cheery voice of my mother would call me into the house to amuse my brothers and sisters, or do some work. Dear Mother! she did not like my always having a book in my hand or pocket, and would have been better pleased if I had been equally fond of the brush or needle.[70]

Even though Mrs Hearne's determination to ensure that Mary Anne would behave in a feminine way involved suppression of parts of her daughter's character, Mary Anne did not resent her. As was the case with Frances Buss, this eldest daughter also developed an intense loyalty to her mother, even as a small child.

The Hearne family were devout Particular Baptists, and their commitment to this austere, Calvinist form of Protestantism permeated every area of life. The need for God's grace was impressed on the children from the time they could talk. One of Mary Anne's earliest memories was of contracting smallpox as a very young child. She remembered her mother 'wringing her hands with tears running down her cheeks', in grief for her 'poor little dying child'. Her mother's grief was as much caused by the child's spiritual state as by her physical condition: in her delirium, Mary Anne had refused the minister's prayers.[71]

As a devout adult, Mary Anne Hearne's intention was to explain that religious belief was not only the centre of her life, during childhood, but was also a great solace. However, she was forthright in her criticisms of the excessive gloominess of early-Victorian Calvinist Dissent. It was not necessary, she says, that she and her companions should have had to sing hymns with lines about the 'everlasting pains' of 'a dreadful Hell'.[72] And she recalls with the satisfaction that she and the other children in the village were able, on occasion, to subvert the more sombre aspects of the faith in which they were being raised. She describes, for example, a game that she and her friends played, in which they pretended to 'baptise' objects in the river. Mary Anne was the ringleader, climbing out on a limb of a tree overhanging the water:

> I stood upon the extreme edge of the [branch] and the boys on the bank, who represented the deacons, passed the candidates on to

me, and with more or less difficulty, I dipped them, while the other children on the bank sang Hallelujah.[73]

Mary Anne's joyous days as a tomboyish girl came to an abrupt end in her twelfth year, when her mother contracted tuberculosis, and went into a decline that ended in her death. It was Mary Anne, as eldest daughter, who went to London with her mother, and cared for her while she consulted a specialist: 'I used to sit and sew in her bedroom, and read her from a book called "The Dying Christian." The depth of the child's attachment to her mother is revealed in the prayer she repeatedly uttered:

> She was so much more to us than our father that again and again I sobbed out this beseeching petition, 'Oh Lord, if you must have one, please take our father to heaven, and leave us our dear mother'.[74]

Mary Anne was just twelve when her mother died, and the death was not only a emotional blow, it brought her own childhood prematurely to an end, because she had to become a little mother to the household herself:

> Of course I had to leave school and do the 'house-keeping' and the work of the house, and I am sure that it was done very badly. We were left very much to ourselves, and I still think it was a bad time for a girl to pass through. . . . My father often said that I never had a girlhood, but grew at once from a child to a woman.[75]

Being robbed of her girlhood caused her a considerable amount of bitterness, and an important ingredient in her sense of having been wronged was a feeling that her life was being stunted because of her sex. Her 'chief consolation' during this difficult period of her life was reading, but even that could add to her anger. She recalls that her father took two Sunday School monthlies for his children's amusement and improvement, and one ran a series that added to her sense of injustice:

> In one of these was a series of descriptive articles on men who had been poor boys, and risen to be rich and great. Every month I hoped to find the story of some poor, ignorant *girl*, who beginning life as handicapped as I, had yet been able by her own efforts and

the blessing of God upon them to live a life of usefulness, if not of greatness. But I believe there was not a woman in the whole series.[76]

To Mary Anne's father, her duties as eldest daughter were clear: she must stay at home, and take her mother's place in the family. But in spite of her father's disapproval, the girl was determined to improve herself, and obtain an education. Defying his injunctions about early bedtime, she studied late into the night, after the household chores were done, drinking tea dregs to keep herself awake. Eventually, her father realised the seriousness of her determination to educate herself, and he allowed her to help him in his business so that she could make a little money and go to school part-time.

During these bitter years, Mary Anne's religious faith wavered for a time. In a Baptist household such as the Hearne's, a loss of faith was probably the most effective act of defiance possible. As she puts it: 'I was very bitter and naughty at that time. I did not pray, and was not anxious to be good.'[77] Mary Anne regained her faith because of the friendship of a Sunday School teacher who loved her and sympathised with her difficulties. The concern of this woman helped her to transcend the difficulties of her early adolescence, and accept her lot as a female. At some time between fourteen and fifteen, she underwent the experience of 'conversion' and became a full-fledged member of the Church.[78]

Also important in helping her to value rather than chafe against the feminine role were the sisterly bonds that developed between herself, Rebecca, the second eldest girl, and Hephzibah, the youngest. As they too grew towards adolescence, both younger girls supported Mary Anne's desires to extend her experience beyond the little village of Farningham. Mary Anne's first opportunity to do so came when she was seventeen and Rebecca offered to take over the duties of the household so that the elder sister could accept a teaching post in Bristol. Mary Anne did not remain very long in Bristol, however, because Rebecca fell seriously ill, and she felt obliged to resign her post and return home: 'With a heavy heart, I said goodbye to Bristol, and as I then thought, to all my best prospects in life.'[79]

When Mary Anne returned home, it was clear that Rebecca was dying. During the last month of her life, Rebecca's character developed that redemptive spirituality that, as we saw earlier, figured in imagery about ideal girlhood. Rebecca apparently accepted her approaching death with patient resignation, and for Mary Anne, caring for her in her last months was a spiritually enriching experience: 'Those months have always seemed to me a most sacred time. She was so bright and patient, and even happy.'[80] Rebecca's death brought Mary Anne and Hephzibah closer together than they had ever been before. Hephzibah, who was a better housekeeper than Mary Anne, took over the cares of the household leaving Mary Anne free to resume her progress towards a career: 'She cared for me with almost more than a sister's love, and gave me time to write and study.'[81]

Mary Anne Hearne went on to develop an independence and autonomy that allowed her to pursue a career as a teacher, and later as a writer. While she was sympathetic to a widening of opportunities for girls and women, hers was very much a 'womanly' career.[82] As was the case with Frances Buss and Anne Jemima Clough, duty, religious conviction, and an acceptance of the Victorian conception of femininity were all integrated in her life and work. Her relationships with the female members of her own family — with her mother and her sisters — were influenced by the strengths of that conception of femininity, and it is perhaps for that reason that she accepted it so whole-heartedly, in spite of an awareness of the injustices which women suffered.

The five women whose early-Victorian girlhoods have figured in this chapter were diverse in temperament, in the nature of their personal relationships, and in social status. This analysis of their experience has demonstrated that while their society's conception of correct feminine behaviour was one factor that contributed to the shaping of their personalities, it was only one of several interacting factors. All five women were, however, affected by the early-Victorian definition of femininity and of the female role. Florence Nightingale, from an upper-class family, and Mary Anne Hearne, from the lowest level of the lower middle class, both felt conscious anger abut the limitations that the feminine role imposed. So too did Anne Clough. Emily Shore and Frances Buss appeared not to have experienced such conscious anger as girls. Emily, living in the isolation afforded by a country house, was able to live a life centred on private scholarship, during her brief life. She never confronted the fact that, as a woman, it would be difficult if not impossible for her to practise that scholarship in the public arena in any way other than as a writer. Frances Buss, it appears, was able from the beginning to integrate into her personality both an inner strength and resourcefulness, and an acceptance of feminine self-abnegation.

The four of these five women who lived to adulthood all had professional careers that were, to a greater or lesser degree, unusual for women born in the 1820s and 1830s. Nightingale's career was unique among nineteenth-century women. Her high social status, and the fact that she became a national heroine, enabled her to have an influence on male politics that was equalled during the century only by the Queen herself. Through her work on behalf of the nursing profession, her career contributed towards the development of new patterns, patterns that would open up career possibilities for middle-class girls in succeeding generations. Buss and Clough both contributed to the creation of these new patterns through their work in education, and in a more obscure way, so too did Mary Anne Hearne. But as they shaped their own lives, they themselves did not benefit from the models that they and others helped to establish; in adulthood all four of these early-Victorian girls were pioneers.

Notes

1. Florence Nightingale, 'Cassandra', printed as an appendix in Ray Strachey, *The Cause* (Port Washington, NY: Kennikat Press, 1969), p. 396.

2. Ibid., p. 414.

3. Ibid., p. 404.

4. For Florence Nightingale's parents, see Cecil Woodham-Smith, *Florence Nightingale: 1820 – 1910* (London: Constable, 1950), pp. 2 – 5, and Edward Cook, *The Life of Florence Nightingale* (2 vols. London: MacMillan and Co., 1913), I, pp. 1 – 7.

5. We know something of the reading matter given to the Nightingale children, because the Osborne Collection of Early Children's Books, Toronto Public Libraries, contains a collection of books that belonged to Florence Nightingale as a child. It includes, for example, copies of *The Child's Companion or Sunday Scholar's Reward* and Maria Edgeworth, *Moral Tales* (1802).

6. Woodham-Smith, *Florence Nightingale*, p. 5; Cook, *The Life*, I, pp. 10 – 12. Frances Power Cobbe offers another example of a well-to-do family of the 1820s in which the mother was closely involved in child-care, even though the routine care was left to servants.

Frances Power Cobbe was born into a well-to-do Anglo-Irish family in 1822. In the Cobbe household, the nursery, presided over by an 'Irish' nurse, was 'so distant from the regions inhabited by my parents that I was at full liberty to make any amount of noise I pleased.' *Life of Frances Power Cobbe*, I, pp. 31 – 2. But Frances did see her mother regularly: 'I was brought to her continually; first to be nursed, – for she fulfilled that sacred duty of motherhood to all her children . . . Later, I seem . . . to have been often cuddled up close to her on her sofa, or learning my little lessons . . .' (I, p. 34).

7. On the relationship in childhood between Florence and Parthe, see Woodham-Smith, *Florence Nightingale*, pp. 9 – 11 and *passim* for its subsequent development.

8. Ibid., p. 7.

9. Ibid., p. 11.

10. Ibid., p. 12.

11. Ibid., pp. 38 – 9.

12. Ibid., p. 31 and Cook, *The Life*, I, pp. 2 – 27.

13. Woodham-Smith, *Florence Nightingale*, p. 17.

14. Ibid., pp. 45 – 6;

15. Florence Nightingale, 'Cassandra', p. 397.

16. Woodham-Smith, *Florence Nightingale*, pp. 487 – 9.

17. *Journal of Emily Shore*, (London: Kegan Paul, Trench, Trubner & Co., 1898), p. vii.

18. Ibid., p. 1.

19. It should be pointed out that, while Emily Shore's journal reflects an unusual maturity and intelligence, it was not unusual for middle-class and upper-class girls to keep diaries, although they were usually undertaken in the teen years, rather than at the age of ten. Other diaries of young girls born in the first three decades of the nineteenth century which survive include: Mary Helen Bingham, see John Bustard, *A Memoir of Miss Mary Helen Bingham Who Died on the 8th of June, 1825 in the Seventeenth Year of Her Age* (London: John Kershaw, 1827); Emily Hall, born in 1819, and Ellen Hall, born in 1822, see O.A. Sherrard, *Two Victorian Girls* (London: Müller, 1966); Louisa Montefiori, born in 1821, see Lucy Cohen, *Lady de Rothschild and her Daughters: 1821 – 1931* (London: John Murray, 1935).

20. *Journal of Emily Shore*, p. vi.

21. E.g., in her entry for 8 July 1831, while on a journey: 'The wild mignonette, which I never saw before, is plentiful on the rocks, as well as another flower, called the little Barmedick. It is a papilionaceous flower, of a yellow colour, and unbranched . . .' Ibid., p. 6.

22. Ibid. For the *Quarterly Review*, see entry of 20 October 1835, p. 127; for the *Boy's Own Book*, see 6 July 1833, p. 61.

23. On the cook and mice, see Ibid., 9 February 1833, pp. 34 – 5.

24. Ibid., pp. 9 – 10, entry for 4 November 1831.

25. Ibid., p. 32, entry for 21 January 1833.

26. At the time the family was moving from Potton to Woodbury, she writes, on 23 December 1832: 'The little girl whom I teach has been here every day for the last week . . . came this evening for the last time . . . she is too young to go as far as Woodbury . . . I have some thoughts of having a few little girls from Everton, if Mamma and Papa approve of it, which I believe they do.' Ibid., p. 27.

27. Ibid., p. 1, entry for 30 December 1831.

28. Ibid., p. 27, entry for 19 December 1832.

29. Ibid., pp. 31 – 2, entry for 21 January 1833.

30. Ibid., p. 130, entry for 1 December 1835.

31. Ibid., p. 28, entry for 25 December 1832.

32. Ibid., p. 87, entry for 10 December 1834.

33. Ibid., p. 76, entry for 23 June 1834.

34. Ibid., p. 142, entry for 5 July 1836. Unlike some young victims of consumption, Emily Shore never came to long for death. See, for example, the journal entry of Mary Helen Bingham for 16 November 1822: 'I long to go to my Redeemer . . . but I believe the strong ardent prayers of my dear parents, for my recovery, hold my soul in its frail tabernacle.' *A Memoir of Miss Mary Helen Bingham*, p. 88. See also the diary of Mary Ann Gilpin, a Quaker girl, 1813 – 37. Although she did not die of consumption until 1837, she had already contracted the disease by 1829. When she was making a partial recovery, she wrote in her diary: 'As I get stronger I feel more and more the danger of a return to the active duties of life, as being so liable to engage my thoughts too much. If it had been consistent with the divine will, oh how willing, how glad should I have been to be taken . . .' *Memoir of Mary Ann Gilpin of Bristol Consisting Chiefly of Extracts from her Diary and Letters* (2nd edn; London: Edmund Fry, 1841).

35. *Journal of Emily Shore*, pp. 174 – 5, entry for 25 December 1836.

36. See Athena Blanche Clough, *Memoir of Anne Jemima Clough* (London: Edward Arnold, 1897), pp. 2 – 8 on the Clough family and on their Charleston years. See also Katherine Chorley, *Arthur Hugh Clough, The Uncommited Mind: A Study of His Life and Poetry* (Oxford: Clarendon Press, 1962), pp. 9 – 11.

37. Clough, *Memoir*, p. 5, and Chorley, *Arthur Hugh Clough*, p. 11.

38. Athena Blanche Clough includes extensive extracts from the diary in her *Memoir*.

39. Anne Clough, quoted in Clough, *Memoir*, p. 9.

40. May 1840, Ibid., pp. 23 – 4.

41. Anne Clough, Ibid, pp. 13 – 14.

42. Ibid.

43. Maria Lance to Anne Clough, Ibid., p. 19.

44. See entry from Anne Clough's journal, Ibid., p. 29.

45. From Anne Clough's journal, Ibid., p. 34.

46. Entry for April 1841, Ibid., p. 38.

47. E.g., 'Have had a great many idle, foolish thoughts about marriage. I cannot always keep myself steady about that. Foolish show-off thoughts will come up and bother me . . . My mind wants a good steady hard working, it is getting flimsy. That would drive out all this nonsense.' Entry for October 1840, quoted in Ibid., p. 31.

48. From her journal, 1839, Ibid., p. 22.

49. Entry for January 1841, Ibid., p. 34.

50. Entry for February 1841, Ibid., p. 37.

51. Entry for May 1840, Ibid., p. 23. Anne did study Greek, but she records that her best friend disapproved of women learning the Classical languages. 'Had some nice talks with Margaret about various things: about women learning Latin and Greek, Euclid, etc.; the use of learning to women; also about doing good in the country, factories, etc. She does not approve of Latin and Greek; in other things we are pretty well agreed.' Entry for July 1840, Ibid., p. 27.

52. Ibid., p. 23.

53. Entry for August 1840, Ibid., p. 29.

54. The entry for August 1841, marks the event: 'Father's letter arrives with the news that all is up with him.' Ibid., p. 41.

55. Ibid., pp. 20 – 1.

56. As Katherine Chorley puts it: 'he was the kind of youth who would imbibe Arnold's doctrines of moral responsibility without any admixture of the light-hearted boyishness which allowed other youths a little moral relaxation.' Chorley, *Arthur Hugh Clough*, p. 30.

57. For example, when Arthur Hugh Clough was still at Rugby, but his brother George was at a much less satisfactory school, the former sent the latter a series of letters urging him to take on a responsible role in the school. In one such letter he wrote: 'You are now in a very important situation; you are the only one it seems of a set of boys, who knows God, and wishes to serve him. So that you are in some manner responsible; I mean you will have to answer for some of their sins, if you do not exert yourself in their behalf, to make them better . . .' The letter is quoted in Chorley, *Arthur Hugh Clough*, p. 32.

58. For example, she wrote in her Journal in June 1841: 'Arthur comes home . . . there has certainly been a quantity of show-off nonsense and attempt at talking finely about poetry, etc., which A. did not seem to approve of, and put off. I want praise too much, yet he is the only person from whom I really desire it.' Quoted in Clough, *Memoir*, pp. 40 – 1.

59. E.g., a journal entry for March 1841: 'Have heard from Arthur — very much pleased. He is my best friend and adviser. He often keeps me from falling into foolish ways, talking of foolish things, etc. I do not like to do or say anything that he would not like, because I believe he is wiser than I am.' Ibid., p. 38.

60. For example, when Arthur, who was at Balliol, received only a second class degree, she wrote: 'Was most exceedingly put out of the way last Sunday on hearing

Arthur was only in the second class in the examination. I could not endure he should be beat by anyone.' Entry for June 1841, Ibid., p. 40.

61. For the Buss household, see Annie E. Ridley, *Frances Mary Buss and her Work for Education* (London: Longmans, Green & Co., 1895), pp. 29 – 37.

62. Ibid., p. 39.

63. 'At that date it was considered necessary that every girl should work; and before I was ten years of age I had made a shirt for my father, all the parts being cut out and arranged by my mother, sewing machines not being then invented.' Ibid., p. 37.

64. Ibid., p. 43. In fact, the Buss boys helped in the family school as well, Septimus teaching when he was only fourteen. See notes by Frank Fleetwood Buss on the North London Collegiate School for Ladies in 'History of the School, 1850 – 1875', North London Collegiate School Archives.

65. 'Queen's College for Women' came into existence in 1848. It was a benevolent scheme that grew out of the combined efforts of the upper-middle-class women who founded the Governesses' Benevolent Institution in 1841, and men like Frederic Denison Maurice and Charles Kingsley, who lectured at King's College, London. In these years, Queen's College's affiliation with the University of London was more honorary than substantive; the teaching it offered was at the secondary level, rather than at a university level. See Strachey, *'The Cause'*, pp. 60 – 3.

66. 'She was teaching all day in her own school, so that she could take only the evening classes. There were at that time no omnibusses, and night after night . . . the enthusiastic girl walked from Camden Town to Queen's College and back.' Ridley, *Frances Mary Buss*, p. 52. The fact that Frances Buss, a middle-class young woman from a respectable family, could take this walk by herself, at night, presumably across Regent's Park (the College premises were in Harley Street) is evidence that among modest middle-class families girls and young women could go out in the world unchaperoned. Compare this with Constance Maynard's experience: Maynard, whose life is discussed in the next chapter, was not allowed to go outside the grounds of the family estate unchaperoned until she was well into her twenties.

67. Ridley, *Frances Mary Buss*, p. 93.

68. Marianne Farningham [Mary Anne Hearne], *A Working Woman's Life: An Autobiography* (London: James Clarke & Co., 1907), p. 117 for family background and early life.

69. Ibid., p. 18.

70. Ibid., p. 23.

71. Ibid., p. 18.

72. Ibid., p. 39.

73. Ibid., p. 27.

74. Ibid., p. 40.

75. Ibid., p. 44.

76. Ibid.

77. Ibid.

78. Farningham, *Working Woman's Life*, p. 57.

79. Ibid., pp. 66 – 7.

80. Ibid., p. 67.

81. Ibid., p. 69.

82. She became editor of *The Sunday School Times*, and under her pseudonym of 'Marianne Farningham', wrote several improving books for young people, including *Girlhood*, an advice book for girls that enjoyed successful sales for several decades, running to two editions, the first in 1869, and the revised, in 1895, which claimed that 25,000 copies of the first edition had been sold.

Chapter 8

MID-VICTORIAN GIRLHOOD EXPERIENCE

The mid-Victorian decades have been characterised as the period when English prosperity was at its height, and when the dominance of middle-class values was most visible and least subject to question. The worst of the misery, dislocation and class antagonism that accompanied the first phase of industralisation had passed, giving way to relative prosperity, and to a consensus about moral, social and political values. In the words of one historian, the mid-Victorian period was 'The Age of Equipoise.'[1]

Like most historical generalisations, much of what has been said about mid-Victorian England was more true for males than for females. The lives of middle-class women during this period were shaped by the prosperity and self-confidence of the class to which they belonged, but at the same time, their situation has a history independent of that of their fathers, brothers and husbands.

Three features were of particular importance in influencing the lives of middle-class women born in the mid-Victorian decades. The values of domesticity, the sanctification of family life and of femininity were at their most pervasive during these years. And yet the period also witnessed the birth of the Women's Movement; moreover it provided a woman born during the mid-Victorian decades with the possibility of benefiting from the educational and professional opportunities that became available to middle-class women in the 1860s. The early-Victorian women who achieved success in the 'public sphere' did so as isolated individuals; for the mid-Victorian generation, there was the possibility of participating in educational and professional enterprises expressly designed to benefit middle-class women as a group.

This discussion of mid-Victorian girlhood experience will focus on six women. Two of them, Constance Maynard, born in 1849, and Lilian Faithfull, born in 1865, came from upper-middle-class families. Both received a University education and then went on to become educators of women. In contrast, Alice Whichelo, born in 1855, came from a much less affluent middle-class family. In comparison to the other women included in this analysis, her life history was more typical of the lives of the great majority of middle-class women of the nineteenth century, who left no individual mark on history. She had no aspirations toward public achievement, married when she was twenty-two and lived her life as a conventional Victorian woman, devoting herself to motherhood. She is remembered not for her own achievements, but because she was the mother of the novelist E.M. Forster.

Sara Burstall, Molly Hughes and Sarah Marks were all from lower-middle-class families and all, in different ways, benefited from the educational opportunities that became available in the 1870s. Sara Burstall, born in 1859, attended both of Frances Buss's schools, went to Girton and later became Headmistress of Manchester High School for Girls. Molly Hughes was born in 1869, also attended the North London Collegiate School, and had a career before marriage as an educator. Hughes is remarkable because of the tenacity with which she embraced the conventional values of femininity, in spite of her considerable professional achievements. Sarah Marks, known in adult life as Hertha Ayrton, was born in 1854. In several ways, her circumstances and her achievements were atypical, even among nineteenth-century women who achieved professional success. In nineteenth-century England, the fact that she was Jewish set her apart from her contemporaries, to begin with; and she achieved success in science, a rare field of endeavour for nineteenth-century women. Most unusual of all was the fact that Ayrton combined marriage and motherhood with a professional career.

Throughout her life, Constance Maynard's personality exhibited two opposing sides. On the one hand, she was ambitious; on the other hand, she was deeply religious. The nature of the conflict between the spiritual life and ambition was not markedly different for this woman born in the mid-Victorian period than it had been for such early-Victorian women as Florence Nightingale or Anne Clough; for her, as for them, the conflict was complicated by the limits and demands of femininity. But in contrast to the early-Victorian women, Maynard was born late enough in the century so that when her desire for independence became acute, there was a ready-made outlet for her ambition: Constance Maynard became one of the earliest students at Girton College. After Girton, her adult life work represented an attempt to provide, for succeeding generations of young women, a compromise between the ambitions that led her to Girton, and her religious faith. Westfield College, which she founded in the 1880s, was deliberately designed to amalgamate the intellectual values of

Girton, and the self-sacrificing, other-wordly values of evangelical Christianity.[2]

Constance was the daughter of a successful businessman. The second youngest in a family of six children, the Maynard nursery and household style were well established by the time she was born in 1849. The family home, 'Oakfield', was a large country house in Kent, surrounded by fourteen acres of land. As befitted the family's level of affluence, the house contained a wing devoted to 'nursery' and 'schoolroom', and a head nurse, nursery maids and governesses were employed. The children were bathed, fed and dressed by the servants, and spent most of their time with them.[3]

But the children were not left entirely to the staff. Their mother Louisa was intensely involved in the rearing of her children. Although she saw them only at controlled intervals, she both designed and oversaw the nursery pattern, and it was she, rather than any of the servants, who had the greatest moral and emotional impact on her children. In Louisa Maynard's case, concern for her children's welfare sprang from deep religious belief. As Constance later put it, her mother had 'a profound depth of puritanism, a genuine contempt for "the world".'[4] All her children were influenced by the strength of her personality and by her rigid, unbending nature. The children were not physically punished, moral disapproval being sufficient to control them, but they were repressed: 'In the Nursery and Schoolroom all teasing and quarrelling were suppressed on the instant, even to an impatient word.'[5]

Louisa Maynard was influential in her children's lives, but remote and even frightening; their father, Henry, who did not enjoy the company of small children, remained a shadowy figure in each of their lives until they reached adolescence; the servants, although everpresent, seem to have made no deep impression on any of the six children. In consequence, the Maynard children were more intimate with each other than they were with any of the adult figures in their lives. Constance, in early childhood, was closest to her brother George, and as his senior by a year she was the dominant child of the two. In typical mid-Victorian fashion, however, they were separated in the middle years of childhood. George was sent to school at ten, whereas Constance remained at home until she was fifteen.[6] After the separation, George quickly became the dominant one in their relationship, the person who, through his experience at school, could expose his sister to information that would not otherwise have been accessible to her.

With George away at school, the foreground of Constance's world was occupied by her three sisters. Josephine, born in 1839, Gabrielle, born in 1845, Dora, born in 1846 and Constance formed a close-knit unit, although the group was not without its tensions. Constance commented later:

> The home-life we four sisters lived is easy enough to describe in its external form, but in its bearing on the mind and the spirit . . . it is almost impossible to give a correct impression . . . It was extremely smooth and cheerful and orderly on the surface, and sometimes it was rough and hard underneath.[7]

Constance attributed many of the underlying tensions to the difficult character of her sister Josephine. The eldest child in the family, Josephine was expected to take on, from an early age, the 'responsibilities of the elder daughter';[8] her mother intended that she should be gentle, submissive and willing to help serve the needs of the younger children. Above all, she was expected to take the lead in deferring to Harry, the eldest son, whose nickname — 'Fatted Calf' — reflected his status in the family. The problem was that Josephine was not only a year his senior, she was also more intelligent and more forceful than the charming but feckless Harry. Consequently, during her childhood and adolescence she was 'exceedingly clever, inventive and tiresome', with a 'talent for mockery', which she directed against her sisters.[9] According to Constance, her character did not change until she was in her twenties, and underwent the experience of 'conversion', after which she became dutiful, gentle and accepting of feminine responsibility.[10]

For a brief period in adolescence, all four sisters were sent to school, but in their childhood years, they were educated in the 'schoolroom' by a succession of governesses. The routine provided the girls with little intellectual stimulation. Constance later described it:

> Think of a bright, pleasant, schoolroom in a country house 'five miles from everywhere', a room containing many things, but witnessing to no real teaching . . . The governesses might change from time to time, but the system never. So many pages of 'Mrs. Markham' to read aloud . . . A French verb to repeat . . . six questions of Mangnall to answer . . . I do not think I remember a spark of real interest being elicited.[11]

For two years during Constance's early childhood, the boredom of the schoolroom was in a measure compensated for by a once-weekly session with her mother. Louisa devoted Thursday afternoons to her four youngest children, letting them learn 'exactly what we liked, printing and willow-plaiting, heraldry . . . the Greek alphabet — and all else.' Louisa's methods were haphazard, but stimulating, and unlike the governesses she 'was able to instill a love of knowledge for its own sake.'[12]

During Constance's childhood and adolescence, much of her energy was channelled into introspection, in which religious enthusiasm played a major part. While Constance's religious feelings had been inculcated by her mother, in this area of life, as in others, she did not succeed in entirely winning Louisa's approval. Louisa Maynard wished her children to be devout, but she did not wish to 'rouse religious emotion', of which she was suspicious. But her youngest daughter's primary response to religion was through the emotions. For Constance, a love of God was bound up with her feelings of joy and sorrow, with her love of nature, as God's creation, on the one hand, and with her feelings of inadequacy on the other. By eleven or twelve, she was longing for 'conversion':

> Once, having an afternoon to myself, I climbed up a tree, that overlooked the sunny walled garden and said I would not come down until I was a *true* Christian. For an hour and a half, I went over texts and hymns and prayers and finally slid down again a little comforted.[13]

The loneliest years of Constance's girlhood were those between twelve and fourteen, when Gabrielle and Dora were both at school, but she remained at home. During these years, no governess was employed to teach this last daughter of the family. Instead, she was told that she must become a 'self-student', but as she later said rather bitterly, 'nothing very definite was proposed' for her to do. The most important event in these years was a change in her relationship with her father, whom she had always feared. When he returned from an extended business trip when she was thirteen, and greeted her warmly, she suddenly realised that, in fact, he loved her, and 'from that moment on we began to be friends'. Soon she was reading aloud to her father, helping him in the garden, and going for long walks with him.[14]

Finally, in 1863, Constance was sent to school. Brief though the experience was — she was removed a year and a half later — it was crucial to her spiritual and psychological development, although only of minor importance from an intellectual point of view. The school, 'Mrs Umphelby's at Belstead', was an establishment of an early-Victorian type.[15] It was small and informal, being run by Mrs Umphelby and her mother, both of whom were fervent Evangelicals. Mrs Umphelby's establishment, like the Maynard's own household, was unworldly, but there were subtle but distinct differences in character between them. Indeed, given Louisa Maynard's distaste for emotional excess, one wonders why this school was selected. At Mrs Umphelby's, emotion was approved of rather than repressed, and the school experience was decisive for Constance, because it sanctioned her natural impulses: 'As I got away to Belstead a sort of pressure was lifted off me, and I could be myself.'[16]

At Belstead, Constance did not undergo 'conversion' — indeed she never had such an experience — but she was confirmed there, and this was a religious landmark for her. Moreover, she made two schoolgirl friendships. Both of these relationships were intense, and continued even after she left school. After her return home, she wrote continually in her diary about both girls and corresponded with them.[17] These friendships, and her love for the Umphelbys, were the first opportunities she had to extend her emotional horizons beyond the sphere of her own family.

Constance was abruptly removed from school when she was just sixteen. It appears that the decision was her father's:

> Father said he didn't see why he should go on paying for an expensive school when I should do quite well at home with three sisters above me who had been educated till they were eighteen.[18]

In fact, Henry Maynard could well have afforded the school fees, and proved more than willing to spend money on his daughters in other ways. But Constance was a girl, not a boy. There was no real need to educate her further, and in any case, the Maynards clearly felt that it was the duty of the elder girls, as sisters, to help the youngest girl prepare for adult life. The Umphelbys encouraged her to accept the decision as a dutiful daughter. At parting, Mrs Umphelby's mother said to her:

> 'You've been taken from us very suddenly, child, but I think that makes it seem all the clearer, that it's His doing . . . go, darling, go

and be a sunbeam in your home, a blessed sunbeam that gladdens all as it comes near. And remember a sunbeam won't do good shining by fits and starts, but patiently . . . Your father and mother are getting old and one never wants the sunshine so much as when one is old.'[19]

From the age of sixteen, until she was twenty-three, Constance, in the company of her three sisters, lived the 'life of a grown-up daughter'. The sisters' activities were shaped by the family's 'unworldliness'. They did not engage in the usual social life of people of their income and position. There were no parties, few trips, and with the exception of the works of Scott, the girls were not even allowed any novels. Instead, in addition to the ritual of family life, the girls had two main activities: their studies and charitable visits to the surrounding cottagers.

In their devotion to private study, the Maynard sisters could have served as models for those advice book writers who emphasised the middle-class girl's obligation to use her time in an 'improving' fashion: 'We started to be very industrious, we made time-tables of the hours for reading and learning and drawing, and at the end of each week counted how much had been done.'[20] The reading they did was serious and high-minded. As Constance says, she often devoted herself to books 'demanding so much attention that each one required several months of the allotted time.'[21]

The motives for the second engrossing interest of the sisters, charitable work with the poor, came partly from emotional needs of their own, and partly from a sense of duty: 'Youth will not be balked of the give and take of human society, and seeing we were debarred from our equals, we made friends with the village people.'[22] For the village poor, Constance and her sisters provided the standard Lady Bountiful amalgam of soup and religious exhortation. Constance believed that she was doing her duty — a duty that she often found difficult to perform — but she never, either as a girl, or later in life, analysed the social significance of such activity. In contrast, for example, to Anne Clough, who was troubled by the limited usefulness of the charitable teaching that she did in Liverpool in the 1830s, Constance never confronted the fact that her unorganised charity could not contribute to lasting remedies for poverty. Nor did it occur to her that a seventeen-year-old girl might be intruding on the privacy of an old farm labourer when she exhorted him to give up drinking,[23] or that it was meddlesome and condescending to assign religious texts for memorisation to an old woman who was in no position to refuse her visits.[24]

At sixteen, Constance began to keep a regular diary. During her years as a 'grown-up daughter at home', the entries reveal the doubt, dissatisfaction and anxiety of her inner life. She felt guilty that in spite of her comfortable home she was not happier; she confessed to insufficient sympathy with others; and she worried about continuing underlying bad feeling between herself and her mother. In short, she was restless and uneasy with the limited life open to her.[25]

Yet, until she was well into her twenties, Constance felt obliged to obey her parents. Although she corresponded with friends, for example, she continually consulted with her mother about the suitability of writing such letters.[26] She and her sisters accepted severe limitations on their physical movements as a matter of course; until they were in their early twenties, the sisters were not allowed to venture alone outside the confines of the estate.[27] And the wishes and needs of her parents took priority over all other activities. Study and charitable works, for example, were always put aside if either parent wanted the company of one of their daughters.

Given the circumscribed nature of their lives, it is not surprising that two of the four daughters never moved on from the position of 'daughter at home' to an independent life. Of the four sisters, only Dora married, and then not until she was thirty.[28] Constance was to escape the confines of home through her professional career, but only after a struggle. Josephine and Gabrielle never did leave home. The barriers to the usual avenue of escape — marriage — were both situational and psychological. Barred from social life, not by income, but by their parents' moral convictions, it was extremely difficult for the sisters to meet suitable men. Moreover, unconsciously, the parents not only kept their daughters within the home circle, they raised them to be spinsters, encouraging them, either overtly or covertly, to suppress any budding feelings of sexuality.

Constance did receive an offer of marriage, in 1869, when she was on a visit from home. The suitor was not ineligible, but her rejection of him was swift and spontaneous, and she suffered guilty feelings that she may even have provoked the 'offer'. Her feelings of revulsion towards the man himself, and towards marriage, are reflected in her diary entries, which indicate that it was not only that she did not find Henry Colliston attractive, but that the idea of sexuality itself was both frightening and repugnant to her.[29]

The turning point in Constance's life came in 1872, when she was twenty-three years old. In that year, she made an extended visit to cousins who lived in Scotland. Lewis Campbell was a Professor at the University of St Andrews and his household was both more worldly and more intellectual than that of the Maynards. It was in St Andrews that she first heard of the enterprise of a woman's college that Emily Davies had founded at Hitchin. With Lewis Campbell's encouragement, Constance decided that she would go to the future Girton if at all possible, and she returned home determined to persuade her parents to let her do so.

Even at twenty-three, Constance could not have determined to attend college without her parents' approval. She was financially dependent on them and she was still tied to them emotionally, still obedient to their wishes. Significantly, it was her father, rather than her mother, with whom she first broached the request:

> Father was always easier than Mother to manage when a request was on hand, so I looked for a suitable opportunity . . . There was a frowning and a smiling and 'I say, Conse, this is something new', and then a pinch on the cheek . . . and 'But where's the *use*? What's it for?' and a murmur or two about staying at home and being like my sisters, and he offered to get me a new pony if I would give it up. But I think dear Father always gave in if rightly and carefully approached, and at the close he said, 'Well, well, I suppose these things must be. The Mother knows more about it all than I do. If you can get her consent, the bills shall be paid, Dear, the bills shall be paid.'[30]

Fortunately, her mother did agree that the experiment could be tried, and after taking the entrance exams, Constance went off to Hitchin in the autumn of 1872. In taking this step, her adult life began. Initially, her parents agreed to send her to the college for one year only, and would not hear of her sitting for the Degree examinations. But her successful achievements softened their resolve and she was allowed to complete the college programme. In preparing her for a good teaching career, Girton rendered her financially independent of her family, and although the psychological bonds remained powerful, Constance never again became a 'daughter at home'.[31]

Constance Maynard found her way to Girton and an independent career largely through her own determination, and with only reluctant support from her family. The path that led Lilian Faithfull to Somerville College, and then to a career in education, was smoothed for her by her own family, a fact that is surprising, given the nature of that family. The Faithfull parents, and Lilian herself, held views about femininity and about social class that were in no way radical: they were conventional upper-middle-class people. Lilian Faithfull's girlhood experiences and subsequent career are revealing, because they illustrate the fact that support for the higher education of middle-class girls was not confined to a small, radical minority.

Born in 1865, Lilian grew up in a large country house in Hertford-shire, her father being a 'professional man' with a substantial income. Lilian was the second youngest in a family of eight. There were six girls and two boys; as with the Maynard family, the sisters formed a com-munity and during their childhood were closer to each other than they were to any adults.

The household arrangements for child-care conformed to the affluent mid-Victorian pattern. There was a 'nursery' and a 'schoolroom', and the primary responsibility for the physical care of the children was in the hands of the nursery staff, the parents remaining remote, if benevolent, figures. Reminiscing about this arrangement in later life, Lilian stressed its benefits: 'Nursery life had its definite delights, and children have missed much who have not had the perfect playmate and kindly autocrat often found in a nurse.'[32]

Of her mother Lilian later said: 'My Mother's activities knew no bounds . . . She made our clothes, taught us, kept elaborate accounts, wrote a diary, contributed articles on the ethics of daily life to magazines.'[33] But, as was usual in such families, the mother's contact with her eight children was limited and formal. Until adole-scence, the children did not eat with the parents. After nursery break-fast, they visited them, briefly, each morning. And then, tidied up, with their hair brushed, and wearing their best clothes, they spent an hour each day, between six and seven, with their mother. Under the influence of this controlled but regular contact, Lilian Faithfull says that she and her siblings viewed their parents with 'awe and reverence', but that they suffered from 'no repression' when they were with them.[34]

As in most other middle-class families formal religion constituted part of the fabric of life in the Faithfull household. There were daily family prayers, and on Sunday, the activities of the household were restricted, the children only being allowed to play games connected with Bible stories. Although Faithfull describes her family as 'Evangelical', religious belief did not have the depth of meaning for this family that it had in a household like that of the Maynards. The Faithfull children were, indeed, raised to have a sense of duty, but duty was more connected with worldly matters than it was with the inner state of the soul.

In the children's regime sharp differences were drawn between the duties of males and the duties of females. The Faithfull girls were taught to be feminine in a variety of ways. As little girls, they were taught to do housework, although in this affluent family their tasks were not meant to contribute to the household routine. The sisters had a playhouse of their own in the garden, fitted up with furniture, and each week the youngest girls gave the playhouse a 'weekly cleaning', under the watchful eye of an elder sister. They did 'scrubbing, washing, ironing and cleaning of knives . . .' In addition, as little girls, they also helped out by waiting at table, when the parents entertained: 'We were dressed in caps and aprons, and with immense seriousness we played our part and learnt our business.'[35]

But the Faithfull girls were not being reared to be domestic servants. The training in housewifery ceased after early childhood, to be replaced by the cultivation of feminine skills more directly suited to their future station in life. They were, for example, taught to be good conversationalists. This was one of the obligations that their mother impressed upon them during those formal daily sessions they spent with her: 'No mercy was shown to the elder girl who would not play her part in the social game. It was not fair, my mother urged, to take everything and give nothing.'[36]

In the Faithfull household, the boys were sent off to school in middle childhood, whereas the girls were kept in 'the schoolroom'. They were taught by governesses, none of whom were satisfactory, and sometimes by their mother. As was the case in the Maynard family, the Faithfull parents exercised considerably more control over the reading habits of their daughters than was exercised by families of similar status and outlook during the early-Victorian period. For example, Emily Shore, it will be remembered, read anything she could find, from the *Quarterly Review* to periodicals designed specifically for boys. In contrast, the Faithfull girls as children were largely restricted to pious and didactic evangelical tales.[37] In adolescence, the girls were allowed, and enjoyed, the novels of Charlotte Yonge. Among Victorian novelists, no one more fully reflected the values of middle-class domesticity and femininity than Yonge. Lilian and her sisters not only enjoyed the stories but identified closely with the characters:

The boys and girls of Miss Yonge's huge families were indeed ourselves — people of like passions, emotions, hopes and fears, and we were as intimate with every detail of their lives . . . as with the lives of our sisters, cousins and aunts.[38]

The fact that these girls saw themselves so clearly reflected in Charlotte Yonge's works indicates the extent to which, by adolescence, they had internalised the values that permeate those tales. It was the Faithfull girls, not the boys, who read Charlotte Yonge, and childhood tales of death and redemption like *Jessica's First Prayer*. As Faithfull herself noted, 'the gulf between boys and girls at that time was strongly marked in the books provided for them'. 'No boy', she says, 'would have endured our mental pabulum'. Instead, the boys were given tales of adventure, tales their sisters also enjoyed reading, surreptitiously, whenever they were lucky enough to lay hands on such unauthorised reading matter.[39]

In spite of Lilian's conventionally feminine girlhood, in 1883, she entered Somerville College as one of its earliest students. Apparently it was her mother who decided that she should go to Oxford; Lilian's father was at first reluctant, but finally 'gave in to' his wife's wishes, although he regarded the experiment merely as a 'harmless amusement', None of the other Faithfull sisters received the academic education given to Lilian. It appears that Lilian showed an unusual aptitude for intellectual work in the 'schoolroom', and for this reason her mother decided that she should receive a more rigorous education than that of her sisters. To prepare her for Somerville, an unusual expedient was arrived at. Lilian, in her mid-teens, attended a select boys' preparatory school, 'The Grange', of which her uncle was Headmaster. Being the only girl among some twenty-five boys was 'rather overwhelming at first', she recalls: 'I was older than the boys and very ignorant, but very keen and intensely conscious that it was a great concession on the part of my uncle and an experiment that must not fail.'[40] As an adult woman educator, Faithfull firmly believed that girls had less creative capacity than boys, less desire for independence, and less real intellectual ability. In her autobiography she explains that it was at 'The Grange' that she first realised the innate and immutable differences between boys and girls. She worked diligently there, developing the capacity for sustained application that she retained all her life, but she saw herself as typically feminine both in her docility and capacity to follow direction, and in her lack of creativity. In comparison to her fellow pupils, she says, 'my general level was, perhaps, higher than theirs; my best was nearly always less good'.[41]

Lilian none the less achieved a level of competence sufficient to gain her admission to Somerville. When she went up, in 1883, the college was in its fourth year. The experience made its mark on her. She worked hard and played hard — she was the Somerville tennis champion — but she did not believe that Somerville, or the women's college movement, was designed to offer any radical challenge to the balance between the sexes. Nor did she recognise any hostility towards the education of women on the part of the Oxford community. Somerville, she says, was accepted by Oxford, because Somerville behaved in a ladylike fashion: 'It was the spirit of unobtrusive receptivity and deference to University traditions and prejudices rather than a demand for rights which the Principal . . . took pains to instill into the first students.'[42]

It was in the spirit of unobtrusive receptivity and deference to tradition that Lilian Faithfull embarked on her career as an educator of girls, a career which began as soon as her three years at Somerville were completed. For much of her career, she served as Headmistress of Cheltenham Ladies College. Cheltenham catered exclusively to 'the daughters of gentlemen', and for the most part, gentlemen sent their daughters there, not so that they might become women professionals, but because, by the last decades of the century, a good education had become one of the assets that a marriageable young lady was supposed to possess. Faithfull and Cheltenham were well suited to each other; her goal was to educate her pupils not to present any challenge to the male world, but to adapt to it in a feminine manner. She, and other educators with similar views, merely modernised the conception of femininity that was considered appropriate for upper-middle-class girls.

The remaining four women whose girlhoods will be examined in this chapter all experienced childhood in more modest middle-class circumstances than those of Maynard and Faithfull. All four families employed at least one servant most of the time, but in no case was there sufficient income to create the formal separation of parents from children that characterised the style of life of the upper middle class. The houses they lived in were modest; a separate wing for the children was no more possible than were specialised servants. For the most part the children, both boys and girls, were educated in day schools, rather than boarding schools, so that the abrupt rupture between brothers and sisters that characterised the experience of many upper-middle-class children did not occur. Finally, these were urban, rather than rural, childhoods.

Alice Whichelo, known as 'Lily', the first of these women, was born in London in 1855. She was the third child and first daughter in a family of ten children. Lily's father was an artist who made his living as a drawing-master, teaching in several schools in Clapham, the neighbourhood in which the family lived. During his lifetime, his income was sufficient to maintain the family in relatively secure middle-class circumstances. However, Henry Whichelo died in 1867, leaving his widow Louisa with virtually no money and ten children to support. Fortunately, Louisa was resourceful: 'a sensible breezy, witty woman, with a great zest for life.'[43] As her grandson, E.M. Forster later put it:

> She had to take lodgers, Germans, whom she undercharged, and to employ a sorry series of maids-of-all-work, whom she scolded and spoiled . . . But there were good looks about and good taste and good spirits, and . . . the Whichelos muddled through.[44]

As Forster describes it, his mother's family was so poor that 'the children had to earn their living almost in their childhood, the boys as clerks, the girls as governesses'. Lily shared this fate with her brothers and sisters, but a fortunate stroke of luck allowed her to be better prepared for it than many a middle-class girl similarly situated. In 1867, after her father's death, she was introduced to two well-connected and well-to-do ladies, Marianne Thornton and her niece, Henrietta Synnot. Lily charmed the two ladies, who became her benefactresses. Knowing that the girl must be prepared to earn her own living, they improved her chances to do so by providing her with a better education than Mrs Whichelo herself could have afforded. At first, Miss Synnot taught Lily herself and then sent her to boarding school for a brief period at seventeen. Finally, when Lily was nineteen, the two ladies found her an excellent place as a governess. While living in her employer's household, Lily met Edward Forster, one of Marianne Thornton's nephews. The two fell in love, and were married in 1877, and Lily's brief interlude as an employed young woman came to an end.[45]

In January 1872, Lily bought herself a little pocket diary in which she recorded her activities throughout that year, and during the early months of 1873. An eventful year in her life, it included the beginning of her boarding school career. Its entries provide insight into Lily's place as a second mother to her younger siblings, and as helpful daughter; we learn about her occupations and amusements; about her feelings for the opposite sex; about the place of religion in her life; and about the schools she attended.[46]

In 1872, Mrs Whichelo employed two servants, but they by no means relieved her or her eldest daughter from household responsibilities. Lily's main task was the care of the four youngest children, beginning with Nellie who was ten, down to Harry, whom she refers to as 'baby', who was five. Lily records that she bathed them, took them on outings to places like the Zoo or Kensington Gardens, gave them lessons and played with them. There is no indication that she found these duties onerous. Like the rest of her family, Lily was intelligent and charming, and in addition 'she had one quality which some of them lacked: a sense of responsibility'.[47] She loved her little sisters and brothers, enjoyed their company and was concerned about their welfare. She would for example devote hours to projects like making clothes for Nellie's dolls.[48]

Mrs Whichelo entrusted her daughter with considerable responsibility for the children. For example, from February to July of 1872, the five year old 'baby' was boarded out with a woman in Tunbridge Wells, and it was Lily, not Mrs Whichelo, who took the child there on the train, settled him in, and made sure that the caretaker was satisfactory. 'Very nice place', she records in the diary. 'I hope he will be happy, dear boy.'[49] And in July, she took the younger children on an extended holiday to Margate, staying in lodgings with them, taking them to the beach, and being totally responsible for their management and welfare during a holiday that lasted for several weeks.[50]

In addition to caring for her younger sisters and brothers, Lily also helped with the housework. She mentions doing mending, sorting linen, helping out in the kitchen and even with the cleaning. Again, as with her child-care responsibilities, she appears to have taken these duties as a matter of course, and did not feel burdened by them.[51]

Although she was continually busy with the affairs of the house, she also had many outlets for enjoyment. The Whichelos may have been short of money, but they entertained, went to parties, to the theatre, to concerts, and on frequent excursions. Several entries indicate that, at seventeen, Lily obviously enjoyed clothes and was a good seamstress. She mentions constructing a bustle, buying fabric, and on one occasion, being taken by her mother to a dressmaker to have a dress professionally made.[52]

In the first half of 1872, Lily was still doing lessons with Miss Synnot. In her diary, she records that she worked at her lessons, struggling to improve her German and her musical skills.[53] She often visited Miss

Thornton and Miss Synnot, and thoroughly enjoyed herself there. While her contact with these ladies does not appear to have made her value her own family less, neither did she feel uncomfortable in the more affluent surroundings of her benefactors. The fact that she was able to move freely between these two environments indicates that even at seventeen she had considerable personal self-confidence.

Her diary also indicates that in this year her interest in the opposite sex was awakened. She had no serious romance, but it is clear that she was attractive to men and found the experience of meeting them pleasurable. For instance, in April, the Whichelos gave a party: 'Enjoyed myself immensely. Did not go to bed all night, a Mr. Taylor here; like him very much'.[54] In January, 1873, just before her eighteenth birthday, she describes a party to which she was taken by Miss Thornton:

> Dance at Harley St. Very nice indeed . . . We had children first and Punch and Judy. I was not dressed in time, my petticoats were too short . . . Mr. Tom Latham gave me a fan in the morning, the first present I ever had from a gentleman. I was dressed at last and although I did not look nice, I enjoyed myself very much indeed. Danced every time.[55]

At seventeen, Lily's attitude towards religion was entirely conventional. She attended Church regularly, unless she had a cold or the weather was unpleasant, but there is no inkling of the religious turmoil that affected the lives of many of her contemporaries in adolescence. Church attendance would sometimes cause her to make 'good resolutions', but at seventeen Lily Whichelo was a happy girl with a cheerful, uncomplicated outlook on life, and a ready acceptance of her own circumstances. Neither family practice nor her own disposition led her to experience a spiritual crisis at this time in her life.[56]

In the autumn of 1872, Lily's benefactors sent her to a small boarding school in Brighton. As E.M. Forster later wrote: 'The school chosen was one kept by a Mademoiselle Collinet at Brighton, and was not altogether successful, but my mother enjoyed herself, picked up some French, acquired social assurance, and made friends.'[57] At the time that this school was selected for Lily, the first Girls' Public Day School Company school was opening, and of course, the Buss schools, the North London Collegiate and the Camden School already existed and had received considerable publicity. It is likely that Marianne Thornton, who was involved in charitable endeavours to educate

working-class girls, had at least heard of these middle-class institutions. But there is no indication that they were considered as possible
schools for her protege. Instead, Lily was prepared for her future at a
typical, unreformed, Victorian 'Young Ladies' Academy'.

If one of the pioneering middle-class schools had been selected, Lily
herself probably would not have enjoyed it; from her diary entries, it is
evident that it was the old-fashioned aspects of the Brighton school
that she enjoyed most. She wrote on her arrival, for instance: 'It is a
very nice place. The schoolroom is just like a drawing room.'58 The
girls followed the typical mid-Victorian young ladies' curriculum.
They learned French, German, drawing and music, and studied
literature. There is no indication that they learned Latin or
mathematics. For exercise, they went for sedate walks on the beach;
there is no mention of the callisthenics that formed part of the curriculum of the new girls' schools. This polite, conventional education
was probably the best preparation possible for her immediate future: a
good place as a governess, and an early, upwardly mobile marriage. A
more solid education might have left her better prepared for the fate
that befell her in 1880, when she was left a young widow, by no means
penniless, but with the responsibility of raising her only son, Morgan,
alone.

In contrast to Lily Whichelo, who received a conventionally
feminine education, Sara Burstall, born in 1859, was educated at the
new type of girls' school and women's college. Indeed, her educational
and professional career, from the time of her entry into the Camden
School for Girls at the age of twelve, until her retirement, in 1924,
after many years as Headmistress of Manchester High School for Girls,
can be seen as a paradigm of the benefits that the 'renaissance in girls'
education'59 could provide for a woman from lower middle-class
circumstances.60

Sara's parents were English, but she was born in Aberdeen where
her father was the agent for a London firm of granite exporters. Sara
was the eldest of three children, and the only daughter. During the
first eleven years of her life, the family was relatively affluent, living in
middle-class comfort, and employing some domestic help. But while
her father was employed in a conventional business occupation, the
most important quality that both parents had to offer was their unconventionality. According to Sara, her mother was a 'woman of great
natural ability, of strong physique and independent mind'. She came,
most likely, from an artisan's family, had been a Chartist in her youth,
and while she had had little opportunity for education as a child, she

attended lectures at Birkbeck College, as soon as they were open to women. While she was an excellent housewife, she was even unconventional about dress: 'she had never followed fashion, or . . . worn a crinoline', her daughter says.[61]

Sara's father, also a strong, independent character, had considerable influence on his daughter because he was more involved in the day-to-day care of his children than were most Victorian fathers. For example, when Sara was still the only child in the family, her mother 'who had no nursemaid', would often take the little girl to her husband's office, where she would be 'perfectly happy playing in a corner with filing cards'.[62]

Most of Sara's early childhood was spent in the home. Both parents had great faith in education, but 'no great belief in schools', and although the child was sent briefly to a 'little ladies' school' when she was five, she was soon removed, and did not attend school for some years.[63] While a governess was employed for a brief period, the parents were the chief teachers for all three children. In this urban, middle-class family, there was none of the compartmentalisation that characterised more affluent households. The three children's days were spent together in the garden, where their favourite toy — a sand heap — was provided for them. Indoors, in the playroom they shared, Sara did play with dolls, but she also played with her brothers' toys. She was particularly fond of their model railway set.[64]

In 1870, when Sara was eleven, her father lost his job, and, as his daughter says, 'he had to begin the world again at nearly fifty years of age'. While the experience was a 'terrible blow' for her parents, Sara was in fact to benefit from the family's downward mobility. The Burstalls moved to London where the father set up as a builder in Camden Town. The change to the lowest levels of lower-middle-class status allowed the family to assume a more unconventional style than had been possible in Aberdeen.[65]

Like the Whichelos, the Burstalls used the amenities of London to the full: they went to the British Museum, to the National Gallery, and to the threatre, and they all played in Regent's Park. Sometimes, after one of these outings, the whole family would have a 'modest supper' at a restaurant. Burstall points out that it was only because of her parents' progressive views that such pleasures were part of their lives. In the 1870s, normally, 'women and children ate at home'.[66] Sara's father would take his daughter on a horse omnibus, again something that middle-class girls did not do, and even allowed her to ride in a hansom 'which was a thing no lady did'. In summing up her relatively unconfined girlhood, Burstall commented many years later:

> The modern age does not need to be told about Victorian con-
> ventions. They were oppressive to many girls and women, but they
> did not oppress us partly because we were poor; partly because we
> lived in a rather Bohemian quarter where artists and actors
> abounded, but chiefly because of the principles of my parents.[67]

But even given such unusual parents, without education Sara's life
might well have been little different from that of her mother 'who felt
her own life to have been a failure': 'There have been many like her,
women of great natural ability, but with no education and little
opportunity for the exercise of their powers'.[68] Sara's opportunities for
education came to her in 1871, when she was twelve:

> My going to the Camden School [came] about by an accident, and a
> girlish impulse . . . I was always a great newspaper reader, and
> running through the column of the *Daily Telegraph* in July 1871
> . . . I came upon an account of the Distribution of Prizes by the
> Lord Mayor of London . . . and I said to my father, 'Oh, Papa, do
> let me go to that school, and someday I may receive a prize from the
> Lord Mayor.' The school was within walking distance, and the fees
> were within my father's means; so I became a pupil in September,
> 1871.[69]

The Camden School for Girls, then in its infancy, was founded by
Miss Buss to serve girls from families who could not afford the fees at
the North London Collegiate. Some of the girls would go on to the
more expensive school, but the Camden's curriculum was designed to
prepare its pupils to take the Junior Cambridge Local Examination at
fifteen whereas the North London Collegiate would prepare girls for
University. At the Camden, the girls studied academic subjects in the
morning; after lunch they played in the garden; in the afternoon they
did needlework and drawing. They also had callisthenics and swim-
ming lessons. Sara did well.[70]

Her success at the Camden was such that she earned a scholarship
that paid her fees at the North London Collegiate, which she entered
in 1875. She also did well there. Both Frances Buss herself, and Sophie
Bryant, the school's excellent Mathematics Mistress, recognised Sara's
abilities and did everything possible to encourage her. On completing

her school career, she won one of the North London Collegiate's scholarships to Girton.[71]

Sara went up to Girton in 1878, when she was nineteen. For her, the opportunity to attend Girton filled her with a sense of privilege, but in contrast to her near contemporary, Lilian Faithfull, who entered Somerville just a few years later, it was not the male University establishment to which she felt grateful, but the women's movement. For her, all the early women University students were 'members, however young and obscure, in a great forward movement for the women's cause'.[72]

From the evidence available, it appears that any adolescent emotional crises that Sara Burstall experienced were absorbed by the energies she gave to her studies. The majority of her contemporaries who attended good girls' schools and were in the first group of women university students came from affluent families. Their achievements, while never easily won, were perhaps not as difficult as Sara's, nor did they make as much difference for the girl's future. The relative poverty of Sara's family meant that working at being a good student was not only a way of overcoming the limitations imposed by her sex, but also those imposed by her economic status. Sara Burstall is an early example of a woman for whom educational opportunity was a path to upward social mobility.

The girlhood experiences of Molly Hughes, who was born in 1867, and who grew up in a middle-class household in the North London suburb of Canonbury, provide a number of sharp contrasts, as well as a number of similarities to those of Sara Burstall. Molly Hughes, like Sara Burstall, benefited from the opportunities that opened up for women in the late-Victorian decades. Like Sara Burstall, she too attended the North London Collegiate School. She went on to become one of the first students at the Teachers' Training College established at Cambridge in 1885, took a University of London Degree, and in 1891, when she was twenty-four, assumed a responsible post as first Head of the Training Department at Bedford College. Yet when she married Arthur Hughes in 1897, not only did she give up her career without a moment's regret, she appears to have welcomed assuming a subordinate position within the marriage. Of her wedding ceremony she says:

There had been a great deal of argument in the press as to whether a woman ought to promise to obey her husband, and some brides had omitted the word. So I said my 'obey' firmly, feeling the pleasure of having no longer to order other people's lives, but to be ordered myself.[73]

Molly Hughes provides a good example of a woman who could benefit from and contribute to woman's 'widening sphere', but at the same time challenge in no fundamental way the Victorian conception of femininity. She achieved this seemingly contradictory combination because she was very early and very thoroughly trained to accept female inferiority. In the 1930s Hughes published an autobiographical account of her girlhood. Her intention was to present her childhood as an unusually happy one. In fact, what she achieved is a picture of the way in which a mid-Victorian family defining itself as close and happy could induce a girl to accept willingly her second-class status.

Molly Thomas was the youngest child and only daughter in a family with five children. Her father was a dealer on the Stock Exchange, and the family income fluctuated sharply between what she herself described with some exaggeration as 'great affluence and extreme poverty'.[74] During Molly's first twelve years, they lived in the same house in respectable, suburban Canonbury. The house itself was a large one, bespeaking affluence, but at times, the money was not available to maintain the style of life that the size of the house suggested.

The Thomases were wise enough not to expand their style of life to lavish proportions when times were good, and for this reason they were able to live fairly comfortably with the fluctations in income. Although they usually employed servants, Mrs Thomas never employed a nurse or set up a formal nursery.[75] Consequently, even during the periods when the family had a substantial income, the Thomas children never experienced the formal childhood that usually characterised affluent families. Molly, especially, as the only girl, was extremely close to her mother.

Molly Hughes began her autobiography with the statement that 'a girl with four brothers older than herself is born under a lucky star'.[76] But what she goes on to record is a childhood in which she was always forced to take second place to those brothers. It was her father, even more than her mother, who insisted that the activities of his only daughter should be severely limited, in contrast to those of his sons, but it was her mother who actually ensured that these limits would be imposed. The mother and daughter formed one unit in the family, and the three boys and the father formed another. The mother and daughter were confined to the house, whereas the father and sons enjoyed pleasures away from home: 'My father's slogan was that boys should go everywhere and know everything, and that a girl should stay at home and know nothing.'[77]

Young Molly's life was so restricted that, as she herself put it, 'my outside amusements were mainly pale reflections of what the boys told me about theirs'. But she recalls protesting her limited lot once during her childhood:

'How I wish I were a boy!' Mother caught me saying this aloud one day, and promptly told me that this was a wicked thought. She did not go on to give a reason, but merely insisted that it was splendid to be a girl, and with such exuberant enthusiasm that I was quite convinced.[78]

Molly Hughes was determined to remember her childhood as happy, and in no way deprived, even though it is clear that she had neither the privileges nor the experiences to which her brothers had access. She achieved this state of mind by identifying with her brothers and thus overlooking or suppressing the fact that she was not one of them. For example, in her autobiography, she describes the children's special room. Instead of a nursery, she says, 'we were given a room to ourselves — *all* to ourselves'.[79] In fact, this room, which was called the 'study' belonged to the four boys. Molly was allowed to help dust and clean the study, but at other times, she was only permitted to enter when she was invited by her brothers.

The Thomas boys were all sent when 'quite small' to a day school, and then to good Public Schools.[80] Molly herself was not sent to school until she was almost twelve. Until then, she says, 'I was saved from the stupefying influence of such a place.'[81] 'Mother undertook all that she thought necessary for me . . .' Molly and her mother did lessons in the morning, reading from the Bible, memorising poetry, doing sewing, French, some Latin and a little arithmetic.[82] When she was sent to school at twelve, it was to an 'Establishment for Young Ladies', which while it provided her with companionship was, from the point of view of instruction, almost as haphazard as the lessons she had received from her mother.[83] Had her father lived, and the family's relative affluence continued until her adulthood, there is little question that the home training and the 'Young Ladies' ' school would have been all the education she would have received.

It was, in fact, her father's sudden death in 1879 that gave her the opportunity for an independent career in the years before her marriage. With Mr Thomas's death, the family's financial position at once became insecure, and when, at sixteen, Molly was given a choice between the prospect of living with her mother, in reduced circumstances, dependent on her brothers, or preparing for work herself, she chose the latter alternative. The obvious choice of occupation was that of teacher: 'In those days it was not considered the thing for a girl to "earn", although she might toy with a little work. Any other career than teaching was practically unknown.'[84] Molly received her excellent preparation for teaching through the kindness of an aunt, who offered to send her to 'the very best school that can be found', and pay the fees. The 'very best school', it was decided, was the North London Collegiate, which she entered in 1883, when she was sixteen.

Unlike Sara Burstall, who as a schoolgirl adapted smoothly to Miss Buss's routine, and as an adult had almost unqualified praise for her methods, Molly Thomas disliked both the school and its founder. All that mattered to Miss Buss, she claims, was outward achievement. 'Marks were the life-blood of the school', she says; any genuine cultivation of the mind or the spirit interfered with this main object. As an adult, she blamed Miss Buss's conception of the purpose of girls' education:

> She was a pioneer, and almost single-handed, in getting some kind of systematic education for girls . . . all the hitherto satisfactory ideals of accomplishments . . . must be wiped out, but what was to take their place? While the education of boys had been gradually shaped from ancient times . . . that of girls had as a rule no other aim beyond making them pleasing to men. This idea was to Miss Buss anathema, and she failed to see all its great possibilities when really well done. To be deeply pleasing to a husband, and widely pleasing to other men, seems to me as good an ideal as a woman can have. But instead of facing squarely the real needs of future wives and mothers . . . Miss Buss seized the tempting instrument at her hand — the stimulus to mental ambition afforded by outside examinations . . . And thus, for better or worse, the education of girls became a feeble imitation of what the boys were doing.[85]

During her twenties, Molly Thomas Hughes followed the same path as Sara Burstall, Constance Maynard and Lilian Faithfull, but then, like Lily Whichelo, she devoted herself to conventional wifehood and motherhood. Having passed several years of her adulthood as a 'modern' woman — pursuing a responsible professional career; living independently — when she came to write about her life, she evidently felt the need to develop an ideological position that would reconcile the seeming conflicts between her independent life before marriage, and her dependent and subordinate position after marriage. The ideological position she adopted was that of anti-feminism, an anti-feminism that was conscious and deliberate. Hughes is an example of a woman who, having tasted the freedom that an autonomous life could offer, rejected it completely, and consciously embraced the view that women are unalterably inferior to men, and of secondary importance.

Hertha Ayrton, whose experiences provide our concluding example of mid-Victorian girlhood, was the least typical of the six women whose lives figure in this chapter. Sarah Marks (her name in childhood) was born in 1854, one of two girls in a family of eight children. Sarah's father had a small business in Petworth, Sussex, as a clockmaker and jeweller, but he died in 1859, leaving his wife to face a difficult widowhood.[86]

Sarah's mother was the most important influence in her childhood. Unlike her husband, who had been a first-generation immigrant from Poland, Mrs Marks came from a family that had settled in England for several generations. She herself had had seven sisters, and the girls had all been raised in a sheltered, restricted environment influenced both by English concepts of femininity and by Orthodox Judaism with its narrow conception of the feminine role. The girls were, however, given extensive exposure both to English and to Jewish culture.[87]

Once a widow, Mrs Marks eked out a living both through assistance from her relatives, and by doing needlework. As in other families similarly situated, the mother depended on her daughter, and since Mrs Marks's second daughter was a life-long invalid, Sarah was, effectively, the only daughter. Sarah learned very early to be an aid and comfort to her mother. At the age of six, she had made all of her youngest brother's clothes, and throughout her early years she helped to tend to her siblings, in order to free her mother to do the needlework on which the family's income largely depended.[88]

But although Sarah had to assume considerable responsibility, her childhood was not only happy, it was unconstrained, in spite of the family's poverty. Mrs Marks's views on childrearing were most unusual for a mid-Victorian, and they had an important influence on the formation of her daughter's character. Mrs Marks believed in treating children as beings amenable to reason, rather than in the use of arbitrary authority, and apparently she succeeded. Sarah was never disciplined 'otherwise than by kindness and the appeal to reason',[89] even though she was never a gentle, retiring little girl. She had a passionate, active nature, was a fearless 'tomboy', and her appearance was unruly — she had thick, curly hair, and the fact that she could not keep it neat caused her continual difficulties with adults other than her mother. Sarah's vivid assertiveness got her into trouble at the little dame school to which she was sent at the age of five. When the teacher caned her on the hands, she at once ran home. Mrs Marks was as upset as Sarah, and promptly removed her from the school. In contrast, thus, to a girl like Molly Thomas, Sarah was early taught to question authority.

The little dame school was the best in the way of formal education that Mrs Marks could afford for her daughter. However, when the girl was nine, one of Mrs Marks's sisters, who ran a good girls' private school in London, offered to take her niece into her home and educate her. Although it was not easy for Mrs Marks to part with her daughter, she believed that Sarah had unusual abilities, and moreover, she felt that a daughter, if anything, needed a better education than a son because 'women have the harder battle to fight'.[90]

Thus, at the age of nine, Sarah left her mother's home, but the close bond between the two remained, and the parting was difficult. Sarah's unusually free upbringing did not fit her for life with her relatives, who expected her to become a 'docile little schoolgirl',[91] but she did adjust to her aunt's family, and benefited both from the education she received and from the atmosphere of the household. The Hartogs were cultured intellectuals with a wide and interesting circle of friends and it was in this fortunate environment that Sarah grew to maturity.

In early adolescence, Sarah went through a religious crisis. Her closest friend at the time was her cousin, Marcus, and it was with his help that, at sixteen, she was able to bring her religious thinking to a resolution. The Hartogs, in spite of their status as intellectuals, practised a 'strict and narrow Judaism',[92] as did Sarah's mother. But Marcus Hartog, who was somewhat older than Sarah, was an undergraduate at Cambridge, where he imbibed a rationalist outlook. It was through Marcus's influence that Sarah, at sixteen, became an agnostic, and while she never renounced a cultural attachment to Judaism, her agnosticism was permanent.

It was also Marcus who introduced her to her first close female friend, Ottilie Blind, who came from a family similar in character to that of the Hartogs. Ottilie and Sarah developed a 'spontaneous and romantic admiration' for each other;[93] it was at Ottilie's suggestion that Sarah adopted the poetic name 'Hertha'. During her late teens, Hertha spent much of her time at the Blind's Hampstead home. For several months, she and Ottilie spent every evening studying together for the Cambridge Higher Local Examination, which Hertha took and passed in 1874.

By this time Hertha was in fact self-supporting. Although reared in her aunt's home, she never severed her ties with her own family, and when she was sixteen, she felt an obligation to discontinue her own formal education so that she could help support her mother. Accordingly, she became a governess, making enough money to support herself, and even to send money home.

Hertha continued to do this work for six years, but already in 1873 she had heard about Girton, and had determined to become a student there if possible. She owed the fact that she was able to attain this goal to the friendship and generosity of Barbara Bodichon, the wealthy and influential activist in the women's movement. Hertha was introduced to Mme Bodichon in 1873, and soon became one of her protégés. Cambridge was not immediately possible; her own family was too much in need of her help and support. But Barbara Bodichon organised a fund to pay for Hertha's fees and support, and in 1876, she began her Girton career.[94]

Hertha's adult career, after Girton, was atypical. The majority of the early university women became teachers, but Hertha became a scientist. She achieved a distinguished reputation as a physicist, becoming an authority on the electric arc, and achieving such awards as the Hughes Medal of the Royal Society which she received in 1906. Moreover, not only did Hertha marry and continue her professional career — in itself an unusual combination — she also had a child, a daughter with whom she had a close and egalitarian relationship. Finally, Hertha Ayrton was an active feminist; in the years 1911 – 14, both she and her daughter participated in the militant wing of the suffrage movement.[95]

In comparing the experiences of the six women who are included in this chapter with that of the five early-Victorian women who were the subject of the preceding chapter, contrasts in girlhood patterns between the two periods do emerge. For example, there is a contrast between the level of parental control exercised over the daughters in both the Maynard and the Faithfull households and the relative freedom that Emily Shore enjoyed. The contrast suggests that by the mid-Victorian period, the belief that children were beings of a different order from adults, and that girls had unique needs, had gained in influence among upper-middle-class people.

In both the Maynard and the Faithfull households, the life of 'nursery' and 'schoolroom' was separate from the world of the adults; in both cases, the reading matter of the children was closely controlled. In the Faithfull family, moreover, there is clear evidence that the reading matter and the play experience of the daughters were selected to reinforce their status not only as children, but as girls. The books they were given were deliberately and consciously selected to encourage femininity, as were toys like the playhouse in the garden, through which they practised housewifery. In contrast, Emily Shore read what she pleased, and was encouraged to build model steamships. Faithfull and Maynard on the one hand, and Shore, on the other, are not isolated examples; other girlhoods, not included as a central focus in either chapter, reflect similar patterns.[96]

The most striking contrast between the early and the mid-Victorian experience of adolescence and young womanhood that emerges from the examples presented is that the six mid-Victorian women, unlike their predecessors, had open to them the possibility of acquiring higher education through institutions, and of pursuing careers in professions that had a collective organisation. The contrasting responses to these opportunities displayed by the six women underline once again the fact that sex was only one factor in determining both girlhood experience, and the pattern that the individual's adult life would take. Social status and individual temperament and circumstances were also of importance.

Constance Maynard and Lilian Faithfull, the two upper-middle-class women, were both early University students, both went on to careers in teaching, and both remained unmarried. However, the personal motives that led each to these similar futures were dissimilar. Constance Maynard's childhood developed in her both an evangelical conscience and a desire for independence. While her support for the organised women's movement was passive rather than active, and while she retained a belief in the values associated with femininity, her life work was designed to contribute to the development of female autonomy. Lilian Faithfull, on the other hand, appears to have combined a commitment to professional work, with belief in women's inferiority. No compelling personal ambition appears to have influenced her decision to attend Somerville, nor during her adult career did she present any challenge to prevailing notions about the secondary role of women in middle-class social, economic and family life.

In the lives of Sarah Burstall, Molly Thomas Hughes and Hertha Marks Ayrton, the opportunities available for higher education and fulfilling professional work made a greater difference than they did to Maynard and Faithfull. Both of the latter women could have achieved lives of comfort, dignity, and even of achievement had they remained permanent 'daughters at home'. No such option was open to the three women from less affluent circumstances. In all three cases, had they been born a generation earlier, their preparation for work would, in all probability, have been inadequate. Their working lives, most likely, would have offered them little in the way of money, status or satisfaction.

Sarah Burstall did not marry, so that a conflict between marriage and career did not arise in her case. Like Faithfull and Maynard she is representative of a new type of woman, a type that emerges at the end of the nineteenth century — the life-long professional woman. While only a small minority belonged to this group, it was, none the less, by the end of the century, both a recognised and respected one.

Molly Thomas and Hertha Marks, on the other hand, did marry. These two belonged to the first generation in which a group of women, rather than an isolated few, were faced with the conflict between professional career and wifehood and motherhood. Their choices represent two opposing solutions. On marriage, Molly Thomas abandoned her career, and developed an anti-feminist outlook; Hertha Marks, on the other hand, combined professional work with marriage and motherhood, and, in contrast to Thomas, was a committed feminist.

Lily Whichelo Forster was the only one of the six women included in this chapter who was not influenced by the changes in women's education and employment opportunities that began to make themselves manifest in the 1860s. The education she received and her choice of employment in the brief period before marriage would not have been markedly different had she been born in 1820, rather than 1855. Her experiences in girlhood and young womanhood should serve as a reminder of the way in which older patterns continued to be influential, even as newer ones were beginning to emerge. Indeed, in the mid-Victorian period, the girlhood pattern and adult life choices of Lily Whichelo Forster were still, without question, more common and more widely accepted than the opportunities provided by 'the widening sphere'.

Notes

1. W.L. Burn, *The Age of Equipoise: A Study of the Mid-Victorian Generation* (London: Unwin University Books, 1968).

2. This analysis of Constance Maynard's girlhood has been drawn from her unpublished diaries and autobiography in the Westfield College Archives, and also from C.B. Firth, *Constance Louisa Maynard, Mistress of Westfield College: A Family Portrait* (London: George Allen and Unwin, 1949).

3. For the Maynard nursery, see Firth, *Constance Louisa Maynard*, pp. 15 – 19.

4. Maynard, ms autobiography, p. 62, Westfield College Archives.

5. Firth, *Constance Louisa Maynard*, p. 19, quoting a cousin, Mary King, who was a frequent visitor to the household.

6. Ms autobiography, p. 25, and typescript fragment, p. 2. Westfield College Archives.

7. Ms autobiography, pp. 61 – 2.

8. Firth, *Constance Louisa Maynard*, p. 15.

9. Ibid., p. 15, quoting Constance. For Henry as 'F.C.', see ms autobiography, p. 36.

10. Ms autobiography, p. 22.

11. Maynard, Constance L., 'From Early Victorian Schoolroom to University', p. 1,063.

12. Firth, *Constance Louisa Maynard*, p. 23 (quoting Constance). The distance even a conscientious upper-middle-class mother would keep from her children is revealed in Firth's description of these lessons: 'For two or three years she laid aside Thursday afternoons to spend with her four younger children' (p. 23).

13. Ms autobiography, p. 27.

14. Ibid., p. 30.

15. For Mrs Umphelby's, see ms autobiography, typescript fragment, pp. 2 – 3. For a description of a similar sort of school, see Frances Ridley Havergal's description of the school to which she was sent in 1850. It was run by 'Miss Teed':

> That none might leave her roof unimpressed [with religion] was her desire, and it was to a great extent fulfilled. She prayed and spoke with us, together and individually, with a fervour which I have never since seen equalled, and seemed a very St. Paul in the intensity of her yearning over us. The result was what might be really called a *revival* among her young charges. There may have been, and probably was, some excitement; but that the Holy Spirit was, even then and there, sent down into many a young heart, and that many dated from that time their real conversion to God, and went home that Christmas rejoicing in a newly and truly found Saviour, I have no doubt.

Memorials of Frances Ridley Havergal, p. 32.

16. Ms autobiography, p. 47.

17. For example, see the entry for 15 June 1866, in the 'Green Book', Maynard Papers, Westfield College Archives.

18. Ms autobiography, pp. 53 – 4.

19. Constance recorded this memory of Mrs Umphelby's mother (whom she called 'Grannie') in her diary, at the time of 'Grannie's' death. 2 May 1866, Constance Maynard's Green Book, Westfield College Archives.

20. Ms autobiography, p. 55.

21. The books included 'Milner's "Church History", Stanley's "Life of Dr. Arnold,", with Tom Brown thrown in! — and the eight volumes of the "Life of Wilberforce", with the whole history of the Abolition of Slavery involved.' Ms autobiography, p. 56.

22. Ibid., pp. 57 – 8.

23. The farm labourer in question was Joseph Igglesden; several entries in the 'Green Book' for 1867 refer to him and his family. E.g., 'The time of Joseph Igglesden's pledge is gone, and he has begun to drink worse than ever' (17 July 1867, Green Book).

24. 'I want to try what knowledge poor Harriet Boxall has of religion, and if she can learn a text and understand it'. Ibid., 20 December 1867.

25. Her doubts, fears and anxieties were almost always expressed through the medium of religion. E.g., 'I should be much happier and better if I had more of a true spirit of self-denial. I do not mean the least better in God's sight, only it would be easier to run along the narrow way, because self denial is just the letting go of all the earthly things we so cling to.' Ibid., 20 October 1869.

26. E.g., see entry for 3 January 1867, Green Book.

27. Ms autobiography, p. 34.

28. Dora met her physician/husband when she was doing nursing training. Perhaps because Constance had paved the way by going to Girton, perhaps because the family financial circumstances had altered for the worse, when Dora wished to take up nursing, in her mid-twenties, the family did not oppose her plans.

29. She records when Henry made his offer:

> I am ashamed to recollect, that the first flush of feeling was one of pleasure mixed with great trembling, then a sense of utter bewilderment, and then an overwhelming feeling that it must not be allowed for an instant . . . I could only feel the bitterest distress for what had happened and remorse of mind, for I felt the Lord would not have sent so great and sad an affliction, except as the punishment and (if I received it rightly) remedy, for some great evil within me.'

17 August, 1869, Green Book.

30. Firth, *Constance Louisa Maynard*, p. 102.

31. Even in 1879, when she was thirty, Constance was still subjected to pressure from her family to be a 'daughter at home'. In that year, when she wished to start a Boarding House for some of the girls attending the school at St Andrews, where she was then teaching, her father wrote: 'I *cannot* think of it as a suitable line of life for my dear daughter whose prospects of inheritance *ultimately* are still such as will render her entirely independent.' Henry Maynard to Constance, 17 February 1879, Maynard mss, Westfield College. She was still being pressured to come home in June 1879, but she resisted: 'My health really is *no* reason. Girton was a *little* bad for me . . . but now I have wonderfully recovered . . . I suppose I was born to work, for I always vaguely longed after it . : . I would do *anything* for dearest father, but there again, while he has Gazy [her sister, Gabrielle] he does not *want* me in the least and I know that . . . were I married here at St A . . . he would be perfectly contented.' Constance Maynard to 'Dearest Tissy' [her sister, Josephine], 24 June 1879, Maynard mss, Westfield College Archives.

32. Lilian Faithfull, *In the House of My Pilgrimage* (London: Chatto & Windus, 1924), p. 15.

33. Ibid., p. 17.

34. Ibid., pp. 17 – 18.

35. Ibid., pp. 22 – 3.

36. Ibid., p. 18.

37. The same kind of control was exercised over the childhood reading matter of Janet Hogarth Courtney. Janet Hogarth, born in 1865, was the daughter of a Church of England clergyman; like Faithfull, she attended Oxford. In the large Hogarth family, as in the Faithfull family, the girls spent the afternoon sewing, and 'reading aloud in turns'. The books included Miss Yonge's novels. See Janet Courtney [*née* Hogarth], *Recollected in Tranquillity* (London: William Heinemann, 1926), p. 26.

38. Faithfull, *In the House*, pp. 32 – 3.

39. Ibid., p. 34.

40. Ibid., p. 39.

41. Ibid. Faithfull is an example of a woman educator who had an unconscious contempt for women. Her writings on girls' education reflect a belief that girls were more shallow and less honest, as well as less creative, than boys. E.g., 'Girls have a fatal facility in expression . . .' 'It is generally said that girls are unselfish and boys selfish. If you mean that a boy wants to go his own way, yes. But if you mean he is self-centred, an egotist, no. He is interested in the things he is doing, not in himself. Girls on the other hand are interested in themselves.' Lilian Faithfull, *You and I: Saturday Talks at Cheltenham* (London: Chatto & Windus, 1927), p. 49.

42. Faithfull, *In the House*, p. 53.

43. P.N. Furbank, *E.M. Forster, A Life; Volume I; The Growth of the Novelist* (London: Secker & Warburg, 1977), p. 2.

44. E.M. Forster, *Marianne Thornton, 1797–1887; A Domestic Biography* (London: Edward Arnold, 1956), p. 250.

45. Furbank, *E.M. Forster*, p. 6.

46. The diary is in the E.M. Forster Papers, King's College, Cambridge.

47. Forster, *Marianne Thornton*, p. 251.

48. Lily Whichelo's diary, 12 January 1872. Lily's given name was Alice C. Whichelo, but she was known by her nickname, Lily.

49. Ibid., 5 February 1872.

50. Ibid., see entries for 15 July to 6 August 1872.

51. For example, 'All the morning cutting sandwiches. Fetched Nelly [her little sister] Juvenile party.' Ibid., 1 February 1872.

52. Ibid., 5 April 1872.

53. E.g., this typical entry: 'Went out, worked, did my lessons, practised, made a bustle to wear.' Ibid., 6 March 1872.

54. Ibid., 18 April 1872.

55. Ibid., 17 January 1873.

56. 'Went to Church. Good resolutions and I hope I shall keep them. Took Lizzie to Church. Went to see the decorations at St. Pauls: played all evening.' Ibid., Sunday, 25 February 1872.

57. Forster, *Marianne Thornton*, p. 252.

58. Lily Whichelo's Diary, 5 November 1872.

59. The phrase 'renaissance in girls' education' comes from the title of an early history of the subject: Alice Zimmern, *The Renaissance of Girls' Education in England: a record of fifty years' progress* (London: A.D. Innes & Co., 1898).

60. Information about Sara Burstall's life comes mainly from her autobiography, Sara A. Burstall, *Retrospect and Prospect: Sixty Years of Women's Education* (London: Longmans, Green & Co., 1933).

61. Ibid., pp. 33–4.

62. Ibid., p. 3.

63. 'Fortunately, just as I began to attend a little ladies' school, I caught measles very badly, and was so ill that I was ordered off school for — it seems to me — years.' Ibid., p. 12.

64. Ibid., pp. 12–15.

65. Ibid., pp. 22–4.

66. They went to a type of restaurant called an 'à la mode beef shop'. Ibid., p. 30. 'It was unusual for a man to take his family there, as my father did.' p. 31.

67. Ibid., p. 33.

68. Ibid., p. 42.

69. Ibid., pp. 46–7.

70. On the Camden school, see Doris Burchell, *Miss Buss' Second School* (London: Frances Mary Buss Foundation, 1971). Sara Burstall discusses the routine during her time there in Burstall, *Retrospect*, pp. 46–53.

71. For Sara's career at the North London Collegiate, see Burstall, *Retrospect*, pp. 53 – 7.

72. Ibid., p. 65.

73. M. Vivian Hughes, *A London Family, 1870 – 1900: A Trilogy* (Cumberlege: Oxford University Press, 1946), p. 530. Information for Molly Hughes's life comes from this trilogy, originally published as three separate volumes: *A London Child of the Seventies* (1934); *A London Girl of the Eighties* (1936); *A London Home in the Nineties* (1937).

74. Ibid., p. 13.

75. Ibid., p. 4. And she describes a 'lean year' as 'devoid even of servants'. p. 19.

76. Ibid., p. 3.

77. Ibid., p. 33.

78. Ibid.

79. Ibid., p. 4.

80. The eldest boy was sent to Shrewsbury, the others to Merchant Taylors, pp. 54 – 6.

81. Ibid., p. 41.

82. 'Mother's arithmetic was at the level of the White Queen's' Ibid., p. 43.

83. Ibid., p. 58.

84. Ibid., p. 151.

85. Ibid., p. 179.

86. Evelyn Sharp, *Hertha Ayrton, 1854 – 1923: A Memoir* (London: Edward Arnold & Co., 1926), pp. 4 – 6.

87. Ibid., p. 4.

88. Ibid., p. 7.

89. Ibid.

90. Ibid., p. 11.

91. Ibid., p. 13.

92. Ibid., p. 24.

93. Ibid., p. 27.

94. Hertha met Barbara Bodichon in 1873 (Ibid., p. 30). In that same year, Mme Bodichon introduced her to George Eliot, who was immediately taken with Hertha's vivid, passionate character. Hertha became a regular visitor to the George Eliot-George Henry Lewes household, and Hertha became an inspiration for the character of Mirah, in *Daniel Deronda*, at which Eliot was then at work. Ibid., pp. 36 – 9.

95. On Hertha's relationship with her daughter, see Ibid., pp. 237ff.

96. Girls from early-Victorian middle-class families who experienced an intellectual freedom similar to Emily Shore include Frances Power Cobbe and the Brontë sisters. Frances Power Cobbe, in her childhood years, was educated by governesses, but she had lessons only in the mornings, and was left to herself in the afternoons:

> When the weather was too bad to spend my leisure hours out of doors I plunged into the library at haphazard, often making 'discovery' of books of which I had never been told, but which, thus found for myself, were doubly precious. Never shall I forget thus falling by chance on *Kubla Khan* in its first pamphlet-shape . . . My mother did very wisely, I think, to allow me thus to rove over the shelves at my own will.

Life of Frances Power Cobbe, I, 47.

The intellectual and emotional milieu inhabited in childhood by Charlotte, Emily, Anne and Branwell Brontë has been the subject of much discussion. Because Charlotte and Emily both produced works of major importance as adult writers, critics have perceived their intense intellectual life in childhood as being extremely unusual. The quality of their juvenilia is unusual, and in style and theme it does relate to the later Brontë works: Charlotte's Byronic hero Zamorna, who figures in her *Angria* tales, does prefigure Rochester in *Jane Eyre*, for example. But the fact that the Brontës read widely as children, and spent much of their time producing juvenile literary works, did not set them apart as unique. For the Brontë childhood experience, see Winifred Gerin, *Charlotte Brontë*, (London: Oxford University Press), pp. 35 – 6; Margot Peters, *Unquiet Soul: A Biography of Charlotte Brontë* (Garden City, New York: Doubleday and Co., 1975), pp. 1 – 44 *passim*; Charlotte Brontë, *Legends of Angria*, compiled by Fannie E. Ratchford and William Clyde DeVane (New Haven: Yale University Press, 1933).

The mid-Victorian pattern of a controlled and deliberately childlike childhood similar to that of Maynard and Faithfull is reflected, for example, in the following accounts:

Janet Courtney [*née* Hogarth], born 1865, whose father was a Church of England clergyman. Janet Hogarth was an early Oxford student. Description of her controlled childhood is found in her autobiography, *Recollected in Tranquillity*.

Louisa Innes Lunsden, born 1840, daughter of a lawyer. The family was Anglo-Scottish. Louisa attended Girton, then had a career as a teacher. She describes her childhood in *Yellow Leaves: Memories of a Long Life* (Edinburgh: Wm. Blackwood, 1933), pp. 1 – 25.

Chapter 9

LATE-VICTORIAN EPILOGUE

In the two preceding chapters, girlhood experience in the early and mid-Victorian years has been analysed through the method of group biography. To conclude the composite portraits, this chapter will focus on the experience of three women who were born in the 1880s: Phyllis Bottome and Helen Corke, both born in 1882, and Marie Stopes, born in 1880. In her autobiography, Helen Corke declared that she belonged 'indisputably to both nineteenth and twentieth centuries', and, as that comment suggests, it is the bridging during their formative years of two radically different periods that distinguishes these women from the mid-Victorian generation. While all of the women included in the analysis of mid-Victorian experience lived past the watershed of the First World War, they were, unlike those born after 1880, essentially Victorian: they had experienced childhood and youth at the pinnacle of Victorian prosperity and the dominance of Victorian ideology, and they had lived a considerable portion of their adult lives before they were affected by the changing circumstances of the new century. In contrast, women who experienced girlhood in the 1880s and 1890s were, first of all affected by the considerable changes in social, intellectual and sexual mores that had begun to be evident even in the last decades of the century, and second, they experienced their early adulthood in the years when the foundations of the Victorian liberal consensus were crumbling.

As girls, the three women provide individual illustrations of both change and continuity. One notable contrast, in comparison with the lives of our early and mid-Victorian examples, is the fact that all three women came from families that were smaller than those of the earlier generations. The size of the families indicates that in the three cases, some form of family planning was being practised. A second contrast is that in comparison to the mid-Victorian generation, these girls, as they experienced adolescence in the nineties, were affected by the late-Victorian concept of the 'modern girl'. Along with these changes, the girlhood experience of the three also provides evidence of the continued influence of Victorian ideas about sex roles. Mid-Victorian conceptions of femininity and of feminine duty continued to affect, in varying degress, both the character development and the life choices of these women while they were girls.

Phyllis Bottome, in adulthood a minor novelist, was born in 1882, and grew up in an upper-middle-class family. Her girlhood illustrates the continuity between the late-Victorian decades and the years that preceded them; in most respects the milieu of her childhood was not different from that of a mid-Victorian upper-middle-class household; the education and training that she received reflected few of the changes that had by that time altered the structure of middle-class girls' education. But because so much of Bottome's life was lived in the twentieth century, she offers a radically different perspective on such a girlhood from that which can be gained from the evidence available for women of the mid-Victorian generation. In adulthood, Bottome underwent intensive psychoanalysis with Alfred Adler, and in her autobiography she attempted to apply the insights of Adlerian psychology to her understanding of the family dynamics of the late-Victorian household in which she grew up. The perspective of psychoanalysis is, in its own way, as limiting and confining as the world view of the Victorians, but it is, at least, different from it. Bottome's approach does allow her to perceive circumstances that otherwise she might not have noticed or remembered.[1] She displays, for example, little reticence about discussing her early responses to sex, a subject rarely alluded to by women of the mid-Victorian generation.

Phyllis Bottome was the third daughter in a family of four. Her parents' last child, born when she was three, was a boy. Her father was a Church of England clergyman of American origin. The family moved frequently during the years of Phyllis' childhood, both within England, and in America, where they spent the years 1890 – 5, but throughout all their movements, they maintained an affluent life style.[2]

Bottome's analysis of her father and mother was influenced by her psychoanalytic perspective. She says that her mother was totally devoted to her husband, children and household, and to the practice of religion, but that she avoided the social contacts appropriate for a woman of her social position:

> She went to church constantly, she read enormously; she was the loving, gentle and beneficent background of our lives . . . all her rare intelligence, her sparkling humour, her perfectly sweet, sound temper were confined to the home.[3]

The mother's excuse for shunning outside contacts was her delicate health. Each of her pregnancies gave her considerable difficulty, and she was, throughout most of her life, a semi-invalid. Bottome suggests that this invalidism was psychosomatic. Her mother, she says, had suffered from a lack of love in her childhood, and, as a result, her 'unconscious' wish was to keep her husband from making any contacts outside the home, and invalidism was one weapon with which to do so. 'There was never really anything at all seriously the matter with my mother', Bottome concludes.[4] Her father, on the other hand, she describes as 'warm and openhearted'. As a girl, she was able to perceive his faults more clearly than those of her mother, but in many ways she felt closer to him.[5]

During Phyllis's first eight years, when her father held two successive country livings, the family lived in conventional upper-middle-class country-house style, although, except during periods of acute illness, Phyllis's mother was more closely involved with her children than many Victorian upper-middle-class mothers. After the birth of George, in 1885, a nurse was employed, but the children's care was shared more equally between the mother and the nurse than was often the case in upper-middle-class families. As with so many girls with a brother close in age, Phyllis's earliest companion, the person she felt closest to, was George: 'this strange creature that shared my nursery — a child but not a girl — a fellow baby.'[6] Later on, again typically, George would move into the masculine world of school, and Phyllis had more to do with her sisters; Mary, six years older than she was, and Wilmett, who was a year older than Mary.

Until she was eight, Phyllis's world was limited by the boundaries imposed by her sex and class. Although George was sent to school in early childhood, the girls were all educated at home during the family's initial English phase, the two eldest being sent away to boarding school only when they were twelve and eleven. The Bottomes maintained a 'schoolroom' for the girls; for several years, Phyllis, although she was a bookish child, was not officially allowed to participate in the schoolroom lessons. However, she would sit under the table while they were in progress, and benefit from them unofficially.

For contacts outside their own family, the Bottome children were restricted to the local 'gentry'. When Phyllis began playing with a little 'village' child, Hannah, who was better company than either of the 'squire's' children, Hannah, wiser than Phyllis, knew that their friendship would be curtailed should the adults discover it. 'Don't ee tell nobody', she said, 'or they'll stop we sure-lye'. Hannah, of course, was correct: the family nurse, when she found out about the friendship, forbade it, saying that Hannah was 'only a village child'. When Phyllis appealed against this decision to her mother, her mother confirmed it, saying: 'Hannah . . . might have things in her head — and you could catch them.'[7]

Although this was a clergyman's family, and religion played a prominent part in the family routine, it appears that belief, for both father and mother, was of 'an institutional rather than a personal kind'.[8] Certainly, throughout her girlhood, religious belief was the medium through which duty and morality were conveyed to the children, but intensity of belief of the kind that formed part of the experience of so many early and mid-Victorian girls was not part of Phyllis Bottome's development.

From the perspective of Adlerian psychology, Bottome later analysed the relationship that existed between herself and her two sisters, and her analysis offers an interesting perspective on the nature of this Victorian group. Wilmett, the eldest, who died in young womanhood, had a passionate, domineering, but at the same time, responsible, nature. Mary was a more shadowy character, the child least loved by the mother. Wilmett controlled the outward and the inward activities of her sisters. Under her aegis they did some things that were amusing — for instance, she would get them up at dawn on summer mornings to go mushrooming — but she would also engineer activities that could be frightening. For example, she invented a game called 'Christian Martyrs', which involved the sacrifice of dolls to the nursery fire; the dolls always belonged to Mary or to Phyllis, never to Wilmett. Looking back on their relationship, Bottome concluded that she and her sisters, in contrast to their brother, suffered permanently from the intensity and exclusiveness created by their childhood situation:

> I often think that had all of us been sent to a nursery school where we should have learnt independence of each other, and true give and take, our whole lives might have been different. These family relationships, and their unhindered sway, are terribly under-estimated, both for good and evil, in the formation of character.[9]

Because the family spent five years in America — her father had a parish first in Yonkers and then on Long Island — Phyllis experienced more freedom in the middle years of childhood and in early adolescence. In the States, she was sent to school: first, to an unusually progressive school in Yonkers, where the children 'danced, sang, moulded in clay and wielded fret-saws'; later to a conventional girls' private day school; and finally, she spent three years as a boarder in the rarefied atmosphere of an Episcopalian convent school in New York City.

It was in America, at the age of nine, that Phyllis first came face to face with sexual knowledge. She describes her lack of awareness up to that time:

> I had no curiosity, let alone knowledge, about my body or its func-
> tions. At nine years old I was both mentally and physically unaware
> of the existence of sex . . . When George was born I had discovered
> that his body was slightly different from my own; but as mine
> seemed to function just as satisfactorily, I felt no sense of dis-
> advantage . . . nor had it occurred to me to ask why we should not
> both of us have been made the same. Many English children with
> sheltered lives like ours grew to adolescence floating about in the
> same sea of ignorance . . .[10]

At the progressive school in Yonkers, Phyllis, the transplanted English child, was laughed at by the other children when she naively revealed that she did not know 'where babies came from': she still believed that an angel brought them. Her teacher talked to her alone, after school, and suggested that she ask her mother to discuss the matter with her. When Phyllis did so, she was given a full and frightening account:

> There unrolled before my horrified eyes, an amazing and tragic
> picture of the life between the sexes. The pains of childbirth — the
> greater physical strength of men — their far from greater moral
> strength — the white slave traffic — nothing was spared me.[11]

The effect of this sudden transition from naive ignorance to an excess of information about the dangers of sex was that she became 'nearly frantic with rage and terror'. Her initial response was that she would live her life 'as if it were *not* true': 'My future — the husband and twelve children I had happily intended to possess — I would now arrive at in a different way from that of Nature's'.[12] Accordingly, between the ages of nine and eleven, she went through what she describes as a 'tomboy' phase. Before that, her main activity in her free time had been reading, and while she still read 'omnivorously', she now spent the greater part of her free time 'practising wild feats of physical strength and endurance. I climbed trees, ran races; I jumped incredible heights . . .' At eleven, however, Phyllis went through what she describes as an early and difficult puberty, the pains of which she apparently could not discuss with any member of her family. In consequence, she endured acute dysmenorrhoea for several years, and had to have a gynecological operation, about which she does not elaborate, when she was seventeen.[13]

When Phyllis was fourteen, the family returned to England, the father taking a curacy first in Bournemouth, and later in the Kentish village of Swanscombe. With the family's return to England, Phyllis's regular education was over. Although money was not lacking for the payment of school fees — George was attending a boarding school at the time — it was the family viewpoint that, for a girl, she had received sufficient formal education. In 1896, she was expected to take up the traditional Victorian role of grown-up daughter at home. Phyllis herself wished for more schooling, and at her own insistent request, her parents did agree to allow her to attend a girls' grammar school for part-time lessons, and she also discovered for herself a series of Oxford Extension Lectures. From one of the lecturers, she received praise for her work, and began to think for the first time of writing for publication.[14]

When Phyllis was eighteen, the family moved from Bournemouth to Swanscombe in Kent, where her father took over a largely working-class parish. In Swanscombe, Phyllis and her elder sister Mary took up what had for several generations been an acceptable activity for upper-middle-class daughters; they visited the poor. Their charitable activities, however, were influenced by late-nineteenth-century ideas about voluntary work, stemming from the 'scientific' charity organisations and the Settlement House movement. Compared with the activities of such early or mid-Victorian girls as Anne Clough or the Maynard sisters, the Bottome sisters resembled social workers more than they did ladies bountiful: their work was both better organised and more effective.[15]

Phyllis was also busy writing her first novel, which was published when she was just twenty. The book provides direct evidence of her late adolescent beliefs about femininity, women's work and relations between the sexes. It reveals that she was both acutely aware of, and troubled by, the choices and the conflicts with which young middle-class women were faced in the 1890s. In the first part of the novel, the heroine, Muriel, forsakes society to work in a Settlement House in

Stepney. Although in real life, Phyllis's own voluntary work was encouraged by her father, in her novel, the heroine's family is distressed by her decision, so distressed that they call in a physician in an attempt to discover why she is so determined on 'slumming'. The physician declares that Muriel is suffering from 'a case of Hysteria . . . in its most patent modern form'.[16] At this point in the construction of her plot, the young author's sympathies are with her heroine's desire for useful work, and against her family's attempt to control and confine her. Muriel goes off to the Settlement House.

As the plot develops, however, Muriel learns that love and motherhood are woman's true vocation, not work in the world. The author provides a suitor for her heroine, a man who shares Muriel's beliefs about social justice, but opposes her views on the 'woman question'. The critical scene in their courtship is a fiery argument about women's rights. Muriel insists that women are repressed by men: 'They keep us from being trained for anything because they want us to marry', she says. Her lover retorts that women 'lack depth and continuity'. Only a tiny minority will ever be capable of sustained work, and their physical incapacity will always handicap them: 'As long as you are labelled women, you'll be labelled weak.'[17] Muriel does not show her lover the door on hearing these sentiments. Although initially she feels 'absurd, snubbed, dissatisfied', she quickly capitulates, and accepts his proposal of marriage. The author's message in the novel is clear; while it was legitimate for a young woman to wish for useful work, rather than the idle role of the daughter at home, only marriage and motherhood could bring her contentment, and fulfill her womanly nature.

Phyllis Bottome, born in the 1880s, was reared in a family that displayed little awareness of the changes in women's roles that were taking place in the last decades of the nineteenth century. The socialisation and formal education she received left her as little prepared for any role except affluent domesticity as a girl born in 1820. However, as she grew into her teens in the 1890s, and began to extend her horizons beyond the family circle, she was exposed to new ideas and new experiences. As her first novel indicates, by late adolescence, she had come to question the inequalities of the late-Victorian social structure, and she had been influenced by the women's movement. But while influenced by early feminist beliefs, she remained still more strongly committed to the Victorian notion of femininity, and it was a traditionally feminine role that she adopted in young womanhood. Phyllis Bottome lived at home, and played the role of daughter at home until her marriage in 1917, when she was thirty-five. Between 1913 and 1917 she was responsible for the care of her widowed mother. As she puts it: 'Women of my generation took both their home ties and their chief friendships as primary obligations.'[18] Only after 1917 did the more modern, twentieth-century phase of her life begin. Then, as a married woman, she became involved in the psychoanalytic movement, and after her own analysis, she not only pursued an active career as a writer, but also became a lecturer on Adlerian psychotherapy.

Helen Corke, like Phyllis Bottome, was also born in 1882. In contrast to Bottome, her family was lower-middle-class. Corke's recollections of her childhood and adolescence provide a detailed description of family life in a lower-middle-class family experiencing downward mobility. Her account of her struggles in adolescence poignantly illustrate the difficulties faced by a girl of the 1890s whose aspirations collided with barriers imposed as much by the class system as by sex.[19]

Helen was the eldest child and only daughter in a family of three children. Her father was a small shopkeeper in Tunbridge Wells, and during the first eight years of Helen's life, he did well in business and her family lived in solid lower-middle-class prosperity. The Corkes employed a servant, Emily, who stayed with them for many years, and they lived in a substantial four-storey house, the ground-floor front of which was occupied by the shop.[20]

Helen's father Alfred, as the son of a a draper, had been brought up in the retail trade business. He had also received a solid, if not extensive, education, and had widened his knowledge and understanding by serious private reading. All his life, Alfred Corke loved and respected literature and the world of ideas; the example of his capacity for self-culture was the most important gift he was able to bestow on his daughter. Helen's mother Louisa was a woman of much narrower interests than her husband. She had received only the briefest sort of 'young ladies' ' education as a girl. She was an attractive young woman at the time she met Alfred Corke, and while she was intelligent, her main interests were clothes and social intercourse.[21]

In her early childhood, young Helen and her brothers were cared for both by her mother and by the maid. Mother and maid shared the housework as well as the child-care responsibilities. One of Helen's earliest memories is of the household kitchen which was situated on the ground floor behind the shop. A swing had been rigged up to hang from the kitchen ceiling, and Mrs Corke used the swing the way a twentieth-century mother would use a 'jolly jumper' or play-pen: each morning, after breakfast, Helen was placed in the swing, along with her doll and a picture book, and she amused herself by watching her mother do her morning work; sometimes it would be the ironing, at other times it would be cooking.[22] Emily, the maid, also figured in her early memories: it was Emily who dressed her each morning, and Emily who put her to bed, after bathing her by the kitchen fire.[23]

In summing up her memories of the trio of adults who made up her early childhood world, she says that first of all there was 'Mamma, dominant, always at hand'; then, there was Papa — 'not so omnipresent, less insistent, beneficent and wise; the ultimate authority'. Finally, there was the maid, Emily, who figured in her recollections primarily in a physical way. The child found her '*tightness*' unpleasant: 'her hair sticks tightly to her head on either side of a white parting . . . she is buttoned tightly into her black dress'.[24]

As Helen grew from babyhood to early childhood, her world expanded, but only to a small extent. Louisa Corke was a careful rather than a spontaneously loving mother, and one of her main concerns was that her children should enhance the family's respectability by being neat, tidy and well-behaved. As little children, Helen and Arthur (the brother closest in age) both conformed to the pattern that was set for them. For both the boy and the girl the scope of life was limited, and they played almost exclusively with each other as small children. Inside the house, they were allowed to play alone in the store-room on the top storey. Outside the house, they were confined strictly to their own garden and only went farther afield when taken for their afternoon walk by Emily. Often, they would simply accompany her when she went shopping. Sometimes, they would be taken to the Common. There, they could watch the other children playing in the sand: 'We are forbidden to touch the sand, which Mamma says is dirty; we linger on the grass edge, envying, but feeling superior.'[25]

Helen Corke's early childhood was, from a physical point of view, neat, tidy and confined. It was limited and confined from an intellectual and emotional point of view as well. Later, her father's intellectual curiosity would have an influence on her, but during her first eight years, it had little effect. Louisa Corke had been raised as a Congregationalist, and her spirit of narrow, non-Conformist respectability pervaded the household. Religious belief, while integrated into daily life, was fundamentally a matter of outward ritual. The family went regularly to Chapel on Sunday, the children accompanying their parents even before they were five, but displays of emotion, about religion or about any other matter, were not encouraged. Self-control and respectability were what mattered.[26]

The reading matter the children were allowed was strictly controlled. Helen, who learned to read early — before she went to school at seven — was given the *Line Upon Line* books, and pious tales that were borrowed from the Sunday School library. As she puts it, 'the theme of saintly death occurs *ad nauseam*'[27] in the majority of tales she was allowed as a child. The only 'storybook' that did not 'feature religion' was Susan Coolidge's *What Katy Did*.

What Katy Did is a girls' story. That she read it, provides one indication of the way in which Helen's sex made a difference in her upbringing. She read girls' books, and she played with girls' toys. Dolls were of special importance to her. While it appears that she accepted her sexual identity without protest as a child, she does mention that, in doll play she did not always take the role of the mother:

> Doll-play took no small place from babyhood to my thirteenth year. It was serious play; the dolls were my real children . . . I was always the mother of my dolls when the play was social — yet when daydreaming or inventing situations alone . . . my part was that of the husband and father.[28]

Although her toys and some of her books were explicitly feminine, and she was taught to develop a feminine love of dress, sex differences played a less explicit part in Helen Corke's early upbringing than they did in more affluent families. In contrast to the upper-middle-class pattern, Helen and her brothers were brought up in the same milieu; indeed, except for a brief period, they attended the same schools. The chief means by which Helen would have learned appropriate sex role behaviour would have been through observing the adults in the household. In this respect, implicit sex role differentiation may have had a greater effect on her than it would have done on a girl from a more affluent middle-class family; in a family where neither mother nor father did housework, a girl might have been led to believe that only *servants* performed such tasks. In Helen's much more confined family setting, the sexual division of labour was more obvious.

Helen's first contact with the world outside her family came when she was sent to school at seven. At school she quickly developed a sense of social status. She knew that her family was not like those of the 'rich' children, who came to school wearing velvet and talked about their ponies. But she learned, also, that her family was not poor: 'poor people live in "hovels" or "slums" . . . It is kind to throw them pennies.'[29]

Helen's sense of her family's status as solid and respectable, if not affluent, was soon to be shaken. While the Corkes were never to sink into the working class, her father's business troubles began when she was eight. Driven near to bankruptcy, he was forced to sell the goodwill of his Tunbridge Wells shop, and the family moved to a country village where Alfred Corke attempted to re-establish himself as a grocer on a much more modest scale. In this village, there was no fee-paying school, although the family could still have afforded one, and Helen and her brother were sent to a Board School. For her mother, the fact that her children had to attend the Board School was one of the most painful indications of the family's loss of status, but Helen, in fact, adjusted to the school and did well there.[30]

Alfred Corke's shop did not do well, however, and from this time on, the Corke family's circumstances declined irrevocably. After two years, the family moved again, this time to the London suburb of South Norwood. After a final unsuccessful attempt to succeed as a grocer, Alfred Corke gave up shopkeeping and eked out a living selling insurance. The failure of their prosperity broke the spirit of Helen's parents, and from the age of eleven, she was aware of the sense of defeat that pervaded the lives of both of them. Helen adapted to the dispirited atmosphere of the household by escaping from it whenever she could, into the world of books. Perhaps because she was older, perhaps because her mother was too unhappy to attempt to exercise much control, she was allowed to read much more widely. She took full advantage of the local public library, and would lose herself in works of fiction at every possible opportunity.[31]

From the time of their move to South Norwood, there was no longer any possibility that the Corkes could afford a fee-paying school for their children, and so Helen was educated in the State elementary school system until she reached the age of fourteen. Intrinsically, the education she received was adequate, but it left her, at fourteen, at what seemed to her to be a dead end. In 1896, there was no provision for secondary education, even for the most successful of elementary school pupils.[32] Thus, Helen, who had been as successful as possible — she had reached Standard 7 — had to show for this achievement nothing but 'four ornate certificates' she had been awarded for passing the special examinations the Borough Council set for senior pupils. As she says, with justifiable bitterness, 'The certificates [were] worth just as much as they cost to produce — no more.'[33]

Helen, who read periodical literature both in the library and in her own home, had, no doubt, read some of the articles directed at the 'modern girl' which suggested that in the world of the 1890s, opportunities abounded for girls in her position. But she had learned, by adolescence, that 'poverty governs life', and she knew that there was only one option for her. By means of the pupil-teacher apprenticeship system, she could train to be an elementary schoolteacher herself. At fourteen, having read books as diverse as Olive Schreiner's *Story of an African Farm* and Bulwer Lytton's *Last Days of Pompeii*, and having tried writing, in secret, she was not ready to settle for such a narrow future. Therefore, to the surprise and dismay of her parents and teachers, she did not immediately embark on the pupil-teacher course of training.

Instead, for eighteen months, she stayed at home, attempting to plan a future for herself. She knew what she wanted: a life of 'freedom, opportunity, education, varied experience', but she could see no way to get them, even though her parents allowed her the time to try to do so.[34] During this period, she helped her mother with the housework in the morning, and in the afternoons, she spent her time at the South Norwood Public Library, reading books and scanning the columns in periodicals 'headed Educational and Personal — hoping for I know not what vague opportunity'.[35]

During this eighteen-month period, Helen experienced the onset of menstruation. Throughout her childhood, all matters to do with sexuality had been treated with 'the greatest secrecy and intimacy', and in spite of the fact that she had read widely, at fifteen, she did not realise what had happened to her. When her mother explained and then gave her directions about the 'personal hygiene' necessary during menstruation, her reaction was one of revulsion:

> I hear what she has to tell me with impatience and disgust. What an odious, limiting state of things! Are boys, as well as girls, subjected? No, boys are not. This is, I object, unfair! For the first time I wish, heartily, that I were a boy. My mother ignores this, and proceeds, hastily, to advise me of all the precautions and prohibitions relative to the monthly period that she had herself received at my age.[36]

Of the 'sexual act itself', she remained unaware, until, on seeing the neighbour's cats mating, she was 'enlightened by her own sensations'. She explains that her knowledge became more 'accurate' when she found a book called *Esoteric Anthropology* hidden in her mother's chest of drawers. The book described 'in simple terms, the whole sequence of coition, conception, generation and birth'.[37]

At sixteen, Helen realised that she would have to find a wage-earning job. After a nine-month interval, in which she was employed at two dead-end, unrewarding junior clerk jobs, she met a woman who had taught her at Board School, and with her help, Helen retraced her steps to begin apprenticeship as a pupil-teacher. She completed the training successfully, and at twenty, received her first full-fledged appointment.

Helen Corke's childhood and girlhood experiences reflect both the possibilities and the limits afforded by the 'widening sphere' of opportunity that opened up to middle-class girls and women in the final decades of the century. In spite of the loss of prosperity that her family experienced over the course of her childhood, Helen did receive an adequate education, and was able to expand her horizons through reading. It was the State system of education and the Borough Council's free library that provided these opportunities for her; had she been born in the 1850s, they would not have been available to her.

On the other hand, her formal education and her own reading caused her to develop ambitions that could not be fulfilled. As she would have learned from glowing articles in periodicals designed for girls, some young women did attend University in the 1890s, and enter professions like medicine, but such options were not in fact open to a girl like Helen Corke. The barriers imposed by sex were formidable enough; those imposed by class were even more insurmountable. Like Sue Brideshead or Jude Fawley, the main characters in Thomas Hardy's *Jude the Obscure*, a novel which deeply influenced her,[38] the future she could build for herself was a limited and dreary one, when compared to her inner vision of life's possibilities. Still, she was able to become an elementary school teacher, and humdrum as this occupation was, it did offer more independence and dignity and better remuneration than any that would have been readily open to her had she been born in the early or mid-Victorian decades.[39]

The final late-Victorian girlhood we will examine is that of Marie Stopes. As an adult, Stopes was the only one of our late-Victorian women to achieve widespread public recognition. In adulthood, she became Britain's best known advocate of birth control and sex education. Her experiences in childhood and adolescence provide a telling contrast with those of Corke and Bottome. Unlike Helen Corke, who was cramped by the narrowness created by poverty, Marie Stopes came from a family with sufficient affluence to provide her with an education and a cultured environment. And unlike Phyllis Bottome, who received a limited formal education, not because of her family's lack of income, but because of their traditional views about the education of women, Marie's parents held advanced views on the subject. In consequence, Marie received the very best possible education available to a girl of her period.[40]

Marie Stopes was born in 1880, and was the first of two children. Her mother, Charlotte, who was forty years old at the time of her birth,[41] was an Edinburgh woman who was herself a product of the mid-Victorian women's movement. She had attended Edinburgh University, was a supporter of Women's Suffrage, and continued, after her marriage, to write and lecture on such subjects as Rational Dress. Henry Stopes, her father, was eleven years younger than her mother. The son of a prosperous brewer, he became an architect and engineer who designed breweries. He shared an interest in reform with his wife, as well as a passion for palaeontology.

At the time of his marriage, and for several years thereafter, Henry Stopes was in very comfortable financial circumstances. The family had two houses: one London house, in Upper Norwood, and a country place in Kent. Charlotte and Henry kept the usual upper-middle-class establishment of servants, including a cook and a nanny — or rather, a succession of nannies. Although later in his life, Henry's amateur interest in fossil collecting drained their income, Marie and her sister Winifred, who was born in 1884, experienced comfort and financial security throughout their childhood.

The most distinctive feature of Marie Stopes's childhood was her mother's attitude towards her. Charlotte Stopes was a conventional woman in many ways — for example, she retained, and transmitted to her daughters her own Calvinist religion, and she expected her daughters to acquire feminine skills and feminine manners in addition to the other attributes she encouraged. However, the driving ambition she had about her elder daughter, was not that of a typical Victorian mother. As the diary she kept of the child's infancy attests, she was always concerned that the girl should be an achiever, and it was intellectual achievement on which she set her sights. Even when her daughter was only seventeen months old, she was competitive about her achievements. On a visit to a sister, she comments:

> Nelly's twins are 6 months younger than Marie, but are much farther back for 11 months, than Marie was at that age. I feel so thankful she is so far on — it makes it so much easier to me.[42]

In rearing her daughters, Charlotte Stopes avoided praise, lest it spoil the girls, and she imposed her own views on the children even when it meant setting them apart from others. For example, as a member of the Rational Dress Society, she did not dress the girls in the fashion of the day, but in knitted dresses. Although this garb was comfortable, its peculiarity caused the girls considerable embarrassment. Above all, she always treated Marie, especially, as more of an adult than a child. Until Marie was twelve, she taught her at home, herself: she started the girl on Greek and Latin when she was five, and became impatient with her when she found these languages difficult.[43] And she expected her to be emotionally and morally mature as well. For example, in September 1887, when she was away in Manchester giving a lecture at the British Association for the Advancement of Science, she wrote to her daughter, then six, in the following fashion:

> I arrived here safely, have nice rooms and have seen many friends. I thought of you yesterday very much when I was eating my dinner alone in the train. I trust you were both good girls and ate your dinner. I trust that you will remember that I have left Winnie partly in your care, and that I expect you will be extra kind and careful of her while I am away as you must be little mother and big sister at the same time.[44]

In contrast to the precocity encouraged by Charlotte Stopes, and to her relatively cold and distant style of mothering, Henry Stopes was a warm and loving father. It is generally agreed that Marie 'adored' him, and that she spent a considerable amount of time with him on his fossil-collecting expeditions. Certainly the written correspondence between father and daughter is indicative of affection. However, that affection was of a kind that may have been as distorting for Marie's development as her mother's coldness and exaggerated expectations for her. In his letters, at least, Henry assumed towards his daughter a mawkish, sentimental tone that was designed to infantilise her. In the same year that Charlotte wrote to Marie enjoining her to be a 'little mother' to Winifred, Henry sent the following letter to her, when she was at the sea-side:

> Be kind to the cockatoo and to winnietoo. Play with the sand and the tiny little waves. The mightiest force on earth loves to play in the sunlight with little girls . . . when you grow big, papa will tell you many things they said to him when he was little before his ears were

hurt by the hard harsh words of cruel men and women. Listen, and play and think for each year as it speaks to you the tales will change and the day may come when it is mute to you.[45]

The underlying message in this letter is clear; if you can avoid it, don't grow up. Throughout Henry's life, his relationship with his daughter was always tinged with whimsicality. In much of their correspondence, little jokes about the succession of family cats appear continuously, but a serious note is almost never present. Even in 1902, when he himself was fatally ill, and his daugher was a young woman of twenty-two, and a student at University College, he still addressed her as 'My Dearest Mariekins'.[46]

From Marie's point of view, the most damaging feature of this aspect of her relationship with her father was that she may, without realising it, have taught herself to assume a deliberately childish façade. Her letters to him are, at the same time, sentimental, and strikingly empty both of emotion and of intellectual content. Their childishness, and the childishness of her first attempts to keep a diary are in marked contrast to the written efforts of gifted early or mid-Victorian girls.[47] The contrast may partly be a result of individual differences in temperament and rates of intellectual development; but in part, as well, they can be attributed to the growth, in the late nineteenth century, of a tendency to value childishness for its own sake, a tendency that in Marie's case was encouraged by the parent from whom she received the most affection.[48]

Whatever internal pressures were created by the contrast between Marie's relationship with her mother, and that with her father, resolved themselves during her teen years, when she went to school. Although success did not come to her without a struggle, she succeeded at both the schools she attended, proving herself to be diligent, efficient and ambitious. The first school to which Marie was sent, when she was not quite twelve, was a boarding school in Edinburgh, selected by her mother. St George's High School for Girls conformed to the model of the modern, goal-oriented girls' school. Its Committee of Management was comprised of five women, and in 1893, it was in its fifth year of operation. The Headmistress had the Edinburgh University Certificate in Arts and, as well, a Teacher's Certificate from the Training College at Cambridge. Most of the staff had Degrees or Certificates of Degrees, and they frequently had teacher training as well. The curriculum was wide: Latin, Greek, mathematics were all included — as was needlework — and the school had a Gym Mistress who had been trained to teach Swedish callisthenics.[49]

In spite of her mother's ambitious attempts at home education, Marie was not well prepared for St George's and it took her some months to catch up with the other girls. During this period, the impulse to succeed came both from her mother who wrote urging her to work hard and to overcome her tendencies towards 'carelessness and inexactitude' and from herself. The diary she kept at the time indicates that she disliked the school at first, but that she was determined not only to overcome her dislike, but to become, as quickly as she could, an acceptable, achieving schoolgirl. Her school reports from St George's indicate that she achieved her goal.

Marie and her sister Winifred spent two years at St George's High School. The girls were then brought back to London and sent to the North London Collegiate School where Dr Sophie Bryant had succeeded Miss Buss as Headmistress. The Stopes family moved to Hampstead, so that their daughters could be close to the school. During her four years at the North London Collegiate, Marie did very well. She adapted to the routine of the school, her school reports reflecting that she was not only a most satisfactory student, but that her conduct conformed to the norms of the school as well. She regularly won prizes throughout her school career and in the Sixth Form she became a school prefect. As a pupil, in short, Marie exhibited none of the vivid unconventionality that was to characterise her as an adult.[50] One can surmise that, in adolescence, all of her emotional and intellectual energies were directed towards living up to the standards set for her by her mother: doing so involved the suppression of many parts of her personality that would only later emerge.

Some of them began to emerge as soon as she left school. Although her parents wanted her to attend one of the women's colleges affiliated with the University of London, she took the courageous step of enrolling at University College in the Science Faculty. Her supplementary decision to obtain her degree in two, rather than three, years was not merely courageous, but audacious. The fact that she succeeded in doing so attests both to her ambition and diligence, and to her possession of unusual intellectual gifts.[51]

In adolescence, Marie Stopes exemplifies some of the aspects of that 'modern girl' whose merits and defects were so hotly debated in the last decades of the century. While Marie was no 'hoyden', she did exhibit the emotional flatness and one-dimensionality that many of the more sensitive critics of the new girls' education believed to be characteristic of the 'high school girl'. In adolescence, Marie did not have time for the kind of introspection that characterised the experience of girls of similar intelligence during earlier periods of the century. On the other hand, as an adult, she was able to make excellent use of the educational foundation laid in her youth. Unusually unhampered by the need to exhibit feminine self-sacrifice, Stopes built, with her single-minded ambition, an achievement from which she herself benefited, but which also was of genuine benefit to society.

For Emily Shore, born in 1819, girlhood in a middle-class country house provided ample scope for the development of her personality. Her intelligence, curiosity and creativity all flourished, during her brief life, within the family circle. Neither the stereotypes of femininity, nor those of childhood intruded on her consciousness to any marked degree. She could study Latin, build a model steam packet, and read the *Quarterly Review*, while at the same time she could learn needlework, and play with her sisters and brothers. But Emily Shore was unusually fortunate in her girlhood; her interests, contemplative and creative as they were, needed no institutional structures through which to express themselves. Moreover, we do not know what conflicts might have confronted her had she lived into adulthood.

For Constance Maynard, born in 1849, girlhood in the 1850s and 1860s was in some essential ways similar to that of Emily Shore. Like Emily, Constance's emotional, social and intellectual development all took place within the confines of an affluent middle-class family. But for this mid-Victorian girl, girlhood experience was more constrained than it had been for Emily Shore; the role of daughter-at-home more clearly shaped by mid-nineteenth-century conceptions of the feminine role. But if Constance's experiences exemplify the constraints of the mid-Victorian years, they also illustrate the new possibilities that characterised those years. When Constance was thirty, she wrote: 'I suppose I was born to work, for I always vaguely longed after it . . .'[52] Fortunately for Constance, by the time she grew to adulthood, institutions existed through which she could express that need to work.

The girlhood of Marie Stopes, born in 1880, provides a sharp contrast to that of Emily Shore and of Constance Maynard. Like Shore and Maynard, Marie Stopes grew up in an affluent family. Unlike them, her girlhood was defined as much by her school experience as by life within the family setting. From early childhood, Marie was encouraged to work for measurable achievement; for a late-nineteenth-century schoolgirl, such achievement meant, in girlhood, conformity to a rigid atmosphere of outwardly imposed tests and measures. Emily Shore could shape her own intellectual development in childhood; Constance Maynard devoted much of her girlhood to inward contemplation of a religious nature. Marie Stopes had little time for either sort of experience, in girlhood. Only in adulthood did her unconventionality and creativity flourish. Then, of course, her excellent education, and her emotional preparation for a life of goal-directed ambition enabled her to achieve unusual professional success.

Shore, Maynard and Stopes all had the benefits of an affluent girlhood. Mary Anne Hearne and Helen Corke exemplify lower-middle-class girlhood. The similarities in the experiences of the two women, the one born in 1834, the other in 1882, underline the fact that social and economic barriers, as well as those of gender, continued to limit opportunities for the great majority of English women even in the last decades of the century. In childhood, both Mary Anne and Helen were bookish girls who developed, through reading, a vision of a life less narrow than that of their own families. As adults, they both were able, in some measure, to live lives of dignity and independence, if not of adventure. Both did so through work as teachers and as writers. Achieving such a life was easier for Helen Corke than it had been for Mary Anne Hearne. The Board School and the library of a late-nineteenth-century South London suburb did offer more scope for personal development for an intelligent girl than did the environment of a Kentish village of the 1830s and 1840s. But the difference was one of degree, not of kind.

Like Helen Corke and Marie Stopes, Molly Hughes, born in 1869, grew to adulthood during the period when 'woman's sphere' was widening — at least for those whose social and economic status allowed them to benefit from the new opportunities. But while Molly Hughes benefited from woman's 'widening sphere', she fundamentally rejected it. Molly Hughes's anti-feminism, her willingness to accept a subordinate role in relationship to males, and to treat her own considerable professional achievements as unimportant, illustrate the fact that Victorian girls could be trained to perform like men, but at the same time to accept the limits that society imposed on women. Her girlhood experience exemplifies the remarkable tenacity of the hold that the Victorian definition of the feminine role could have on the development of a female personality in childhood, adolescence and adulthood.

Notes

1. Information about Phyllis Bottome's life comes from her autobiography, *Search for a Soul* (London: Faber & Faber, 1947); from a later autobiographical work, *The Goal* (London: Faber & Faber, 1962); and from her first novel, *Life, The Interpreter* (London: Longmans, Green & Co., 1902).

2. During their early years in England, the household was staffed with Cook, Parlourmaid, Gardener and Nanny. See Phyllis Bottome, *Search*, p. 13 and p. 18.

3. Ibid., p. 22.

4. Ibid., p. 21.

5. Ibid., pp. 39 – 41.

6. Ibid., p. 13.

7. Ibid., p. 55. Phyllis's experiences were typical. Eleanor Acland, born in 1878, who grew up in an upper-middle-class family in a Westmorland village, was told that 'young ladies and gentlemen didn't play with village children because you never knew what you might pick up'. Eleanor Acland, *Good-Bye for the Present: The Story of Two Childhoods, Milly: 1878 – 88 and Ellen: 1913 – 24* (London: Hodder and Stoughton, 1935), p. 56. See also Janet Courtney, *Recollected in Tranquillity* (London: Heinemann, 1926), pp. 20 – 1 and the recollections of Ida Gandy, who was born in the 1860s, and grew up in a Wiltshire vicarage. Ida Gandy, *A Wiltshire Childhood* (London: George Allen & Unwin, 1929), pp. 49 – 51.

8. Bottome, *Search*, p. 38.

9. Ibid., p. 58.

10. Ibid., p. 94.

11. Ibid., p. 95.

12. Ibid., p. 96.

13. Ibid., p. 191.

14. For the Bournemouth period, see Ibid., pp. 221 – 4.

15. Phyllis ran a Boys' Club in Swanscombe, serving boys from 13 to 18 from the families of cement workers: 'These boys, who left school just at an age when they had begun to enjoy their school work, were thrown into the factory on dangerous and tedious jobs. They soon forgot the little they had learned at school, and many became incapable of reading or writing. In the evening there was nothing for them except the streets . . . until the brief moment of their falling in love — before the grim up-hill task of home-making shut down upon them, under its most adverse conditions.' Ibid., p. 272.

16. Bottome, *Life*, p. 40.

17. Ibid., pp. 259 – 61.

18. Bottome, *The Goal*, p. 39.

19. Information about Helen Corke is drawn from her autobiography *In Our Infancy: An Autobiography, 1882 – 1912* (Cambridge: Cambridge University Press, 1975).

20. Corke, *In Our Infancy*, p. 15.

21. On her parents, see Ibid., pp. 1 – 8.

22. Ibid., pp. 9 – 10.

23. Ibid., p. 12.

24. Ibid., p. 14.

25. Ibid., p. 18.

26. Corke recalls that, during her sixth year, when she saw the two boys who lived next door torturing frogs, and became hysterical, her parents were more disturbed by her behaviour than by that of the boys: 'Then comes the realisation, slow but abiding, that to them my loss of self-control is a worse matter than the cruelty of the boys.' Ibid., p. 18.

27. Ibid., p. 35.

28. Ibid., p. 78.

29. Ibid., pp. 34 – 5.

30. Her mother felt that the Board School was 'but a degree superior to a Ragged School'. Ibid., p. 45.

31. 'With *The Last Days of Pompeii* I take the curtain of romance and draw it deliberately across the window of my mind to shut out undesirable reality.' Ibid., p. 65.

32. On the State system of elementary and secondary education during this period, see J.H. Adamson, *English Education: 1789 – 1902*, (Cambridge: Cambridge University Press, 1964), 347 – 86.

33. Corke, *In Our Infancy*, p. 86.

34. Ibid., p. 96.

35. Ibid., p. 90.

36. Ibid., p. 93.

37. Ibid.

38. Ibid., p. 132.

39. Helen Corke's later life had much in it of interest. She wrote several books of fiction and poetry; and, as a young Board School teacher, she became friends with D.H. Lawrence, during the period in which he, too, was a Board School teacher, and she wrote about her memories of him, and of Jessie Chambers, his friend and hers.

40. Information for this analysis of Marie Stopes's girlhood has been drawn from the recent biography by Ruth Hall, *Marie Stopes: A Biography* (London: Andre Deutsch, 1977); from two earlier studies, Aylmer Maude, *Marie Stopes: Her Work and Play* (London: Peter Davies, 1933), and Keith Briant, *Marie Stopes: A Biography* (London: The Hogarth Press, 1962); and from manuscript material in the Marie Stopes Collection, housed in the British Library.

41. On Charlotte Stopes's age, about which there is some dispute, see Hall, *Marie Stopes*, p. 19.

42. Diary of Mrs Charlotte Stopes, p. 35, BL Additional Mss, 58453.

43. Maude, *Marie Stopes*, p. 31.

44. Letter from Charlotte Stopes to Marie, dated September 31 [sic] 1887. BL Additional Mss 58449.

45. Letter from Henry Stopes to Marie, dated July 30, 1886. BL Additional Mss, 58448.

46. Letter from Henry Stopes to Marie, 14 October 1902. BL Additional Mss, 58448.

47. For example, she wrote on 21 October 1893, soon after her thirteenth birthday, thanking her father for her birthday presents: 'Thank you for your letter and presents and kind wishes. I will indeed try to be what you and mother wish me to be. I had a very happy birthday; Mousa is a little pet of a dog.' Four years later, on her seventeenth birthday, 15 October 1897, she wrote: 'Dear Daisy was so happy (you know it is his birthday too) . . . He had fish for tea and while I was saying grace I thought I had better open just one eye, so I saw one sweet little paw laid so gently on my fishtail . . .' Both these letters are in BL Additional Mss, 58448.

Marie kept a diary when she first went to school in Edinburgh, in 1892, when she was twelve. The two following are typical entries: 'Got up early and tidied my draw [sic] . . .' Monday, 7th (no month given); on Tuesday, 11 February, she records that she was very pleased to be put into 'a Higher class at school, with a much nicer form mistress and much more difficult lessons'. BL Additional Mss, 58739.

48. The literary critic, Peter Coveney, has noted this tendency in literature. As he puts it, the literary image of the child changed over the course of the nineteenth century. Whereas the Romantic imagery of childhood did not reflect a desire to perpetuate childhood, the work of such late-nineteenth century writers as J.M. Barrie or Lewis Carroll did do so. In the late nineteenth century, he suggests,

'writers begin to draw on the general sympathy for childhood that had been diffused, but for patently subjective reasons, their interest in childhood serves not to integrate childhood and adult experience, but to create a barrier of nostalgia and regret between childhood and the potential responses of adult life. The child indeed becomes a means of escape from the pressures of adult adjustment, a means of regression towards the irresponsibility of youth, childhood, infancy, and ultimately nescience itself.'

Peter Coveney, *Image of Childhood* (rev. edn; Baltimore: Penguin Books, 1967), p. 240.

49. See the Circular from St George's in the Stopes papers: BL Additional Mss, 58463.

50. Although Ruth Hall suggests that she was only an average pupil throughout much of her school career (see Hall, p. 30), her school reports, which are to be found in the Marie Stopes collection, indicate that she did consistently well. See BL Additional Mss, 58463.

51. Hall, *Marie Stopes*, pp. 31 – 4.

52. Constance Maynard in a letter to her sister Josephine, 24 July 1879. Maynard Papers, Westfield College Archives.

CONCLUSION

Women have served all these centuries as looking-glasses possessing the magic and delicious power of reflecting the figure of man at twice its natural size.

Virginia Woolf, *A Room of One's Own*

Woman . . . is defined and differentiated with reference to man and not he with reference to her; she is the incidental, the inessential as opposed to the essential. He is the Subject, he is the Absolute — she is the Other.

Simone de Beauvoir, *The Second Sex*

The Victorian idea of feminine girlhood provides one example of the way in which women have served as 'looking-glasses' for men. As a feature of Victorian middle-class ideology, the idea of femininity had a life of its own, independent of the individual experience of particular women. As an idea, it reinforced the Victorian conception of masculinity, and helped to maintain the system of dividing the moral, intellectual and emotional universe into separate spheres, a system that was peculiarly well suited to the needs of an emerging industrial capitalist society. As an abstract idea, the image of feminine girlhood found expression in symbols and images that pervaded Victorian literature, art and social commentary. As an abstract idea, it shaped the beliefs of men and women alike.

Images exist in a realm removed from practical problems and day-to-day needs. In a more concrete way, the idea of feminine girlhood also helped to shape Victorian ideas and beliefs about how middle-class families should rear their daughters, from infancy to adulthood. Unlike the image of feminine girlhood, the nature of practical advice about the rearing of daughters did change over the course of the Victorian period. As society's economic structure altered, the middle-class female's participation in the 'public sphere' in adolescence and young womanhood came to be seen as both respectable and necessary, and accordingly, some preparation for the public sphere became acceptable. Yet, even amid these changes, the idea of feminine girlhood retained its force; never abandoned, it proved remarkably adaptable to new circumstances. The 'modern girl' of the 1890s might ride a bicycle, take competitive examinations, or work in an office, but she was still expected to be gentle, non-assertive, and subservient to men.

Patriarchy affects every aspect of women's lives. Patriarchy makes women poorer than men; it has left them more subject than are men to the effects of malnutrition and disease; it has subjected women to physical abuse, simply because they are women. Patriarchy has also deprived women of the possibility of independent self-definition. As 'looking-glasses', as 'the Other', the idea of woman has reinforced and has served the idea of the masculine. All women living in a patriarchal society are affected by the fact that the definition of women serves the needs of patriarchy, not the needs of women. Some women accept the male definition of female personality willingly; others resist. Still others are so situated that the definition affects them less than it affects most women. And while temperament, social status and family circumstances all contribute to the development of individual women in girlhood, the influence of gender is always present. The idea of femininity shaped the development of the personality of individual women in the Victorian period; it continues to shape the experience of girls growing to womanhood in our own time.

BIBLIOGRAPHY

I. Primary Sources, Unpublished

British Library Manuscript Collections, London. Marie Stopes Papers
Girls' Public Day School Trust Archives, London. Register books; pamphlets; miscellaneous letters
King's College Library, Cambridge. In the E. M. Forster Papers, Lily Whichelo's Diary, 1872 – 3
North London Collegiate School Archives, London. Correspondence; notebooks of Medical Inspection; clippings; pamphlets, register books, miscellaneous material
Westfield College Library Archives, London. Constance Maynard's autobiography (ms.); black book and green book diaries (mss.); correspondence

II. Primary Sources, Published

Acland, Eleanor. *Good-Bye for the Present: The Story of Two Childhoods, Milly: 1878 – 88 and Ellen: 1913 – 1924.* London: Hodder and Stoughton, 1935
Abbott, Jacob. *The Mother at Home: Or the Principles of Maternal Duty.* Derby, 1835
Allbutt, Henry Arthur. *Every Mother's Handbook: A Guide to the Management of Her Children from Birth Through Infancy and Childhood.* London: Simpkin, Marshall & Co., 1897
Ashwell, Samuel, MD, *A Practical Treatise on the Diseases Peculiar to Women.* London: Samuel Highley, 1844
Austen, Jane. *Pride and Prejudice.* London: Collins, 1967
Bottome, Phyllis. *The Goal.* London: Faber & Faber, 1962.
_____ *Life, The Interpreter.* London: Longmans, Green & Co., 1902
_____ *Search for a Soul.* London: Faber & Faber, 1947
British Mother's Journal, I – XI (1845 – 57)
British Mothers' Magazine, The. London: J. Snow. I – IV (1845 – 8)
Brontë, Charlotte. *Legends of Angria.* Compiled by Fannie E. Ratchford and William Clyde DeVane. New Haven: Yale University Press, 1933

Brown, I. Baker. *On the Curability of Certain forms of Insanity, Epilepsy, Catalepsy and Hysteria in Females.* London: Robert Hardwicke, 1866

Budden, Maria E. *Always Happy!!! Or Anecdotes of Felix and his Sister Serena. A Tale Written for her Children, by a Mother.* Fourth edition. London, 1820

Burstall, Sara A. *Retrospect and Prospect: Sixty Years of Women's Education.* London: Longmans, Green & Co., 1933

Bustard, John (ed.). *A Memoir of Miss Mary Helen Bingham.* London: John Kershaw, 1827

Child, Lydia Maria. *The Mother's Book.* London: Thomas Tegg, 1832

_____ *The Little Girl's Own Book.* Edinburgh: Robert Martin, 1847

Child's Companion or Sunday Scholar's Reward. London: Printed for the Religious Tract Society. VI – XII (1828 – 34)

Chirol, J.L. *An Enquiry into the Best System of Female Education.* London: 1809

Clough, Athena Blanche. *Memoir of Anne Jemima Clough.* London: Edward Arnold, 1897

Cobbe, Frances Power. *Life of Frances Power Cobbe, By Herself.* 2 vols. London: Richard Bentley and Son, 1894

Cohen, Lucy. *Lady de Rothschild and her Daughters: 1821 – 1931.* London: John Murray, 1935

Corke, Helen. *In Our Infancy: An Autobiography, 1882 – 1912.* Cambridge: Cambridge University Press, 1975

Corkran, Alice. *The Romance of Woman's Influence.* London: Blackie, 1906

Courtney, Janet [*née* Hogarth] *Recollected in Tranquility.* London: William Heinemann, 1926

Craik, Dinah Maria [Mulock]. *Olive: A Novel.* London, 1850

Crosland, Mrs Newton. *Hildred: The Daughter.* London: G. Routledge & Co., 1855.

Dickens, Charles. *Dombey and Son.* London: Oxford University Press, 1950

Drake, Emma F. Angell, MD *What a Young Wife Ought to Know.* London: The Vir Publishing Co., 1901

Edgeworth, Maria. 'Simple Susan'. *Tales from Maria Edgeworth.* Edited By Austin Dobson. London: Well Gardner & Co., 1903

Eliot, George. *The Mill on the Floss.* London: J. M. Dent & Sons, 1972

Ellis, Mrs [Sara Stickney]. *The Daughters of England, their Position in Society, Character and Responsibilities.* London: Fischer, Son &

Co., n.d. but 1843

Englishwoman's Domestic Magazine (1868 – 70)

Englishwoman's Magazine and Christian Mother's Miscellany, New Series. II – IX (1847 – 54)

Faithfull, Lilian. *In the House of My Pilgrimage*. London: Chatto & Windus, 1924

_____ *You and I: Saturday Talks at Cheltenham*. London: Chatto & Windus, 1927

Farningham, Marianne [Mary Anne Hearne]. *Girlhood*. London: James Clarke & Co., 1869. Second edition, 1895

_____ *A Working Woman's Life: An Autobiography*. London: James Clarke & Co., 1907

Fennings, Alfred. *Every Mother's Book: or the Child's Best Doctor*. London, 1856

Gandy, Ida. *A Wiltshire Childhood*. London: George Allen & Unwin, 1929

Garrett-Anderson, Elizabeth. 'On Dysmenorrhea'. Abstract of the Proceedings of the British Medical Association, Friday, 6 August 1875. *The Obstetrical Journal of Great Britain and Ireland*, III (1875 – 6), pp. 469 – 72

Gaskell, Elizabeth. *'My Diary'. The Early years of My Daughter Marianne*. London: Privately printed by Clement Shorter, 1923

Girl's Own Paper (1880 – 99)

Girls, Their Work and Influence. London: W. Skeffington & Son, 1877

Greg, W. R. 'Why are Women Redundant?' *National Review* (April 1862), pp. 434 – 60

Havergal, Maria Vernon Graham. *Memorials of Frances Ridley Havergal*. London: James Nisbet & Co., 1880

Hopkins, Ellice. *The Power of Womanhood or Mothers and Sons: A Book for Parents and Those in Loco Parentis*. London: Wells Gardner, Darton & Co., 1899

Hughes, M. Vivian. *A London Family: 1870 – 1900*. London: Geoffrey Cumberlege, Oxford University Press, 1946

Jacobi, Mary Putnam. *The Question of Rest for Women During Menstruation*. New York: G. P. Putnam & Sons, 1877

Kenealy, Arabella. *Feminism and Sex-Extinction*. London: T. Fisher Unwin, 1920

Lancet, The (January 1866 – April 1867)

Lumsden, Louisa Innes. *Yellow Leaves: Memories of a Long Life*. Edinburgh: William Blackwood, 1933

Lynch, Hannah. *Autobiography of a Child*. Edinburgh: William Blackwood, 1899

Lynton, Mrs Lynn. 'The Girl of the Period'. *Saturday Review* (March 1868)

Mason, Samuel, MD. *The Philosophy of Female Health: Being an Enquiry into its Connection with, and Dependence upon, the due Performance of the Uterine Functions*. London: H. Hughes, 1845

Maynard, Constance L. 'From Early Victorian Schoolroom to University: Some Personal Experiences'. *The Nineteenth Century* (November 1914), pp. 1060 – 73

Memoir of Mary Ann Gilpin of Briston Consisting Chiefly of Extracts from her Diary and Letters. 2nd edition, London: Edmund Fry, 1841

'Modern Matchmaking'. *Fraser's Magazine*. XIII (1836), pp. 308 – 16

Mother (By a). 'Defects in the Moral Training of Girls'. *The Church and the World: Essays on Questions of the Day in 1868*. Edited by Rev. O. Shipley, London: 1868.

Mother (By a). *A Few Suggestions to Mothers on the Management of their Children*. London: J. & A. Churchill, 1884

Mother's Companion, The. London: S. W. Partridge, I – X (1887 – 96)

Mother's Friend, The. I – XI (1848 – 58)

Mother's Home Book, The. London: Ward and Lock, 1897

Mother's Thorough Resource Book, The. London: Ward and Lock, 1860

Nicholson, W. *How to be a Lady: A Book for Girls Comprising Directions for Being Useful and Happy, Accomplished and Agreeable, Loved and Respected in Single and Married Life*. Wakefield: Wm. Nicholson & Sons, n.d. but *c*. 1850

Nightingale, Florence. 'Cassandra'. Printed as an Appendix in Strachey, Ray. *'The Cause:' A Short History of the Women's Movement in Great Britain*. Reprint Edition. Port Washington, NY: Kennikat Press, 1969

North London Collegiate School for Girls: Our Magazine, I – XXIV (1875 – 99)

Our Mothers and Daughters (1892 – 6)

Patmore, Coventry. *The Angel in the House. Poems*. London: George Bell and Sons, 1906

Peacock, Lucy. *The Little Emigrant*. London: 1826

Pullan, Matilda. *Children and How to Manage Them*. London: Darton & Co., 1856

_____*Maternal Counsels to a Daughter*. London: Darton & Co., 1855

Ridley, Annie E. *Frances Mary Buss and her Work for Education*. London: Longmans, Green & Co., 1895

Roe, A. S., *The Star and the Cloud: Or a Daughter's Love*. London and Ipswich: 1857

Roe, Mrs. *A Woman's Thoughts on the Education of Girls*. London, 1866

Ruskin, John. 'Of Queens' Gardens'. *Sesame and Lilies, The Two Paths and The King of The Golden River*. London: J. M. Dent and Sons 1907

Schools Inquiry Commission, P.P. Vol. XXVIII, 13, 1 (1867 – 8)

Sharp, Evelyn. *Hertha Ayrton, 1854 – 1923: A Memoir*. London: Edward Arnold, 1926

Shore, Emily. *Journal of Emily Shore*. London: Kegan Paul, Trench, Trabner and Co., 1898

Simpson, Sir James Y. *Clinical Lectures on the Diseases of Women*. Edinburgh: Adam and Charles Black, 1872

Stoddart, Anna. *Life and Letters of Hannah E. Pipe*. Edinburgh: William Blackwood and Sons, 1908

Strachey, Ray. *'The Cause': A Short History of the Women's Movement in Great Britain*. Reprint Edition. Port Washington, NY: Kennikat Press, 1969

Taylor, Isaac. *Advice to the Teens: or Practical Help towards the Formation of one's own Character*. Second edition. London, 1818

Tilt, Edward John, MD. *The Elements of Health, and Principles of Female Hygiene*. London: Henry G. Bohn, 1852

_____ *On the Preservation of the Health of Women at the Critical Periods of Life*. London: John Churchill, 1851

Toplis, Grace (ed.). *Leaves from the Note-Books of Frances M. Buss: Being Selections from her Weekly Addresses to the Girls of the North London Collegiate School*. London: Macmillan & Co., 1896

Ward and Lock's Home Book: A Domestic Cyclopaedia. London: Ward, Lock & Co., 1866

Warren, Eliza. *How I Managed My Children from Infancy to Marriage*. London: Houlston and Wright, 1865

Weatherly, Lionel, MD. *The Young Wife's Own Book: A Manual of Personal and Family Hygiene: Containing Everything that the Young Wife and Mother Ought to Know Concerning Her Own Health and that of her Children at the Most Important Periods of Life*. London: Griffith and Farran, 1882

Wood's Household Practice of Medicine, Hygiene and Surgery. A

Practical Treatise for the use of Families, Travellers . . . and Others. Edited by F. A. Castle. London: Sampson Low & Co., 1881

Young Woman, The. Vols. I – VIII, (1892 – 9)

III. Secondary Sources

Adamson, J. H. *English Education: 1789 – 1902*. Cambridge: Cambridge University Press, 1964

Atkinson, Paul. 'Fitness, Feminism and Schooling'. *The Nineteenth-Century Woman: Her Cultural and Physical World*. Edited by Sara Delamont and Lorna Duffin. London: Croom Helm, 1978, pp. 92 – 133

Avery, Gillian. *Childhood's Pattern: A Study of the Heroes and Heroines of Children's Fiction 1770 – 1950*. London: Hodder and Stoughton, 1975

Banks, J.A. *Prosperity and Parenthood: A Study of Family Planning among the Victorian Middle Class*. London: Routledge and Kegan Paul, 1954

Batts, John Stuart. *British Manuscript Diaries of the 19th Century: An Annotated Listing*. Fontwell, Sussex: Centaur Press, 1976

Best, Geoffrey. *Mid-Victorian Britain: 1851 – 1875*. New York: Schocken Books, 1972

Branca, Patricia. *Silent Sisterhood: Middle-Class Women in the Victorian Home*. London: Croom Helm, 1975

Briant, Keith. *Marie Stopes: A Biography*. London: The Hogarth Press, 1962

Bristow, Edward. *Vice and Vigilance*. London: Gill, 1977

Burchell, Doris. *Miss Buss' Second School*. London: Frances Mary Buss Foundation, 1971

Burn, W. L. *The Age of Equipoise: A Study of the Mid-Victorian Generation*. London: Unwin University Books, 1968

Burstyn, Joan N. *Victorian Education and the Ideal of Womanhood*. London: Croom Helm, 1980

Carew, Dorothea Petrie. *Many Years, Many Girls: The History of a School, 1862 – 1942*. Dublin: Browne & Nolan, 1967

Chorley, Katherine. *Arthur Hugh Clough, The Uncommitted Mind: A Study of His Life and Poetry*. Oxford: Clarendon Press, 1962

Clark, Alice. *Working Life of Women in the Seventeenth Century*. Reprint edition. London: Frank Cass and Co., 1968

Cominos, Peter. 'Innocent Femina Sensualis in Unconscious Conflict'.

Suffer and Be Still: Women in the Victorian Age. Edited by Martha Vicinus. Bloomington: Indiana University Press, 1972

Cook, Edward. *The Life of Florence Nightingale*. 2 vols. London: Macmillan and Co., 1913

Coveney, Peter. *The Image of Childhood*. Revised edition. Baltimore: Penguin Book, 1967

Crossick, G., Ed. *The Lower Middle Class in Britain*. London: Croom Helm, 1977

Cunningham, Phillis and Buck, Anne. *Children's Costume in England: Thirteen Hundred to Nineteen Hundred*. London: Adam & Charles Black, 1965

Davidoff, Leonore. *The Best Circles: Society, Etiquette and the Season*. London: Croom Helm, 1973

_____. L'Esperance, Jean, and Newby, Harold. 'Landscape With Figures: Home and Community in Engish Society'. *The Rights and Wrongs of Women*. Edited by Juliet Mitchell and Ann Oakley. London: Penguin, 1976

Delamont, Sara. 'The Contradictions in Ladies' Education', *The Nineteenth-Century Woman*, edited by Sara Delamont and Lorna Duffin. London: Croom Helm, 1978, pp. 134 – 63

Dunae, Patrick. 'Boy's Own Paper: Origins and Editorial Policies'. *The Private Library*, LX (Winter, 1976)

Dyos, H. J. and Reeder, D. A. 'Slums and Suburbs'. *The Victorian City: Images and Realities*. Edited by H. J. Dyos and Michael Wolff. Vo. I. London: Routledge and Kegan Paul, 1973

Ellsworth, Edward W. *Liberators of the Female Mind: The Sherreff Sisters, Educational Reform and the Women's Movement*, Westport Conn.: Greenwood Press, 1979

Firth, C. B. *Constance Louisa Maynard, Mistress of Westfield College: A Family Portrait*. London: George Allen and Unwin, 1949

Forster, E. M. *Marianne Thornton, 1797 – 1887: A Domestic Biography*. London: Edward Arnold, 1956

Frankle, Barbara Stein. 'The Genteel Family: High-Victorian Conceptions of Domesticity and Good Behaviour'. Unpublished PhD dissertation, University of Wisconsin, 1970

Frieze, Irene, *et al. Women and Sex Roles: A Social Psychological Perspective*. New York: W. W. Norton & Co., 1978

Furbank, P. N. *E. M. Forster, A Life*. 2 vols. London: Secker & Warburg, 1977

Gathorne-Hardy, Jonathan. *The Old School Tie: The Phenomenon of the English Public School*. New York: Viking Press, 1977

_____ *The Rise and Fall of the British Nanny*. London: Hodder and Stoughton, 1972

Gerin, Winifred. *Charlotte Brontë: The Evolution of Genius*. London: Oxford University Press, 1967

_____ *Elizabeth Gaskell: A Biography*. Oxford: Clarendon Press, 1976

Gillis, John R. *Youth and History: Tradition and Change in European Age Relations 1770 – Present*. New York: Academic Press, 1974

Glass, D. V. *Population Policies and Movements in Europe*. Reprint ed. New York: A. M. Kelley, 1967

Hall, Ruth. *Marie Stopes: A Biography*. London: Andre Deutsch, 1977

Hartman, Mary S. 'Child Abuse and Self-Abuse'. *History of Childhood Quarterly*, II (1974), pp. 221 – 48

Holcombe, Lee. *Victorian Ladies at Work: Middle-Class Working Women in England and Wales 1850 – 1914*. Newton Abbot: David & Charles, 1973

Hollis, Patricia. *Women in Public, 1850 – 1900: Documents of the Victorian Women's Movement*. London: George Allen and Unwin, 1979

Houghton, Walter E. *The Victorian Frame of Mind, 1830 – 1870*. New Haven: Yale University Press, 1957

Johannson, Sheila Ryan. 'Sex and Death in Victorian England: An Examination of Age and Sex Specific Death Rates, 1840 – 1910'. *A Widening Sphere: Changing Roles of Victorian Women*. Edited by Martha Vicinus. Bloomington: Indiana University Press, 1977

Kamm, Josephine. *Hope Deferred: Girls' Education in English History*. London: Methuen & Co., 1965

_____ *How Different From Us: A Biography of Miss Buss and Miss Beale*. London: The Bodley Head, 1958

_____ *Indicative Past: A Hundred Years of the Girls' Public Day School Trust*. London: George Allen & Unwin, 1971

Kleinbaum, Abby. 'Women in the Age of Light'. *Becoming Visible*. Edited by Renata Bridenthal and Claudia Koonz. Boston: Houghton Mifflin Co., 1977

Lister, Raymond. *Victorian Narrative Painting*. London: Museum Press, 1966

Lomax, Elizabeth Raine. 'Advances in Pediatrics and in Infant Care in Nineteenth Century England'. Unpublished PhD dissertation, University of California, Los Angeles, 1972

McBride, Theresa. ' "As the Twig is Bent": The Victorian Nanny'. *The Victorian Family*. Edited by Anthony Wohl. London: Croom Helm, 1978

_____ *The Domestic Revolution: The Modernisation of Household Service in England and France 1820 – 1920*. New York: Holmes and Meier Publishers, 1976

Matthews, William. *British Autobiographies: An Annotated Bibliography of British Autobiographies Written Before 1951*. Berkeley: University of California Press, 1955

_____ *British Diaries: An Annotated Bibliography of British Diaries Written Between 1442 – 1942*. Berkeley: University of California Press, 1955

Maude, Aylmer. *Marie Stopes: Her Work and Play*. London: Peter Davies, 1933

Millett, Kate. 'The Debate over Women'. *Suffer and Be Still: Women in the Victorian Age*. Edited by Martha Vicinus. Bloomington: Indiana University Press, 1972

Neff, Wanda F. *Victorian Working Women: An Historical and Literary Study of Women in British Industries and Professions 1832 – 1850*. Reprint edn. London: Frank Cass & Co., 1966

North London Collegiate School 1850 – 1950: A Hundred Years of Girls' Education. London: Oxford University Press, 1950

Osborne Collection of Early Children's Books. 2 vols. Prepared by Judith St. John. Toronto: Toronto Public Library, 1975

Pattison, Robert. *The Child Figure in English Literature*. Athens: The University of Georgia Press, 1978

Pedersen, Joyce Senders. 'The Reform of Women's Secondary and Higher Education: Institutional Change and Social Values in Mid and Late-Victorian England'. *History of Education Quarterly*. 19, 1 (19), 1979, pp. 61 – 91

Perkin, Harold. *The Origins of Modern English Society: 1780 – 1880*. London: Routledge and Kegan Paul, 1969

Peters, Margot. *Unquiet Soul: A Biography of Charlotte Brontë*. Garden City, New York: Doubleday and Co., 1975

Peterson, M. Jeanne. *The Medical Profession in Mid-Victorian London*. Berkeley: University of California Press, 1978

_____ 'The Victorian Governess: Status Incongruence in Family and Society'. *Suffer and Be Still: Women in the Victorian Age*. Edited by Martha Vicinus. Bloomington: Indiana University Press, 1972

Pinchbeck, Ivy. *Women Workers and the Industrial Revolution*. Reprint edition. London: Frank Cass & Co., 1969

Sherrard, O. A. *Two Victorian Girls*. London: Muller, 1966

Showalter, Elaine. 'Victorian Women and Insanity'. *Victorian Studies*, 23, 2 (Winter, 1980), pp. 176 – 9.

Smiles, Samuel. *Self-Help*. With a Centenary Introduction by Asa Briggs. London: John Murray, 1958

Smith-Rosenberg, Carroll. 'Puberty to Menopause: The Cycle of Femininity in 19th Century America'. *Clio's Consciousness Raised: New Perspective in the History of Women*. Edited by Mary Hartman and Lois Banner. New York: Harper Torchbooks, 1974, pp. 23 – 37

Smythe, Charles. 'The Evangelical Discipline'. *Ideas and Beliefs of the Victorians: An Historical Reevaluation of the Victorian Age*. New York: E. P. Dutton and Co., 1956

Stone, Lawrence. *The Family, Sex and Marriage in England: 1590 – 1800*. London: Weidenfeld and Nicolson, 1977

Strachey, Ray. *'The Cause': A Short History of the Women's Movement in Great Britain*. Reprint edition. Port Washington, NY: Kennikat Press, 1969

Sturge, H. Winifred and Clark, Theodora. *The Mount School: York*. London: J. M. Dent and Sons, 1931

United States Army. *Index Catalogue of the Library of the Surgeon General's Office*. Washington: Government Printing Office, First series, 1880; Second Series, 1911. New York: Johnson Reprint Corp., 1972

Utter, Robert and Needham, Gwendolyn. *Pamela's Daughters*. New York: Russell, 1972

White, Cynthia. *Women's Magazines: 1693 – 1968*. London: Michael Joseph, 1970

Woodham-Smith, Cecil. *Florence Nightingale: 1820 – 1910*. London: Constable, 1950

Zimmern, Alice. *The Renaissance of Girls' Education in England: A Record of Fifty Years of Progress*. London: A. D. Innes & Co., 1898

INDEX

221